NOBODY'S PERFECT

ADVICE FOR
BLAME-FREE LIVING

DR. JOY BROWNE

SIMON AND SCHUSTER

NEW YORK   LONDON   TORONTO
SYDNEY   TOKYO

Published by Simon and Schuster
A Division of Simon & Schuster Inc.
Simon & Schuster Building
Rockefeller Center
1230 Avenue of the Americas
New York, NY 10020
SIMON AND SCHUSTER and colophon are registered trademarks
of Simon and Schuster Inc.

Designed by Levavi & Levavi
Manufactured in the United States of America

10   9   8   7   6   5   4   3   2   1

Library of Congress Cataloging in Publication Data
Browne, Joy.
    Nobody's perfect: advice for blame-free living/Joy Browne.
        p.   cm.
    Includes index.
    1. Life skills—United States.   2. Conduct of life.   I. Title.
HQ2039.U6B76   1988
158'.2—dc19   87-37657
ISBN 0-671-64867-5

Acknowledgments

I suppose it's a bit cynical of me, but whenever I have read flowery acknowledgments, especially when directed to editors or agents, I have blissfully assumed that it was a way of ensuring continuing loyalty, sort of an upscale Brownie point. In my case in particular, nothing could be further from the truth. I give heartfelt thanks to Sally Arteseros, who started me on the path. She contacted me about writing a book (at the urgings of Alex Gotfryd), bought me lunch, and encouraged me to write in my radio voice. In exasperation one day, I wailed, "If you can come up with the questions, I can come up with the answers." It then occurred to me that if I could come up with the answers, I could come up with the questions, and I went home and came up with a hundred in two days. Doubleday passed on the book, but it wouldn't have gotten started without Sally and her enthusiasm.

Thanking your agent seems de rigueur, but Mitch Douglas is no ordinary agent. His sweet southern drawl made his criticisms acceptable and when he finally uttered, "Joyah, you should fayal reahl prawd of yourself," I did, I did. Mitch kept me on the path when I was convinced I was writing in the dark for myself. Ten percent was never better spent. He is also my friend and the person most likely to cheer me up by taking me to lunch.

If Sally started me on the path, and Mitch kept me there, then Nancy Nicholas deserves thanks for making it all happen. For me, writing is lonely and not much fun, and she made me feel a lot less alone and made it as close to fun as it will probably ever be, although each time I sent off a new batch, I was convinced I was going to receive a telegram saying, Please return advance immediately. Nancy is the kind of editor who makes almost no changes and when she does they're either brilliant, the exact right word, or so dumb

ACKNOWLEDGMENTS ————————————————————

they make me furious. How could she have missed the whole point? I think. Aha, if she missed it, it's because I failed to make it, right? Like I said, the perfect editor. Besides which she gives great gossip and can tell the wildest stories with the straightest of all faces.

I also do want to thank those listeners who've been put on hold and still been kind and relatively patient in telling me their stories, and that listener years ago in Boston who asked for a list of my sayings. I wrote back and said I didn't have any "sayings" and he sent me a list which served as the original basis for putting pen to paper. I thank you all.

To my listeners, who have shared with me and allowed me to touch their lives, however briefly, I am truly grateful.

Contents

INTRODUCTION

Growing up in America means growing up insecure. We live in a capitalistic marketplace society designed to sell us things we don't need. By and large this is accomplished by making us believe that whatever we are is wrong. We are too fat, too smelly, too dark, too light, too sexless, too poor, too hairy; but fortunately any one of these horrifying problems can be solved by buying the appropriate product whose use will result in long-term happiness, acceptance and love.

The only way this pitch can work is if we believe simultaneously that there is an ideal or perfect state, that it is achievable and that although we do not currently enjoy this state of perfection, even we can potentially achieve it.

If you think about this for a minute, it is patently ridiculous, yet we swallow it lock, stock and barrel when we buy a pair of eyeglasses advertised by a beautiful woman, a perfume touted by panting nymphets, a diet drink hawked by a hunk, a car based on the assumption that Mustang makes it happen or that we are listening to the heartbeat of America.

Not only do we get suckered into believing in perfectionism on an individual level, we basically believe in Norman Rockwell's view of America: there is a perfect family eating a perfect turkey around a perfect centerpiece without one drop of milk being spilled, one argument or even one drunken uncle making off-color jokes. Even if it's not happening in our home, we're sure it's occurring down the block.

In theory, this asinine set of assumptions would be painful but harmless if we didn't beat up on ourselves as well as everybody else when we come face to face with our imperfect lives. These uncomfortable feelings take hold very early; if not at birth, then very soon thereafter.

The trap of perfectionism begins with the gnawing realization around three or four that we're not perfect and that

Mom and Dad don't appreciate goof-ups, so we begin to lie about who we are or what we did so that our parents will continue to love us. An older sibling who has already started school or learned to tie a shoe or chews with his mouth closed or a brand-new baby who is cuter and softer and everybody likes better increases the anxiety.

When we start school, perfectionism becomes even more of a competitive issue. It becomes vital to have the right answer or at least the right lunch box, cookies and brand-name sneakers. Once we have finally, painfully figured out that we're not perfect at all, it's crucial to hide the fact from ourselves and everyone else—inside and out. Inside by denying not only what we are and how we act but also how we feel; outside by looking right and trying to behave in a way that will not invite suspicion or closer inspection. No one must discover our terrible secret: We're not perfect.

As we move into the teenage years, we guard the secret by staying in the middle of the right crowd, wearing the right clothes. After a few years of this we come to feel that the right accoutrements are fundamental to our survival rather than window dressing. It is a short step to demanding perfection of our friends, our family and our surroundings. Adolescence is a time where other people's ideas of our worth are inseparable from our own feelings about ourselves. Kids who can't make the grade will purposefully, aggressively, even savagely reject all values and paint themselves as disdainful and belligerently opposed to the group whose approval they so desperately seek. There is no middle ground.

Family is a real problem during these years because we're confronted on a daily basis with their imperfections and, by association, with ours. So family becomes the enemy—important to reject and even, if possible, jettison during these years. Values are discarded, noses are fixed, names are changed, traditions are ignored and ties are severed as brutally as possible.

Knowing that our origins are imperfect sets up the terrible search for a new and perfect set of origins, friends and, most importantly, a mate. We seek out the right schools to create a temporary perfect family and environment so we can meet perfect people who will welcome us into their perfect world and make our perfect lives begin.

Any sign that a potential mate is less than perfect or less than perfectly acceptable to our perfect crowd is reason for immediate reflection. On the other hand, we're so busy being perfect ourselves that close scrutiny of someone else's behavior is often obscured by the close scrutiny and monitoring of our own image, lest someone figure out that we're not perfect.

Unfortunately, adolescence does not end this process. Having now acquired a seemingly perfect mate in a perfect wedding with perfect gifts for the brand-new perfect life, we are brought up short by the startling revelation that upon close observation everything isn't perfect. Day-to-day living is real tough on perfectionism. We usually accept this as further evidence of our own imperfection: We haven't been good enough to deserve a perfect mate, the jig is up and we've been found out. We got what we deserved.

At this point everything dissolves and we begin the quest again with image even more polished and facade even more firmly in place, or we decide to maintain appearances and find the perfect house with perfect furnishings and perfect gardens and appliances and proceed to have a perfect family with the right car, dog, recipes and address.

All of this would be exhausting but harmless if somewhere along the line the whole thing didn't become unconscious. Once we begin to believe in perfection, we get angry when someone isn't perfect, because his or her imperfection becomes the crack in the dam and opens up the terrible possibility that everyone will know we're not perfect if the facade and surroundings aren't. Because we never examine the underlying assumption that perfection is obtainable, we continue to accept that everyone or at least someone must be perfect and it had best be us. If we're not perfect and someone else is, then that person will get the acceptance and love that we want. Thus, any tiny blemish, any minute indication that everything isn't right is terrifying.

In a society where being perfect means being strong and silent and independent and sure, it is of obvious benefit to be a man. Thus, being a woman makes things both easier and more difficult. Women start out trying to be something they're not, but they at least feel they can offer some comfort to one another. Women understand very early that girls are second rate and designated to the sidelines as cheerleaders while the boys get to do the fun stuff. Pronouns are masculine, exciting jobs are masculine and principals are men. During the time girls are taught to lose to boys at tennis and talk about things the boys like (what boy ever sued to join a girls' team) they are compensated by the closeness of one another. There may never again be the intimacy attained between twelve-year-old girls. Once boys enter the scene, the girls become competitive for the real prize—the boys—but at least they have learned to confide in one another. They can take some comfort from the fact that they both have breasts that are too small and practice dancing with each other until the "real" thing comes along.

By the time dating is an issue, there are still confidantes, often unattractive and therefore no competition. Most groups consist of one brain, one athlete and a bunch of hangers-on, too fat or tall or skinny or hairy. Once a woman is firmly married, she can confide her less than perfect thoughts.

School is really for boys and careers, while girls shouldn't worry their pretty little heads or try to be too smart the closer they get to puberty. Boys and girls both dress in pants; ever see boys trying to wear girls' clothes except at Halloween?

At work it's okay to gripe about the boss, but most real feelings focus on the imperfection of sports teams, who are always supposed to win and do their best and play beyond pain. It is also okay to complain lightly about women colleagues who aren't perfect and strong like men.

If there are any doubts, television reinforces the idea that everybody else's life is perfect; except for the bad guys, who are always caught and punished and can easily be identified because they look all wrong and drive the wrong cars and hang out with the wrong women on the wrong side of town. The message is very clear: There are good guys who are perfect and rewarded and bad guys who have no redeeming values and are caught and punished.

Who would want to be a bad guy?

Knowing that we're not perfect sets up a terrible conflict. Admitting it would mean being ostracized and unloved, so maintaining the image becomes paramount. The image is based on how we look and act and what we surround ourselves with. The more we surround ourself with perfection, the less likely it is that anybody will pierce through to our imperfect core and discover our terrible secret.

Thus, when any of our surroundings are less than perfect, it means that not only are they failing us but they leave open the possibility that we will be unmasked as frauds. It is crucial that they be perfect, since we already know that we're not. But it's our dirty little secret. This means that when somebody lets us down they don't love us, they're trying to embarrass us or ruin our life. "They" can range from a drunken husband to a wife who burns the bacon to kids who make lousy grades to a son who dribbles too much at two and not enough on the high school basketball team.

As we get older, which of course must be denied, since perfection is young and firm, we also are faced with aging parents who are primary sources of irritation and possible sources of exposure, since they are our roots. They can either behave themselves and act like perfect people or we will jettison them; and acting perfect means not forgetting the rules or spilling the beans. Grandchildren offer a new potential source of perfection if only we can convince their benighted parents of the right way to raise them. Potential in-laws must be carefully scanned for marks of imperfection and criticized to enable them to learn to be perfect.

It must have now become evident that perfectionism is an enormous burden both internally and externally and nearly universally shouldered. Perfectionists are a pain in the neck to live with, for themselves and everyone else—constantly demanding, never satisfied and constantly on guard. They can't handle any criticism yet are constantly critical. No mistake can be tolerated either in their own behavior or in anyone else's. They are always under a time pressure, since they must do everything and do it perfectly and quickly. They are constant jugglers. Perfectionists are everywhere.

This introduction is a long-range perspective of a problem that pervades many nooks and crannies of our lives. It's just that we choose different arenas. It makes us unwilling to take up new challenges with confidence, makes us dislike ourselves and others, allows us to be constantly disappointed and, in general, much less content, happy and serene than we might be. Perfectionism is a distortion of reality perception.

The vast majority of us are victims of this notion of perfectionism. We shoulder the blame and suffer the consequences of years of unrealistic expectations with no benefit at all. On the contrary, this pervasive idea alienates us from one another, from easy interactions, restful sleep, any chance at real intimacy and most tragically from a feeling of peace within and with ourselves.

The chapters that follow offer an overview of these expectations and their consequences. From the abstract material I have discussed here, the focus shifts to specific examples from everyday life culled from recurring questions and situations encountered in my private practice, my radio program and my own personal life. By understanding other people's questions and predicaments, we can often gain a perspective on our own lives and begin to believe and then practice the idea that no one's to blame. I guarantee that once you begin to put this simple concept into practice, a healthier, happier, more relaxed, less angry, more functional you will result.

PART I
FIRST FAMILY

INTRODUCTION
FIRST FAMILY

No matter how old we are, how sophisticated we've become, how far we've traveled, it all gets back to basics: Mom and Dad. Some of us are exceptionally lucky and get assigned great parents, some have lousy parents. For most of us our luck falls somewhere in between, as do our parents. Parenthood is one of those jobs for which nobody feels adequately trained. Few of us believe that our parents did right by us, although most probably they did the best job they could at the time. On the other hand, if we don't think they're the world's best parents, maybe we're not their nominees for the world's best kids either. The problem is that we're all stuck with one another, and for better or worse it's a crucial relationship. We can deny, pretend and finesse lots of things in this life, but none of us was hatched. As adults it's too late to put ourselves up for adoption, so we all might as well face up to the task of at least minimizing the wear and tear on our nerves, heartstrings, pocketbooks, stomach linings and telephone bills by coming to terms with the parents we've got.

It's a good idea to make peace with parents as soon as possible after your adolescence, as they often have an annoying habit of dying just before we mean to tell them how much we love them. This error in timing leaves them without comfort, and we end up carrying an enormous load of guilt and unresolved, undiscussed, difficult thoughts and feelings of which the primary is guilt—difficult to manage between parties, overwhelming alone. The first step in avoiding this burden is to understand that our parents have first names. Relating to a parent as a human being rather than as a function is one of the first major goals of adulthood.

My mother and I have worked out a terrific relationship due mostly to her. In a phone conversation several years ago she said I treated her with sublime indifference. Not only did

I have no idea what she was talking about but neither did she. That isn't the way she talks. She had obviously been coached by someone, and that infuriated me. Not only was she unhappy with me but she'd been blabbing to someone else about it. I did the grown-up, responsible hey-I'm-a-trained-psychologist thing and burst into tears. I explained to her that I loved her, but no matter what I did it never seemed enough. She was always critical; so while I wanted to have a good relationship with her and she's the only mom I'll ever have, this time I get a vote too.

She started calling me a couple of times a month just to chat. (Before this, I'd called and visited her; she called when somebody died.) I told her how much fun it was just to talk and how special it made me feel, especially since private time was always hard to come by growing up—I'm the oldest of six kids. Our relationship isn't perfect, but it's a lot better than it used to be.

I'm still trying to reach my dad. To date he has remained unmoved by my attempts to relate to him as a person rather than an oracle. I keep trying, because he's not getting any younger. I'm stubborn, and I firmly believe that the easiest path to a sane adult love life is to have worked out your relationship with your father. Otherwise you keep picking the same personality type as your dad, hoping this time you can make him love you. Since you choose the same type, the guy will be just as aloof or undemonstrative or unreliable or absent or whatever your dad is or was. If you think about it, it's horrifyingly simple in its logic. Dad is the first man a daughter ever loves, and he's going to set the pattern. Since children assume that adults are perfect, they will assume that lack of loving means they are unlovable. Since it is the kids' fault, they will try to change their behavior, never questioning the adult. As we grow older, we seldom question those early reactions; and that unobtainable, elusive dad who almost loves us continues to tantalize. If we don't examine those feelings left over from childhood, we are apt blindly and unconsciously to recreate that futile and doomed search for a response. We realize Dad isn't an appropriate love/sex object, but the die has been cast, especially if the relationship is flawed and unresolved. It isn't Dad's problem; he doesn't have to work it out, but we do.

Probably the most important thing to remember in dealing with your first family is that even Norman Rockwell didn't have the kind of family he depicted on the cover of the *Saturday Evening Post*. No family sits around holding hands and smiling beatifically at one another on Thanksgiving. Milk is spilled, the phone rings, Uncle George is tipsy. Aunt Charlotte is late, Mom keeps running back and forth to the kitchen and Jimmy pinches Susie. If you're comparing your family to some idealized notion of how everybody else's family functions, you're not only kidding yourself but you're well on the way toward making yourself and your family miserable.

Families are basic, intense, changing, important and infuriating. In the pages that follow, I've chosen some problems common to many families. By reducing situations to questions and offering answers that acknowledge the commonality of the issues, I've offered you an opportunity to fill in some of the blanks and see yourself and your family in the questions and, I hope, the answers. If you can find yourself in the questions, you can apply the answers and better cope with your family, your feelings, yourself and the next family gathering. My guess is that you will see yourself, if not in every situation, then in many and will be able to adopt more appropriate ways to act. You won't be perfect, but you may be a lot happier, less stressed and calmer. How bad can that be?

QUESTIONS
FIRST FAMILY

1. My grandfather died three months ago and everybody's forgotten him but me. How can they be so insensitive?

2. My parents are too strict; they treat me like a baby. I'm at the end of my rope; I'm ready to run away from home and not even finish high school. What can I do?

3. I'm trying to save money to buy a car, so I'm living at home while I attend college. They wait up for me every night and want to know everything that goes on in my life. Aren't I entitled to any privacy at all?

4. My mother is an alcoholic. I hate going over there on Sundays because she's always drunk and Daddy pretends there's nothing wrong. Do I have to continue going over on Sundays?

5. Is it normal to get the holiday blues every year and is there any way of fighting them?

6. My mother verbally abused me as a child and now nothing in my life goes right. My husband left me for his secretary and my kids ignore me. Is it too late for therapy?

7. I often feel overwhelmed and panicky. Is this normal?

8. My dad is dying. Do you think we should tell him?

9. I hate my body. I've tried every diet known to man and I still look like the Titanic. My husband nags, my mother chides and I eat. Short of having my mouth glued shut, is there any good way to lose weight?

10. *I've never resolved my anger toward my father, and now he's dead. I've got to clean up my act; it's time. How do I find a good shrink and what should I expect once I'm there?*

11. *Daddy's ninety-seven, deaf and crotchety. He lives alone and doesn't want to go to a nursing home. He's driving me crazy. What do I do?*

12. *My sister has always tried to run my life. We're both in our seventies and she still opens my mail. Do you think I can have her committed?*

13. *Mom lived with me and I took care of her and now everybody's mad about the will. Should I divide it evenly into three parts even though she left nearly everything to me?*

My grandfather died three months ago and everybody's forgotten him but me. How can they be so insensitive?

Different people mourn in different ways. It sounds like you and your grandfather had a very special relationship. It may be that your parents saw his death as a release from his suffering or from their responsibility to take care of an aging or sickly and maybe even crotchety parent. They may also be a bit more used to losing loved ones, although nobody ever really gets used to death. Or maybe they're acting in a way that they think is grown up, or maybe they're distracted by day-to-day responsibilities. They're probably not being insensitive, but maybe they don't miss your grandfather as much as you do.

Let's start with your feelings. It might be a very good idea to write a letter to your grandfather and tell him everything that you're feeling right now: how much you miss him, how sad you are, maybe even how angry you are at the rest of the family. Don't worry about punctuation or spelling or capital letters. Just write what you're feeling. If you're not comfortable writing, get our your tape recorder and pretend that you're talking to your grandfather on the phone or even in person and tell him exactly what's on your mind and in your heart. You can do this whenever you feel like it, for a couple of days or a week or even a month or longer if you want to. It may even feel very comforting to be able to go visit his grave. This may be a good time to not only get your parents involved in the trip to the cemetery if you can't get there yourself but also to sit one or both of your parents down and tell them how you're feeling. Sometimes grownups feel they have to be strong for the kids, and it might be a real relief for them to be able to talk about some of their feelings too. Once they know you won't be frightened by their tears or their sadness, they might be able to open up a bit.

But even if your parents don't talk with you about their feelings, it's okay for you to feel sad not only because your grandfather was very special to you but because it sounds as though he may be the very first person you've ever loved who died, and that's a really tough experience for all of us. It might also be comforting to you to have something special of his by which to remember him: his favorite tie, his fishing hat, a book, a pipe, a vest, a pair of cufflinks, just something to remind you of him.

Sometimes when someone we love dies, it emphasizes a sadness we were already feeling about something else but that we had been ignoring, so you might also ask yourself if something else might be bothering you as well.

It's okay to remember your grandfather at special times or on holidays or just whenever he pops into your mind, and it's okay to talk about those feelings. There's nothing odd or weird about remembering people we love. You can think of him as having a special place in your heart or sitting on your shoulder advising you. There's a prayer that says the only way any of us ever achieve immortality is by living on in the hearts of those who love us and the thoughts of those who remember us. Your grandfather can be with you in your thoughts whenever you want him to be. Just make sure that he doesn't take up all your thoughts all of the time. Once you know it's okay to think about him and talk about him and even feel sad sometimes, you may find that your life goes on and it feels okay to be happy sometimes and still miss him.

My parents are too strict; they treat me like a baby. I'm at the end of my rope; I'm ready to run away from home and not even finish high school. What can I do?

The teenage years are tough. On the one hand, you're not a kid anymore, easily able to follow someone else's rules, but you're also not really ready to be independent yet, if only because you can't support yourself either legally or financially. Believe it or not, your parents probably love you and are as confused about how to deal with you as you are. You've changed a lot in the last five years and they really haven't. You need to catch them up. But I guarantee the least effective way to make them accept your new image is yelling, screaming "You don't understand me," and bursting into tears. You'll just succeed in convincing them that you're an overgrown version of yourself five years ago—especially if you add the magic words "You treat me like a baby; everybody else gets to stay out till three A.M.; you don't know what it's like today," or the all-time favorite: "I hate you, I wish I'd never been born."

Since you can't divorce your parents (luckily, they can't divorce you either), let's talk about some effective strategies.

Obviously you've got some specific complaints. Start by listing exactly what you want on a piece of paper. Don't say, "I want to stay out later," but, "I'd like to extend my curfew on Friday and Saturday nights from nine o'clock to ten; and if my schoolwork stays high after a month, I'd like to add another half hour; and if I'm not late even once, I'd like to extend it till eleven by Christmas." You've set out a specific request, with a trial period, small stepping-stones, conditions. It may also be appropriate to set up penalties ("If I'm more than five minutes late, I revert to a half hour earlier curfew for a month"). And if you're really smart, you'll even add some trade-offs: "If you're willing to show your trust in me by trying this for a month, I'll babysit my ugly little sister for a total of four hours on the weekend without complaint."

For your sake, before you present your ideas, write out all

the areas of your life that you feel are restrictive and put them in order of importance to you. You're much more likely to get some concessions if your parents don't feel that they're being besieged and asked to relinquish all control over you. I wouldn't pick more than three areas at a time for negotiation (that means curfew, allowance and babysitting, not life, liberty and the pursuit of the opposite sex; keep things specific and reasonable and limited), and I'd wait at least two months before springing the next set.

Then the responsibility is on your scrawny little shoulders. Can you do it? Make your own rules? Negotiate? Take responsibility? Do what you say you'll do? In the long run, we talk people into letting us assume more responsibility by showing we can handle it. Everybody has been fourteen or seventeen. It doesn't have to be unbearable. You may find that your parents are so shocked by your grown-up reasonable behavior that they give in while they're still in shock. If not, ask them for suggestions on what they think is fair, and don't have a temper tantrum if they pull rank. Hang in there.

If you really do have tough guys for parents and you've tried this approach (I mean really tried it, not just assumed they wouldn't go along), think in terms of having an older brother or sister or other relative intervene for you initially. Sometimes parents are more willing to listen to a "disinterested" third party. It may get both you and your parents out of a rut. Understand however that you're your own best spokesperson. You care the most about the negotiations because you are the one trying to gain some privilege. If nothing seems to budge, it may make some sense to think of living with a relative on a trial basis for a summer or a long vacation in return for chores or babysitting. You may find out that your parents are more reasonable than you thought. All grownups have rules.

A job outside the home that doesn't interfere with school can offer some breathing space from feeling completely dependent on a parent. And if worst comes to worst, at some point you will be able to leave, with luck, peacefully and happily; but for heaven's sake if you don't have a high school diploma you are nearly unemployable. When you're young, being unable to support yourself is a temporary situation. Leaving school without a diploma is almost certain to make economic dependency a way of life. Besides, if you stay in school and get good grades, you can go to college, which is a terrific way to run away from home without having to get out there in the big bad world before you're completely ready and able.

Try getting organized and acting grownup, and you may fool not only your parents but yourself and have a terrific time doing it.

I'm trying to save money to buy a car, so I'm living at home while I attend college. They wait up for me every night and want to know everything that goes on in my life. Aren't I entitled to any privacy at all?

Of course you are entitled to privacy, but you may have to get it the old-fashioned way—move out. I used to get asked questions about the empty nest syndrome: "My kids have all moved out, and I'm so lonely I don't know what to do." Nowadays I get lots of questions about the crowded nest syndrome, "My kids won't move out and they're driving me crazy."

Let's look at this logically for a minute rather than trying to figure out who's right and who's wrong and assign blame. You're at home for a reason, i.e., it's cheap and you're trying to save money to buy a car. Not unreasonable, but if you're living under your parents' roof, I guarantee you're going to be treated like a child whether you're fourteen or a hundred and fourteen or anything in between. They pay the rent, so they make the rules. One of the reasons lots of us move out is because we want to set our own rules. You may have to decide how much your freedom and your privacy are worth. Perhaps a bank loan to buy the car?

Even if you do move out, your parents won't have so much firsthand information, but they are always going to be interested in your life: who you're seeing, what you're doing, if you're eating enough, how much money you make. It doesn't mean they're nosy, just that they're your parents and that they love you.

Maybe you could find a job on campus that would pay your room and board so you could move out at no cost to yourself and reduce the need for a car. A college dorm isn't real private either, but the eyes don't belong to Mom and Dad, so they may not feel so prying. Life is always a set of trade-offs. Right now you're trading off cheap room and board for being treated like a kid. If you want to be treated more like an adult, you may have to act more like one, which basically means paying your own way. Everything in this life always has a price tag, and you're finding out that the price tag for free room and board is expensive in terms of personal privacy and independence. But in reality you haven't earned your own independence. You'll be a lot closer to independence when you're paying your own bills.

Think about your alternatives, how you can change your behavior. If you're absolutely unwilling to change your living arrangements, you might be able to effect a compromise with your mom and dad by agreeing to volunteer information about your life if they don't ask. In terms of waiting up, you can promise you'll be home by a certain time and will come in and kiss them when you get home. Lots of parents feel they can't sleep a wink till each chick is home safe and sound.

Obviously, I think your best long-term solution is to earn more independence by taking care of business, which may mean finding less luxurious housing with a friend, forgoing the car temporarily, borrowing money, getting a job or finding campus housing in exchange for some work. Not only will your parents drive you less crazy but, although you may feel a bit more tired, you'll feel a lot more grown up.

My mother is an alcoholic. I hate going over there on Sundays because she's always drunk and Daddy pretends there's nothing wrong. Do I have to continue to go over on Sundays?

You've touched upon the major problem of drug abuse in the United States. We have campaigns about heroin, cocaine, crack, marijuana, prescription drugs, PCP, but the major drug of abuse has been, is and will be for the foreseeable future, alcohol. More Pilgrims drowned on Saturday night in drunken stupors than were killed by Indians. The Saturday night massacres have continued on our highways. Every year we kill some 50,000 people in car accidents and conservatively half are directly attributable to alcohol. Alcohol-related deaths from cirrhosis, heart disease and other accidents further dramatize the problem. When you factor in disturbed family relationships, domestic violence, decreased productivity, lost workdays, hangovers, you can begin to personalize the statistic that one out of every six people in the United States is affected by alcoholism. None of which makes your problem any easier to bear, but it may make you feel a little less humiliated or responsible about your mom's drinking problem.

Let's deal with the problems one at a time. First, you see your mom as an alcoholic. Does she view herself as having a problem? Have you ever talked with her about the problem when she's sober? (It will do absolutely no good to try and talk with her when she's been drinking, as you've already undoubtedly discovered.) There is a tendency to keep quiet when things are going well in an alcoholic family, in the hopes that maybe this time sobriety will last forever. It never does; clinging to hope is a very human but futile and inappropriate tendency.

When your mom is sober, you or a bunch of you might try sitting her down and talking to her specifically about the changes in her behavior when she drinks and when she's sober. Emphasize how much you like her sense of humor or orderly mind or wise counsel or neatness when she's "herself" and how that changes when she drinks. I would seriously think of renting a video camera to augment your discussion with some home movies. Many of my patients and callers have told me it wasn't until they had reached rock bottom that they finally heard a loved one's pain. If you're cringing at this suggestion, you and the rest of the family may have become co-conspirators in your mom's drinking. Like your dad, you may have all decided not to rock a very leaky boat.

You are not going to change either your mom's or your dad's behavior, but you can change your behavior and start a chain reaction. You may want to get in touch with AlAnon or AlaTeen (through AlAnon), which are support groups for loved ones of alcoholics. At least you'll feel that you're not alone and you'll have confirmation about what you can and can't do about your mom's drinking. You can't stop your mom from drinking, but you can make sure that you're not making it easy for her to do something you don't want her to do.

While you're at it, you may want to get in touch with Adult Children of Alcoholics (call your local AlAnon chapter for a phone number or meeting place), another support group that explores the special problems of having grown up with a parent who is changeable and scary and embarrassing and inconsistent and remorseful and angry and depressed, and how to recognize and combat the fear of seeing that same behavior in you, their offspring.

Back to your family. You don't have to convince your mom that she's an alcoholic, just that you are concerned about her drinking and maybe she should be too. Present the evidence to her in the same way a lawyer would to a judge and jury and understand that your mom is both. You're not telling her anything she doesn't know even if it's something she may not want to hear. Be gentle, firm, persuasive and relentless. And then you're going to have to let it go. Give it your best shot once; nagging will only diminish the impact.

And speaking of impact, Sunday may be the easiest day for you to visit, but it's probably the day you're most likely to find your mom soused. Why not try to visit during the week, maybe even invite her out. She may be particularly bored and lonely on Sunday, and she and your dad may be having a rocky time of it, and so she's anchoring herself with the bottle. These aren't justifications. Your mom has a problem, but her drinking behavior is *her* problem. *Your* problem is how to deal with your mom. If you can catch her when she's sober and the two of you can have a pleasant time, you've got a much better shot of having her hear you than when you're tight-lipped and she's blasted.

Finally, you've got some clout. You may want to use it. What would happen if you said to your mom, "I'll visit you on Thursday and I'll come over Sunday. If you're not drinking, I'll stay. When you start, I'll leave. You can choose your behavior and I'll choose mine."

In this way you're not treating her like a child; you're not getting into a wrangle about what constitutes drunkenness. You're drawing a line, setting an arbitrary limit for your own comfort that both you and your mother can understand. At the same time you're reinforcing positive, sober, non-drinking behavior. However, remember not to fall into the traps of lecturing her about drinking when she's sober (you've made your one-time video presentation already) or being jollied into "Well, it's a special occasion; one drink won't hurt." You don't want to become your mother's warden. She may need some help to stop drinking. You can offer her love and company for sobriety, but the drinking behavior is hers to alter. You won't be able to do it for her.

A long answer to a poignant question, but no, you don't have to go to visit your mom on Sundays; but we don't stop loving a parent just because they break our hearts, any more than they stop loving us. Understand what you can do and can't do; give it your best shot and go find an AlAnon meeting, so you're not taking responsibility for problems that aren't yours.

Is it normal to get the holiday blues every year and is there any way of fighting them?

Holidays are the way we humans superimpose meaning on the passage of time. They give us an opportunity not only to celebrate but to project both backward and forward, to consider our history as well as our future. For that reason holidays are tricky for a lot of people.

Most holidays in the United States focus on children, and once we aren't children anymore holidays can seem less grand and wonderful and special. There is nothing like being five years old and getting everything you want for Christmas. Literally nothing. And even if you didn't get everything you wanted at five, it will seem like you did once you're thirty-five. The trick is to remember that it's much more fun to get than give, blessedness aside. Giving means you have to wonder if it's the right size or color, if you can afford it, if they'll like it. Being five and receiving means you only have to remember to say thank you somewhere along the line; and even if you don't, it will probably be forgiven, at least this once.

The expectations of Christmas always seem realized at five; it really was worth the wait, the delicious anticipation. When we grow up it seldom lives up to its billing, because it is more complicated to be an adult than a child, because gifts come with price tags, because we expect a lot as adults and because it can never be the same as when we were five, or at least as we remember it being when we were.

Therefore, the first thing is to beware of expectations. Try and be realistic about what it is reasonable to expect. Think back not twenty years but twelve months. The only Christmas that can live up to a remembered childhood fantasy is the first few months of a passionate love affair that happens to fall around the holidays. Keep your expectations small and neat and reasonable. It's also a good idea not to swallow the Norman Rockwell *Saturday Evening Post* fantasy of what everybody else is doing and feeling around holiday time.

Nobody has all family members sitting around the table cheerfully awaiting grace. Water is being spilled, thighs are being pinched, tempers are being frayed and poultry is being overcooked. Holidays are not a time to buy into the Madison Avenue keeping-up-with-the-Joneses nonsense. Other people are often having a tough time too.

Another way to avoid the holiday blues pit is to change family traditions. If you know there's no way to live up to the celebrations of the past, since not everybody can be there and even those that are around are older and wiser and more cynical, why even try. Set up some new traditions that won't be compared to the good old days. Make the holiday and its remembrance something new and special. Begin a new and less painful family celebration, one with which your children and grandchildren can compete.

It's also a terrific idea not to do too much, socially, financially, gastronomically; you don't have to be a perfectionist and get every wreath hollied, every ham glazed and each piece of silver polished. It's a time to relax and enjoy family and friends. (I've gotten in the habit of sending out spring cards after hearing myself complain one too many times about the stupid Christmas cards that I *had* to finish. Nobody knows when a spring card is late and everybody writes back; they don't get lost in the shuffle.) Eating and drinking and partying too much will also make you feel sad and depressed and tired and unhappy. Bodies need some care around this time of year as well. It's okay to taste rather than gluttonize; making every other drink water will keep things festive and happy.

Remembering somebody less fortunate sounds trite, but it really is a great way to get out of the rut of self-indulgence and feeling sorry for ourselves. It can also be the cornerstone for setting up new family traditions and loftier feelings about self as well as the holiday.

A quiet word of warning. If you intend to help out at a soup kitchen or the Salvation Army or one of the better-known facilities, begin calling them around Halloween; they obviously can't afford to depend on last-minute attacks of conscience if they are to get their work done, so think ahead.

Planning a giggle into all of this—a quiet bubble bath, a serene evening listening to classical music, a jigsaw puzzle by the fire, any way to slow things down a bit—will help. Remember, it's all supposed to be fun and meaningful. It doesn't have to be crazy and commercial unless you want it to be.

The worst that can happen is that you're going to let yourself get sucked into all the traps, but even then any day is only twenty-four hours whether it's terrible or terrific, and you can begin during any particular twenty-four hours to make sure that next year isn't the same if you truly want to change it. If it feels unhappy, don't think season, think day by day. And if you suffer year after year, you need to examine the possibility that you are pleased being miserable—that it suits your purpose to be unhappy as a way of atoning for sins against people who are no longer around, or maybe you feel you don't deserve to be happy and holidays just exaggerate your need to punish yourself. If this is the case, none of my suggestions will work. You're going to have to dig to the source of the problem, because then it's not the holiday, expectations, the memory of departed loved ones, old traditions; it's a fundamental misery in you that needs to be rooted out.

My mother verbally abused me as a child and now nothing in my life goes right. My husband left me for his secretary and my kids ignore me. Is it too late for therapy?

Some of us got terrific parents, some got lousy parents and most of our parents did the best they could given the fact that they probably weren't too crazy about their parents. It has become quite stylish to blame parents for anything that goes wrong in our adult life. The problem with that approach is that while it may offer short-term solace and somebody to blame, there is no long-term solution. What are you going to do—sue your parents, send them poison pen letters, ignore them? None of it will make your life any better in the long run. What happens to us as children is largely out of our control. What we do about it as adults is completely our responsibility.

Before we talk about what we can do, let's distinguish among the various forms of abuse. Rightly or wrongly, many parents spank their kids. I'm not crazy about the practice except in an emergency when a kid is about to light himself, the cat, his baby brother or the house on fire, run out in front of a car or something equally dangerous. Young kids between one year and about two and a half or so are largely preverbal. They're good mimics, but they speak the language better than they understand it; and trying to reason with a two-year-old is dumb. On the other hand, whacking them is hard to avoid but harder to justify. When my daughter was about two, we were out somewhere and she was excited, in fact overstimulated. I asked her what she wanted to eat and she slapped me in the face. She hadn't ever done it before or since. I, without thinking, spanked her on her Pamper and said, "We don't hit." Terrific! It's wrong for her and okay for me?

The standards for what constitutes physical abuse not only change with time but vary greatly from place to place. It is legal to hit women and children with a stick no thicker than the diameter of a man's thumb in some states, and caning was practiced routinely in schools until fairly recently. On the other hand, it is illegal to spank your child in Sweden. I would like to think that we are becoming more civilized in this country and less dependent on violence to make a point, particularly with children. However you look at it, there is a difference between yelling at someone and belting them. Physical abuse is not the same as verbal abuse, and when we use the two interchangeably we are giving tacit permission for the much more dangerous violence. I'm not condoning nasty words spoken in anger. In a perfect world none of us would ever lose our temper and say things we didn't mean. It is better to comment on a child's behavior in calm tones with reference to the behavior, not to the child's personality. But in a real world occasionally even the most loving parent hollers, "That's real dumb, nerdcake." It's not nice, but it's fairly human. But it's not the same as slugging a child.

I'm sure your mother got exasperated with you, said some things she didn't mean, just like you have said some things to your kids you wished you could call back.

It may be time to stop beating up your mom about what she did or didn't do for you and get on with your life. You're responsible for your marriage, not your mom. If you feel that your mom taught you to be docile and hide your anger and your husband got tired of the undercurrents and got involved with his secretary, it might be time for you to learn more effective ways of expressing your anger. If you can't express anger, you probably can't clearly express love or closeness or anything else, since the unexpressed anger will creep underground and taint all the other emotions.

Your kids may ignore you because you don't say what you mean. Either you're not focused or you're not honest. It sounds as though it's a good time in your life to take stock and decide where you want to go from here, what you want from your life and to stop blaming anybody, even yourself.

You may have to unlearn some destructive or inappropriate behavior. Therapy can be a good place to begin sorting through the things that you would like to change or to learn some new techniques if you know what you want to change but aren't clear how or where to start. Therapy is a waste of time and money if you're just looking for someone to agree that you've been treated badly or that your mom is a fink. If you genuinely want to change your life—not have your life changed but change it—find yourself a good therapist and get going. In preparation, write down problem areas, things that are troubling you, recurring ineffective ways of dealing with situations that are common. You may want to find an older woman as a therapist as a way of focusing on some of the issues you have with your mom.

Most of all, decide that you're going to take responsibility for your life regardless of what has already happened. I would encourage you to get started right away, especially if your mom is still alive. If you can work out a better relationship before she dies, both of you, but especially you, will be much better off. If she's not, there's still no time like today— you're feeling terrible and aware and close to the problems. Use that intensity to lessen the pain so it will at least lessen not just for today or tomorrow because you've distracted yourself, but for the long term because you've finally had the courage to work it through and take responsibility for your own life.

I often feel overwhelmed and panicky. Is this normal?

Life is a stressful situation. Without overtaxing the system we never grow or change. The problem is that we can be so stressed, so overtaxed, so stimulated that we don't grow, we freeze. We become overwhelmed. There is something to do when you're overwhelmed: Take a deep breath, take a step back and get specific. Overwhelmed means you're only reacting; and even if you happen to hit upon the perfect solution—by accident, because it is ill-considered and reactionary—it won't feel right even if it is.

Allowing yourself to be overwhelmed means you've lost. So you simply must not allow it to happen. This doesn't mean that you necessarily have to remove yourself from all of life's stresses. The only way to achieve that goal is to be dead, which seems sort of silly. But you can reduce some of the clamor at the moment that you feel it. You can reduce it metaphorically by mentally taking yourself out of the situation. I mean it. Close your eyes for a moment, take deep, slow breaths and see yourself taking a step back. Get yourself out of the situation for at least the moment. Then you've given yourself some operating room. You can get organized and tackle things in an orderly way that allows you to be back in control, at least of your behavior if not the situation. And often the situation.

Let's talk about your panic for a moment. In the midst of an anxiety attack or panic attack you are likely experiencing some of the classic symptoms: Your heart beats fast, you can't quite get your breath, you may feel light-headed and dizzy, your tummy feels rotten, you may feel that you desperately need a bathroom, your palms may feel cold and clammy, you may have trouble focusing your eyes, you may even feel that you're getting goose bumps.

This doesn't mean you're losing your mind; it means your body is responding to emotional danger as if it were physical danger. It's a lifesaving response left over from some of our heartier ancestors who didn't have time to sort out whether that saber-toothed tiger was in a good or bad mood. Our alarm system evolved so we could respond quickly without thinking, the so-called fight or flight response. To run like crazy or fight like hell you need oxygen to fuel muscles, a delivery system to get the oxygen there, a detour from other parts of the body, an efficient airway and a very quick way to get rid of excess heat generated by hardworking muscles. These requirements fit all of the symptoms you feel when you're having an anxiety attack. The clue to the whole system is breathing. Your body is going to kick into overdrive when you're dreaming about a car crash or worrying about your boss's reaction when you're stalled in traffic or missing that old lover or wondering why your kid hasn't come home from the prom yet. If you can calm your breathing, you can short-circuit all of those terrifying symptoms we were just discussing.

Until you get the hang of it, a brown paper sack will do the trick. You don't have to take my word for it. Go into the kitchen and get a brown paper lunch bag. Go sit down in front of a clock with a second hand. Make sure you're sitting down. Pant like a puppy dog for four minutes by the clock. I know that's not how you are when you're feeling panicky, but we're trying to speed up the process. All you have to do to be hyperventilating is increase your respiration once per minute over a period of a couple of hours (most people breathe between fifteen and seventeen times per minute). Subtle behavior, devastating consequence. Now, once you're feeling all of those awful symptoms, open the bag and cover your nose and mouth with it. The whole idea is to rebreathe your own air since you are hyperventilating or over-breathing, taking in too much oxygen for your body to use comfortably under normal circumstances. This isn't going to feel too comfortable for the first minute or two. You'll feel you can't get your breath, and putting something over your nose and mouth doesn't seem to make too much sense, but it really will work. Rebreathe for about four or five minutes.

Once you know you can cure the symptoms, you'll have

time to sort through the underlying cause, and then you'll really be in business. For a lot of people just carrying the brown paper bag is a comfort. Some never hyperventilate again.

Incidentally, if you've never had an anxiety attack, beware. It will feel exactly as if you're having a heart attack. There is no way in this world to distinguish between the symptoms of a heart attack and an anxiety attack, especially the first time, without an electrocardiogram (EKG), which has to be performed by a professional. *Do not assume you are having an anxiety attack. Assume you are having a heart attack.* Nobody ever dies from anxiety. The same cannot be said of heart attack. Call the paramedics; while you are waiting, get out your paper bag. Go to the hospital, have an EKG; and assuming your heart is normal, you're not overweight or on the pill and are under forty, next time try the paper sack first.

When you get a bit more experienced, you can try square breathing. Inhaling to the count of four, holding to the count of four, exhaling to the count of four, holding to the count of four. The count can be increased as you master the technique.

The point of either of these exercises is to control the symptom of your anxiety so you have the time and ability to take a step back and figure out the underlying cause and begin to deal with that.

As you begin searching for an underlying cause, try to remember the first time you ever felt an anxiety attack. It may have been as long ago as childhood or adolescence and may most often occur in response to a specific trigger or an overall state of increased stress.

In this life we cannot afford to be overwhelmed, because overwhelmed means powerless, swept along, out of control. It's your life. You're not responsible for your feelings, you are responsible for your behavior.

My dad is dying. Do you think we should tell him?

If your dad is conscious, he probably at least suspects what is going on, and it is very important that you not withhold information from him. However, there is a difference between telling and jamming information down his throat. If he has the information, he can do whatever he wants with it. He can acknowledge it or ignore it, but it is his information, because it is his life. We obviously don't choose to be born and we usually don't choose to die, but having the information at least offers us the option of planning our final acts, if we choose to. Are you tempted to withhold the information because you're afraid your dad can't handle it or because the rest of you aren't ready to face his death? Could it be that, by telling him, you'd make the reality more apparent to the rest of the family; and it's you folks who aren't ready?

I have helped a lot of people die, and most are not so much terrified of dying as they are of dying alone. Withholding information is the ultimate barrier if you think about it.

Logically and compassionately your dad gets to call the shots. It's his death and he's the one who has the least amount of time remaining. Therefore you folks need to do it his way. You won't know his way until he tells you, and he can't acknowledge his predicament until the rest of you do. You may be burdening him with your silence because he may feel that you don't know and he doesn't want to frighten you. With so little time remaining, isn't now a good time to come together and deal with one another rather than erecting silly little mirrors and facades and stories? You folks just don't have that kind of time.

I'm not sure any of us ever really has that kind of time to waste, but we kid ourselves a lot. Tell him—or have the doctor tell him in a straightforward way—the facts as you now know them, admitting that nothing is ever certain, and let *him* choose how to deal with the information.

You all have an opportunity to plan the perfect Christmas or Thanksgiving together; to make a truly memorable, happy warm time together; to help your dad and the rest of the family live until the moment for him to die. None of us is going to get out of this alive, but you can do your best to make your time together count.

And when it comes time for your dad to die, he won't feel like it's been a charade or he's letting you all down or there are things that all of you wished to say or do but you were caught unawares. The trick is to keep living to the last possible moment. Once we give someone permission to die, we're really giving them that permission to live. Courage is often contagious. By your courage in facing his death, you may make it easier for him to find not only courage but serenity, and vice versa. Tell him now. Set you and your father free.

I hate my body. I've tried every diet known to man and I still look like the Titanic. *My husband nags me, my mother chides and I eat. Short of having my mouth glued shut, is there any good way to lose weight?*

My dear, from the sound of it, you are a professional dieter, you know better than almost anybody how to lose weight. The problem isn't losing weight; the problem is keeping it off, and in order to do that you may want to get a better understanding of why you eat, what you eat, when you eat, how you eat. The first thing you have to understand is that you can't lose weight for anybody but yourself. When it's just you and that jelly doughnut, eyeball to eyeball, there is no amount of Mom or husband that is going to keep you from blinking. It's you and only you. Is it possible you are eating to assert your independence? Are you eating to put a buffer between yourself and the world? Yourself and your sexuality? What are some of the consequences of your eating? Do you get more attention? Do people keep telling you what a pretty face you have? Is your weight allowing you to not find a job or friends or clothes?

All of us move toward pleasure and away from pain. Your eating is either momentarily pleasurable so that you are trading off long-term goals for short-term pleasure, or there is some secondary gain, some reward for you in being too heavy.

If your eating problem is primarily the first issue—getting short-term pleasure while ignoring the long-term painful consequences—there are a number of techniques that can be helpful. Start by writing down everything, and I mean everything, before you put it in your mouth. The very act of writing it down will make you think about it rather than allowing it to become an unconscious act. It will force you to ask yourself whether you really want it; it will interrupt the act of eating itself; and it will help you to document when, why and how you eat. You can also use this opportunity to consider the long-term consequences of your behavior. A picture of yourself thin or heavy on the refrigerator door, a picture of a new dress, any motivation positive or negative will do at this point. You may also want to give yourself the opportunity to wait a half hour to eat whatever it is you were thinking of engulfing.

If you keep only good stuff, that means non-fattening, in the house, you won't snack on trash; and neither your husband nor your kids nor anybody else needs the empty calories of candy and junk food. Throw it all out now and you'll be saving them some lifetime lousy eating habits. Getting out of the house isn't such a bad idea. When we're bored, we're more likely to think about food. (Have you ever noticed how much people think and talk and plan their next meal on vacation? I'm convinced it's because they're bored, with nothing better to do.) If you're not in the house and you haven't taken any money, you're not going to eat.

Which gets us to area number two: Why are you overindulging? Oral gratification is the first way any of us learn to soothe ourselves when we are tiny beings, even before birth. It stands to reason that in times of stress we are going to regress to that basic form of pleasuring ourselves. Could it be that you are trying to fill an inner psychological hunger with food? It won't do any good to try and fill up your life or your soul by filling up your stomach, but then you already know that. Do you know the source of your emptiness? Until you do, you will have a difficult time filling it appropriately and food will literally fill in.

On a more pragmatic basis, we put on weight when we take in more calories than we burn and lose weight when the opposite is true, which means to lose weight you've got to take in less and burn up more. The former means better eating habits, the latter means exercise. We have learned two things in recent years about diet and exercise. A couple of Canadian researchers discovered a few years ago that rats that were starved and then fed overate. They lost all sense of what was enough as compared to their eating behavior before starving. The human interpretation of this horrifying behavior is that the body decides that it's starving and changes the balance between what we store and what we use. Our body decides it's famine time and prepares for starvation by storing more and burning less efficiently so we don't die. Bodies aren't smart enough to understand about diets, so what happens is that when you resume normal eating behavior you're going to eat more, burn less and store more. Bottom line: fat city.

On the cheerier side, exercise not only makes you feel more in control of your body and your life, it gets you away from the demon refrigerator and for about two or so hours following exercise your body is an even more efficient little engine, so you can metabolize food about 25 percent more efficiently. Bottom line: fewer calories stored. Those that do stick around will also look better.

If you think this is an argument for less dieting and more exercise, you've read me loudly and clearly. We're a nation of dieters, which doesn't mean that you can't streamline your eating habits and throw out the junk and eat fewer and smaller portions and more frequently, but then I suspect you know all there is to know about dieting. What you need to know more about is yourself and what makes you tick as well as eat. You're not going to bring your appetite under control until you figure out the whys. Using paper and pencil is a good way to start. A therapist might be a good investment. Once you're ready to do it, hypnosis, Overeaters Anonymous, a weight-loss clinic or rabbit food might all help.

You will lose weight when you take in fewer calories than you burn. You will take in fewer calories when you understand more about yourself and your eating behavior. Don't even try until you decide that this time is going to be different and you will do something different based on what you discover about yourself and your inner hunger as well as your eating behavior.

I've never resolved my anger toward my father, and now he's dead. I've got to clean up my act; it's time. How do I find a good shrink and what should I expect once I'm there?

Good analysis, good question. Your dilemma is one of the reasons we should deal with feelings—especially the negative ones—about our parents while they're still around. We're in real trouble if they die just before we get our nerve up. You're very much on the right track in deciding to get on with it so your life isn't any more encumbered than it has to be.

The reason to seek therapy rather than a good self-help book is that you can interact with a therapist and get help in a way no book can offer (even this one). In theory, what you may be able to do is confront some of your feelings about your dad and yourself with the therapist's help and guidance; and even though the eventual success of your therapy and therefore the resolution of your dilemma will be much more dependent on you than your therapist, there's no reason not to pick a good one to begin with. Which gets us to your question.

You find a good therapist the same way you find a good plumber or hairdresser or physician. You ask around your neighborhood, you call the local professional organization, you look in the phone book for someone near you, you ask somebody at the PTA. If one name keeps popping up, that's a good place to start. If not, once you've become very specific about what you think you need, you can call two or three prospective candidates and chat for ten or fifteen minutes. Most therapists are willing to chat for about that long, but you have to remember that we sell our time for a living, so don't be surprised if after ten or so minutes, he or she begins to get a bit abrupt. After a short phone interview you may want to choose the two or three that sound most likely and arrange an office visit. Expect to pay for this, but therapy is a major investment of time and money, and you may want to do a bit of comparison shopping initially before you settle on your choice.

The more focused you are on what you want to accomplish the more likely a therapist will be able to help you easily and quickly. This doesn't mean you have to have a solution to your problem, just a good idea of what it is or, barring that, a fairly complete list of the symptoms that make you think you have a problem. Your therapist is disposable and professional; all you have to do is show up on time, do some work and pay your bill. You don't have to like your therapist, nor is it necessary that he or she like you. You're there to work; friends are a different relationship. The reason you worry about your therapist liking you is that you want to admit your worst fears and behavior and have somebody accept you so you can accept yourself.

The he/she issue is also something to have at least thought about. Unless the problem is specifically a sexual problem, the sex of your therapist may not make a difference. If it does, think about it ahead of time and figure out why. You don't have to justify it, but you may as well know going in that it's an issue. If you're unclear about the problem or its ramifications, you might be better off at a large mental health clinic with a diagnostic intake worker who can help you to clarify the problem and then refer you to any one of a number of different people on staff who employ different techniques.

If you feel there may be an issue of medication or hospitalization at some point, you may want to seek out a psychiatrist from the beginning, although most clinical psychologists have access to a medical consultation either on staff or through affiliation.

The specific background or philosophy of your therapist may be of less importance to you in the long run than your faith in and compatability with your therapist. You will pay more for your practitioner's education; in general psychiatrists cost more than psychologists, who cost more than social workers. It may be a good idea to find out about your insurance coverage before you make your first phone call, and it is perfectly acceptable and smart and grown-up to talk with your potential therapist about fees. There's no sense going through the interview process only to find out that the person you like the best is beyond your economic capability. Therapy goes on for a while in most cases, and getting yourself in over your head financially isn't good mental or monetary health.

Everybody feels a little silly about admitting that he needs some help solving a problem, but adults get help. Only children think problems will go away if you ignore them. Also understand that there are no magic pills or bullets or solutions. If this problem has been hanging around for a while, it's most likely not going to clear up in ten minutes. If you're like most people, finally getting around to making the call will make you feel so much better that you may question the need for any therapy. Don't be fooled; get in there and get some work done. It's your problem; you're going to figure out how to make your life work. You therapist will guide, hold your hand and hold the mirror up to your life, but it is your life. You're the consumer and the only one who can decide whether therapy is worth it. You and your shrink will determine together how things will work; but the bottom line is that you're paying, so you get the final say-so.

You will know that therapy is really working when after about six months you can think of all sorts of perfectly good reasons not to go to therapy, especially when you're just about to get to something really important and/or you decide you have a huge crush on your therapist. Both are normal and need to be talked about with your therapist.

When I had an active practice, I had the fantasy that sooner or later somebody would knock on my door and say, "Look I've got a couple of thousand dollars and some time, and I decided I could either take a course at Harvard or learn something more about myself." It hasn't happened, and the reality is that people find a shrink not because they think it will be fun or interesting but because they feel unhappy and either don't know what the problem is or don't know what to do about it, so they're willing to tell a stranger things that they don't want anybody to know, most importantly themselves. People do it because it feels rotten not to, and it usually feels better eventually.

Good luck and courage. You're about to embark on a very stimulating, scary, important journey.

Daddy's ninety-seven, deaf and crotchety. He lives alone and doesn't want to go to a nursing home. He's driving me crazy. What do I do?

One of the most difficult parts of an aging parent's crankiness is the distressing reminder that not only have the roles reversed and it is now the child who is taking care of the parent but the parent's days are numbered. There is nothing that makes us feel more alone, vulnerable or mortal. The death of a parent is one of life's traumas, and anticipating it can be almost as frightening as the actuality. Death is specific and unique and a one-time event. Worrying about it in advance can go on for a very long time, which makes the thought not only frightening but ongoingly upsetting as well.

Let's get specific in terms of what you can do and what you can't. You can't do anything about your dad's age, but you can do something about his hearing problem. You can also make things easier by focusing on your fears and, by recognizing them, helping him manage his own. Take him to have his hearing tested and find out about some of the new technology in hearing aids. Once your dad can hear better, he might be more willing to listen and less concerned about being left out, which is what he now fears. When you take him to have his hearing evaluated, it might be wise to combine the evaluation with several other doctors' visits. Many elderly people are frightened of doctors, since they associate them with illness and infirmity. By combining visits you may be able to minimize the wear and tear on both of you. If your dad can't get out because he's not ambulatory or just plain refuses to go out, think about contacting the Visiting Nurse Association, a senior citizens' day-care center, an elderly hotline, or an elderly service outreach or home visit program in your area.

You haven't told me anything about your dad's current living situation, other than the fact that he lives alone. Are you afraid that he is going to want to move in with you? Does he live in housing for the elderly? Does he have a support system? Are there medical personnel available? Between living alone and custodial care, there are a wide variety of alternatives.

Let's first look at the possibilities for him to remain where he is for the time being with some minor changes.

In terms of a nursing home, it's a tough call. Most of us would like to remain independent as long as possible. Change, especially of the basics, is scary. Your dad knows how to get around his place. He has memories and associations; it's his turf. Maybe you could investigate having someone live with him in exchange for room and board. If your father is in good health, think about the possibility of an impoverished student who would be there nights, responsible for some meal preparation and a source of companionship and comfort for your dad and whose presence would be a reassurance for you. If a companion is impossible, there currently exists a little button called Medic Alert that senior citizens can buy and wear around their necks to alert a friend or relative or a central station to summon someone in an emergency. Or the two of you could work out a sentry system where you called him every night at a certain time.

I have helped my family go through this twice, once with a great-grandmother who broke her hip at ninety-four and once with my favorite person in the world, my gram, who is ninety-one. The family decided she needed to be placed in a home for senior citizens. I was furious. She was terrified. We plotted escape. I finally realized that we were both acting like kids, which was okay for her but not for me. I also realized that I was not there to take care of her and I therefore had to defer to those who were. I told her that I would call her every night or twice a day if she wished for the first month, and after that if she still hated it I would personally fly out and bring her back to live with me. After a teary couple of days she realized that she had her friends around, three square meals a day and most of her stuff as well as lots of attention; and I didn't have to play family pirate. And she felt she had some choice.

We've now looked at your dad's hearing and the possibility of various living arrangements. Now let's look at the really scary stuff. It's time for you to focus on your own fears about being left alone, about growing old, about losing power, about trusting your own kids. Until you've recognized and dealt with your own fears, it will be impossible for you to be sympathetic or even patient with your dad, since his fears will resonate and reinforce your own unacknowledged terror. Once you're calmer, you can help him better, not to mention taking a huge leap forward in your own serenity and maturity. He may be less cranky if he feels you're listening to him rather than ignoring him, since it's scary for both of you.

Like the women in my family I have every expectation that I will live to be a rotten little old lady, and I can only hope that my daughter will realize that I need some sense of independence, dignity, choice and security. What I'm hoping is that when she has to decide how to treat me in the waning years of my life she will remember how I treated her when I had all the power and she felt she wanted some. Once the roles have been reversed, all any of us has to fall back on is basic humanity, empathy and, perhaps most terrifyingly, experience.

We teach our children how to treat us when we're old and powerless by how we treat them when they're young and powerless.

It's tough but normal and predictable and as old as human history.

*My sister has always tried to run my life. We're both in our
seventies and she still opens my mail. Do you think I can
have her committed?*

Brothers and sisters disliking each other has been making
headlines since biblical times. Since parents are crucially important to kids, and brothers and sisters compete with one
another for parents' time and attention, it is unusual when
siblings get along. In general, the farther apart sibs are in age
the more likely they are to get along. My guess is that your
sister is just a few years older than you are and has been
telling you what to do for years. The real problem is not that
she tells you what to do but that you listen and in some way
you're still looking for her approval. It sounds like the two of
you not only are competitive but that she has also assumed
in your mind some of the importance of your mother. On the
one hand you're rivals and you have always been, but she's
taken on the added power of not only being older and wiser,
as she has always been, but also of replacing your mom. As
a result you probably flip-flop back and forth between wanting to beat her and wanting her to admire you and mother
you.

The first place to start is with the realization that both of
you probably love each other a lot. You compete, but you
probably share as well, including memories, heirlooms and
maybe even living space. You may need to have some things
of your very own, that are separate and distinct, including
friends, memories, clothes, taste, recipes and maybe even
that living space. It's important not to be totally reliant on
your sister for her approval, let alone her life-style or finances
or social activities.

If you have areas of your life that make you happy and
don't compete with hers, you can enjoy them without asking
for her approval or even interest. If she's opening your mail,
maybe it's because it was convenient for you to have her pay
your bills or read you a letter or keep up with your corre-
spondence when you were on vacation or sick or busy. It is

difficult to relinquish power and privilege and information once you've had them. You understand that the situation has changed, but perhaps she doesn't. Explain it to her patiently and carefully and tell her that you're not trying to keep secrets but it's just a particular hang-up that you've had since second grade when Ms. McGillicuddy caught you passing love letters to Jonathan Singly. If that doesn't work, try getting your mail sent to a post office box or opening her mail "by accident" until she stops opening yours.

I suspect that the two of you are getting a bit crotchety with one another maybe because as you get older your circle of friends and acquaintances is shrinking. The real problem may be that you both are a bit bored and too dependent on one another.

Get out and make some friends of your own, find some activities that you can enjoy without her, so that when the two of you are together you enjoy one another's company. Maybe even invite some neighbors in. Most of us are on better behavior around strangers. Try charming her a bit. Sounds like you do love her and she does love you even if you both occasionally forget.

If your sister's preoccupation with your mail is her only sign of deterioration, not only can you not have her committed but you probably would miss her terribly. Getting someone involuntarily committed, even for evaluation, is appropriately difficult. If you suspect that she is having emotional problems, you may want to contact your family physician or call the Visiting Nurse Association or see if there is an elderly outreach worker who could visit you. All of us get cranky if we're not feeling well, so if you think she's getting unusually cranky all of a sudden, think about having somebody take a look at her and maybe even at you. It may be that you're a little less tolerant these days.

If all else fails, have a surprise party for her for no reason. It may throw her enough off balance for a while to treat you nicely, and both of you could stop bickering about the mail.

In the meantime, it may be a comfort for you to realize that as much as the two of you get on one another's nerves, you would miss each other dreadfully.

Mom lived with me and I took care of her and now every-body's mad about the will. Should I divide it evenly into three parts even though she left nearly everything to me?

People who aren't strange about anything else in the world are often strange about money. When you combine money with Mom and guilt, you've got a very messy situation.

You haven't told me whether anybody contributed time or money to helping you take care of your mom, whether you have kids or the others do, how long you took care of her, the circumstances, how far away everyone lived, whether it was your house or hers. On the other hand, to a certain extent, none of that matters. We're not dealing with fair here, we're dealing with your mom's wishes, and clearly she intended you to have the bulk of her estate. She did what she wanted; now it's your turn to do what you want.

The money is legally yours. Whether you earned it or not is beside the point; money in a will isn't a salary, it's a gift. Your mom may have created a difficult situation, but it was nothing that you did.

Your options at this point are any that you care to exercise, from running away to a Caribbean island, to giving it all to an animal shelter, to endowing a dustpan in her name, to dividing it equally among your family members, to setting up a trust for nieces and nephews, to having a party.

It may be that you would like to invest the money and sign over the interest to the family or endow a park bench in your mom's name or a scholarship fund. Bottom line, my dear, is that it's your legacy to do with as you see fit. Make yourself happy, because it is unlikely that you will be able to make the rest of the family happy anyway.

If you plan to give some of the money up, I would do it in a lump sum fairly soon rather than doling it out over a period of time. You won't engender any friends by the latter technique.

Before you make any decisions about the money, take a bit of time and let your own feelings settle a bit. If you are hoping to offset any jealousy that your sibs feel about your relationship with your mother, you will be disappointed. As the memory of her dying fades, to be replaced by the memories of her life, your selflessness will very likely fade as well. You won't be able to defuse their rivalry by giving them money. The reality is that your mom remembered you and not them.

Your mom has already stated her preference. Keep this in mind when you're thinking about divvying up your worldly goods. You can give it away while you live or feel that you got one final word from beyond by doing what your mom did. It's not your fault and it's not your problem unless you decide to make it one. There is very likely no way for your family's wishes to be fulfilled unless they can figure out a way to bring Mom back for further negotiations. Do whatever makes you feel best. Doing nothing means that your mother's wishes are fulfilled. Doing something means that your wishes are.

FIRST FAMILY
SUMMARY

The family is the basic unit of human society. It is here that we first learn about envy, jealousy, competition, love, trust, sharing, cooperation. It is here that many of the patterns are set for the life to follow. Nowhere is the circularity of life more evident than in the family. We return to the point where we begin. We enter this world and this unit helpless, fussed over, small and dependent. We most often leave it a lifetime later larger, older, wiser but still fussed over, helpless and dependent. During the intervening years, we are supposed to emerge strong, independent, self-reliant but still attached—a tall order in human interactions and one requiring balance, adjustment, sobriety and having head and heart in harmony.

In this section we've looked at family issues from the child's point of view, the seesaw of rules and independence, trading obedience for love in the early years and then trying to forge a more balanced equation as a child struggles against strictness. In pretty much the same household setting we go from somebody whose diapers had to be changed, to adolescents who fret about privacy and privilege, decision making and choice of friends. Schoolwork changes from a gleeful source of gold stars to a symbol of repression, boredom and triviality.

As our focus shifts from inside the family unit to outside, our new perspective moves us from total dependence, complete trust, love and heartfelt infatuation with a parent who responds to our childish whimsical desires and naughty exploits with amusement and acceptance to someone who questions and eventually rebels. We begin to question whether discipline was unduly harsh, premeditated, warranted or even related to our behavior. Was I abused? Was that spanking or scolding done for my good or as a symptom of their neuroses? Was that hug affection or exploitation?

Leaving the nest is both a release and a terror. Sometimes the very contemplation of the act is enough to keep us at home, dependent, but rooted and cared for.

Sometimes the escape is so traumatic that any return is impossible for years—for even a Sunday brunch or an occasional phone call. And all of this is just the first part. Then we get to try on the parental role.

Dealing with our own feelings as a parent can be confounding when we find the parental phrases we most hated as children issuing forth from our very own mouths. We demand obedience violently and then question our own motives and shamefacedly remember questioning how a loving parent could say those things or hit that hard. As parents, we find ourselves demanding a respect that we were loath to offer our parents, whining for thoughtfulness or help around the house or consideration on Sunday morning or more caution with our hard-earned money. Kids who don't help around the house seem disrespectful and disdainful. When it was our unwillingness to help out as a child, we remember feeling that our lazy parent had children as free slave labor for the express purpose of cleaning bathrooms, picking up the living room or clearing the table.

The things we took for granted as children now feel like exploitation when our own children demand them. "What am I made of—money?" seems a phrase destined to echo generation after generation. The irritation of an overprotective parent translates into a son who never calls or a daughter-in-law who has always hated me.

And then comes the real kicker. Our parents dare to get old and childlike and needy and demanding. We then have to be in charge, becoming the very parental figure we resisted in them years before; and they horrifyingly and cunningly adopt the whiny, stubborn obtuseness that served us so well with them.

However, no matter how infuriating an aging parent can

be, it's either do business here and now or beware the over-whelming consequences. Parents, especially difficult ones, have a terrifying habit of dying just before we make our peace with them, acknowledge our love and gratitude or even need for them. If you think it's hard dealing with a lively, annoying, crotchety, demanding aging parent, wait until you try dealing with his or her absence.

What's even worse is that our memory plays an awful trick on us when we remember a lost parent with whom we have achieved no resolution. No matter how hard we try to remain balanced in our thinking, we either remember only the good stuff—making us feel doubly alone—or the bad—leaving us with a nearly unresolvable anger combined with a longing for what might have been. This is the kind of situation that keeps therapists wealthy and mankind miserable. Feelings about parents are not easily resolvable, but in the long run resolving them is a hell of a lot better solution than the alternative.

All of this is not to say that families are blameless. Families are made up of individuals, and no one in this life is without blame. That's not the point. Assigning blame requires a judge, a higher authority, objectivity, impartiality and probably even the ability to punish. None of us are impartial when it comes to our family, nor are we objective. We are left only with the ability to punish. Not fair, not right and not smart. Our responsibility is to figure out what we can do about the anger, the hurt, the resentment, the love, the longing and the imperfections—theirs and ours.

To start, it is crucial to distinguish between the common and uncommon situations that occur in families. Common is not the same as normal, nor is uncommon abnormal. Common behavior may be normal and worth reading or talking about; it's the uncommon that needs special attention. If it's common, it can be talked about with friends without embarrassment or fear of censure. It can be read about, and comfort can be sought and found in its commonness. The purpose of this section has been to set out some of the more common concerns for exactly that purpose. Just because a situation hasn't been included doesn't mean it's not common, but if it has been included, it's obviously not uncommon.

If you can look at a family problem and understand that it's just that—a family problem and not a reason to blame anybody: yourself, your parents, your brother or sister— then stop deciding who's right or wrong and find comfortable, workable solutions. If you can understand why other people behave as they do, maybe you can understand yourself and your own family more easily. It doesn't make the behavior right or acceptable, but it makes it visible, understandable and potentially alterable. You can ask yourself, "What did they do, why might they have done it, would I or do I do the same thing in the same situation, how does it affect me and what can I do about it?" Walking a mile in someone else's panty hose allows for a perspective that is often lacking when we are caught up with our own lives, problems and, most especially, families.

You may notice that the question is not "What can I do about them?" but "How can I change my own behavior, take responsibility for my own life independent of my early years?" "How can I acknowledge the problems of growing up with an alcoholic parent who was unstable, unpredictable and largely unavailable, not to mention untrustworthy and embarrassing?" "How different is this from a non-alcoholic family situation? How does it affect the way I see the world or deal with my kids, and what can I do about it?"

"How can I deal with the fact that my sister and I have always competed for a mother's attention who played us off so as to feel important?" You can't stop Dad from drinking or Mom from puppeteering, but you can cut the strings— maybe not all of them and maybe not all at once. It's okay to leave the ones to your heart intact, but many of the ones to other parts of your body, including your head, your stomach and your genitals, are useless and must be severed so you can get on with your life, your parenting, your loving, your work, your friends.

If all this sounds a little grim, there is always grandparenting to look forward to. It is parenting without the responsibilities, but it does seem to take a couple of generations to get the hang of it, as well as a certain amount of luck in terms of survival.

Families are terrific and terrible and transitory and terrifying and transitional and all the other things that define the human situation. They are also here to stay in one form or another. They are our portal of entry after the first few moments of life, and if we're lucky, only with our last breath we depart their embrace. Everything that happens in our family between these two sets of events is a microcosm of the rest of our existence: power, love, lust, play, money, rivalry, authority, competition, acquisition. It's the first and the last institution we join, and we need to understand it to allow ourselves choice in this life.

The past is unchangeable. No amount of gnashing of teeth, tearing of hair or laying of blame will alter what's already occurred. If your family is still driving you crazy, start with a specific list of the particulars. Saying "Mom's overbearing" isn't good enough. "Mother always calls up the day before a party to tell me what to wear" is a much better start. Then you know what you can do. You can take her suggestion, not answer the phone, argue with her, listen politely and wear the opposite, ask her to bug off, laugh, boycott the party, take her out for lunch and tell her she's color-blind, ask her to help you shop, throw away all your clothes except a pair of jeans and formal attire or divorce your mom. The point is, once you're specific about the problem and focus on your options, you will begin to take control of your own life and secretion of stomach acid.

Get over the idea that there is a guilty and innocent party. You may be correct, but it is irrelevant and will make you intractable, self-righteous and a pain in the neck.

If you truly want to end the blame game because nobody is perfect, the first family is as good a place to start as any. It's the place this whole thing began, so it might as well be the beginning of a new way of viewing yourself, your family and relationships both intimate and impersonal. If you can do it here, you can do it anywhere; and you can do it here. It will just take some concentration, some practice and some commitment to a different way of behaving.

Once you've made your list of problems that trouble you in your own family and gotten very specific, read back over this section beginning to end and see if some of the situations haven't already been discussed. Can you use any of the information? How might you use it to change your behavior? Even if the situations aren't identical, are there sufficient similarities for you to work with them? If not, you either need to get more specific, can't see the forest for the trees or may need a professional to help you sort things out.

This will be the basic format for the sections that follow. The specific questions are guideposts to common problems. If you can find yourself or your situation within them, you at least know you're not alone. If you don't find similarities, it may be simply because this is a limited book or it may be that you could use more guided insight. The point is not where or how the insight is acquired or even the insight itself, the point is ending the blame game so that you have some motivation to change your own behavior and get on with your life. Since the family unit is the first, it's also the most important. It's hard to make other things work until the kinks are worked out in this arena; and once they are worked out, everything else seems to run all that much better. Back to basics.

PART II
FRIENDS AND LOVERS

INTRODUCTION
FRIENDS AND LOVERS

It may be that there has never been more hostility between men and women than exists now. Women are angry at men for being exploitive, powerful and wimpy. If men act out their traditional role, women feel they are being put down, patronized and enslaved. If a man holds a door he is equally likely to be glared at as thanked. If he's successful, he's supposed to be sensitive and willing to help around the house. If he's sensitive and handy in the kitchen, he'll be considered a wimp if he's not wealthy and powerful. What women want from men has never been more confusing or impossible or in its own way exploitive. Henry Higgins wondered why women couldn't be more like men, but women these days seem to want men to be more like women *and* more like John Wayne. Henry Higgins was a misogynist, but today's woman is often a virulent misanthrope.

Men for their part feel that women are out to castrate them. They're convinced that without a snappy car and a powerful wardrobe they will be left in the dust of her wheels and self-determination. What's hers is hers and what's mine is hers is their complaint. Men, at least historically, felt that they got something in return for their willingness to take on the financial burden of a relationship with a woman; nowadays a man doubts even her willingness to bring him a cup of coffee, or iron his shirt, let alone soothe his ego.

Women shorthand their discontent by the statement "They're married, gay or bastards." The hard core suggest all three are a possibility and lesbianism is a rational, if unrealistic, alternative. Men seem too confused to have formulated a nifty slogan but act out their frustrations by moving on to the next relationship rather than the next stage of a going relationship.

The recent and highly controversial, not to mention suspect, study that suggests that there aren't enough men to go around has not eased the crunch between men and women at all. Stir in some terrifying statistics on AIDS, herpes and other little niceties that are genitally transferred, and dating isn't a pretty picture these days.

You may have noticed that all the anger, disease, frustration and publicity haven't exactly banked the fires of passion. And that's the point. A man and a woman together offer the possibilities of some of the nicer, more efficient ways of dealing with a large number of the issues of being an adult human, including a need for closeness, companionship, sex, children, affection, conversation, backrubs and a date for New Year's Eve. This section is a combination "how to" and equally important "how not to." It's important to understand that men will always be men and women will be women, but that's not necessarily bad. We have learned and can continue to learn from one another not only the nasties of stress, whining, abusing power, dependence, smoking and workaholism, but listening, acting, daring, balancing. The best way to accomplish these goals is probably—as in all things—to know who you are first and what you want and what you're willing to offer.

Be willing to take risks early on when there is relatively little to lose and a lot to gain. This is the opposite of the way most of us think about relationships. At the beginning we try very hard to please, then less and less as time goes by. What if we were our real true self at the beginning so that the other person could get a sense of who we really are before committing to any extent, and our partner did the same thing? Once the commitment existed, we could really throw ourselves into the preservation and maintenance and even strengthening of the relationship.

I know it sounds logical and reasonable, and you and I both know why it doesn't happen that way. In a word, sex. It moves us too far and too fast, so that we are committed without structure or knowledge. We're two strangers who know each other's bodies a great deal better than we know each other's minds or hearts or souls or middle names, and that is not the stuff of which long-term comfortable, sane, stable relationships are made. If we were willing to become friends before we became lovers, our love relationships might last.

A good rule of thumb for evaluating love relationships is to ask would we tolerate this same behavior from a friend. Most of us choose friends with our head and lovers with our heart or other organs.

Friendship is based on reciprocity—not necessarily equality but the idea that each has something to offer and each expects to get something in return. The whats of the equation are open to negotiation and explanation as well as change. The issue of control is usually nonexistent once we are past adolescence, and we are usually willing to give a friend some slack based on past performance. If a friend continues to be a disappointment, we either stage a confrontation, drop back a bit in terms of intensity and time spent together or drop the relationship altogether. There are very few temper tantrums between friends or recriminations or blame. We know we can't get away with it in a balanced relationship, so usually we don't even try. Most of us are honest with our friends, responsible and fairly forgiving, because we expect the same in return. Most of us are afraid to sermonize or lecture, because we know that we would be told to take ourselves a bit less seriously. Because no one person is in charge of an adult friendship, we have less fear about being dropped and more of a willingness to try. We show our best self and our worst self but mostly our true self; and if we don't, we're talking about an acquaintanceship, not a friendship. Emotional intimacy is usually based on truth and trust, especially over time. Sexual intimacy is often based on neither and can be very exciting and very painful for the lack. If lovers were friends first, some of the fear and therefore some of the excitement might be lost, but an awful lot of comfort, trust and caring might be gained.

The section on friends and lovers doesn't exclusively deal

with lovers of the opposite sex or friends of the same sex, but most of us have learned about both in those contexts, and combining the two seemed to offer the best chance to understand both. I must admit that when I started writing on friends and lovers I saw them as separate. The questions came before the Introduction and Summary, and I combined them and then tried to separate them again. It worked best in my mind as well as in the book to have the questions combined, and then to write separate summaries.

In the book, as in life, it seems most helpful to think of friends and lovers as part of a continuum. I am terrific at friendships and at best mediocre with lovers. Partially because I am inexperienced—I got married young and am hopelessly monogamous—and partially because I seem to revert to some sort of horrifying Scarlett O'Hara mode when a sexy man saunters by. I am nauseated by my own tendency to bat my eyes, ask carefully constructed questions and surrender all but the most vigorously held belief systems. I become an idiotic seventeen-year-old again.

The only antidote I have ever found for this devastating malady is to try and put the brakes on at the beginning. I have never gone to bed with *anybody* on the first date, no matter how powerful the temptation (if he didn't call me the next day, I'd hate myself and him, not necessarily in that order), and once things got going, I asked myself what I would do if this dude was a friend, not a lover. In my mind, I still have to ask myself that question by turning the lover into a female friend in my own mind to decide how to act; but when I can remember to do it, it works more often than not. I am much more my true self with my friends, and I am trying to learn to be that way with a lover. All I have to do is to overcome years of conditioning, my adolescence and my hormones; but I'm trying, and so might you. This section might help by emphasizing how important and sustaining friends can be. If a friend becomes and remains a lover, you've got the absolute best of all worlds: somebody who knows and loves and lusts after you and about whom you feel the same. Isn't that the best that relationships can offer? Worth a try, but beware the pitfalls of trying shortcuts through friendship. They don't exist, since the hallmark of friendship is to be trusting enough to be able to be our truest, not necessarily our best self. Taking risks at the beginning so we have a firm foundation is a lot easier to say than to do, but worth it in the long run.

QUESTIONS
FRIENDS AND LOVERS

1. I'm so bored I could die. People are dumb and shallow and not worth the time. How come you don't just admit that the world is a lousy place?

2. I'm really lonely. Everybody seems cold and uncaring. Why don't I have any friends?

3. Every year I make New Year's resolutions and every year they're a burden by February. Any way to avoid the New Year's Resolution Blues?

4. All my friends envy my life, but I'm miserable. Am I crazy or ungrateful or what?

5. My best friend and I hang out all the time, and now he's hanging out with a guy who drinks and does drugs and I can't get him back. Should I do drugs too?

6. My friends want me to listen to their troubles, but they get bored silly when I try and tell them mine. Is this fair?

7. My best friend only has time for me when she's not seeing someone. A new man shows up and she dumps me. Should I dump her this time before she dumps me?

8. We've been friends for twenty-five years and all of a sudden she won't speak to me and I don't know what's wrong and I miss her. What can I do?

9. We've been friends since sixth grade. I want more from him, but I'm afraid he just wants to be friends. Any suggestions?

10. *I'm recently divorced and I hate the singles scene. Where can I meet a decent man?*

11. *People are always disappointing me. My mother says I ask too much, but she's not exactly Pollyanna herself. Who's right?*

12. *Women really like bastards. I'm a nice guy and they all think I'm a wimp. Where can I find bad-guy lessons?*

13. *How can I avoid the risk of AIDS and still have a normal sex life?*

14. *I always seem to lose my identity in relationships. Am I trying too hard to please?*

15. *I always seem to find men who need me, but what's in it for me?*

16. *I really like giving in a relationship, but I feel like I'm getting taken advantage of. Do I have to change?*

17. *When my boyfriend and I disagree, I just cringe. He yells and always gets his own way. How can I get him to stop yelling?*

18. *He never calls, but he seems glad to hear from me. Should I call him?*

19. *This may not seem too important to you, but I really like this guy, and he chews with his mouth open. Should I marry him?*

20. *We've been dating for seven years and we're trying to decide whether to get married or not. What do you think?*

21. *She wants to have kids. I've had a vasectomy. Should we get married?*

22. *I know it's awfully quick, but we met three days ago and are thinking of getting married this weekend. Is there such a thing as love at first sight?*

23. *He won't give me his home phone number. Do you think he's married?*

I'm so bored I could die. People are dumb and shallow and not worth the time. How come you don't just admit that the world is a lousy place?

Nice talk, garbage-gums. Did you take your nasty pill today? Look, all of us have bad days. Sounds to me that somebody really hurt your feelings. Are you one of those people who only see the world in terms of black and white—and until recently your world looked like Disneyland? Sounds to me that you've recently had your heart broken. What's really going on with you?

With the world as full and complicated and multifaceted as it is, how could you possibly be bored? Have you shut down your feelings because you were hurt and are turned off and tuned out? If so, it is very likely that people are reading that in your behavior and responding in kind. There are lots of fascinating people wandering around; and surely, with nearly four and a half billion people breathing in and breathing out today, you could find a couple to your liking. People who aren't fascinating about any other thing on the face of the planet are alive and engaging when talking about themselves. Are you interested in other people or do you expect them only to be interested in you? Are you spending a lot of time being angry or complaining? For most people those intense feelings are hard to take, especially if they don't know you very well.

All of us move away from pain and toward pleasure. If being with you is painful, people are going to avoid you or dismiss you or deal lightly with you. Sounds like you need a shot of the cheeries. Have you hugged a puppy lately? Jumped in a puddle? Gone barefoot? Bought a posy? Popped a balloon (let's hope your own)? Smiled at a baby or a little old lady? Said thank you to a bus driver? Licked an ice cream cone (again, your own)? Sounds to me like you're feeling underappreciated. If doing something fun for yourself isn't appealing, how about a good deed to make you feel better? All of us can get wrapped up in our own misery, which feels pa ticularly awful when we have very little if anything to complain about. This is your life, not a dress rehearsal. If you don't like it, change it; but for heaven's sake, man, get on with it and stop complaining.

And just for the record, no I don't think the world is a lousy place. I think there are some wonderful and terrible things here, some people who do unimaginable things, both good and bad. I think the world just is, neither good nor bad, and it's up to each of us to figure out a way to get through the nights and the days with some dignity, some cheer and some kindness. None of us is our best self every day; and with effort we can keep our worst selves to a minimum. The trick is knowing who you are, what you want and how to get it with the least wear and tear on yourself and everybody else. I basically think that our happiness is not based on somebody else's misery, nor the opposite. I think life is lots of things, but boring isn't high on the list. If you're bored, it's because you choose to be; you're opting not to spend the time or energy on yourself to figure out how to make things fun. We all need to feel rooted, that we matter; and if you feel that you don't belong or matter or function very well, do something about it.

Our life is our own blank canvas. If our life matters only to us, we've probably become awfully isolated. If it doesn't matter to us, then who in heaven's name is it going to matter to? Don't die. Allow yourself the courage to try living, even though it does indeed mean that you might get your heart broken one more time at least, but think of the possibilities. You can borrow my crazy glue so the most you have to fear is a bruise here and there, so get on with it, you old optimist you. Off you go.

I'm really lonely. Everybody seems cold and uncaring. Why don't I have any friends?

The best way to have a friend is to be a friend. The reality of our existence is that everybody comes into this life alone and we leave it alone. If we can take any edge off of that aloneness, we're ahead of the game. Assuming that nice people have friends and unnice ones don't becomes a self-fulfilling prophecy.

If you're alone in your house all of the time, potential friends are going to have a hard time finding you. You have to get out there and begin to make not friends but acquaintances. It takes time and patience and communality and reciprocity and a bit of luck to make a friend.

The same qualities that you're looking for in a friend are the ones a friend is looking for in you. We want our friends to be warm and caring and available to us and responsive and sympathetic and just generally there for us. But it takes time to cultivate these qualities, to find out people who can be trusted and can be open. Anybody who is completely open is very likely a babbling fool. We all protect the most private and vulnerable parts of our personality, and it is often those parts that are the most crucial to an enduring friendship.

Some people are more gifted at friendship, just like some people are more gifted at tennis or playing the violin or at business or making pies. If you're not very practiced or skilled, you may have to devote more time to being open, to sharing your feelings, to being available and considerate.

Maybe there's someone you already know whom you would like to get to know better. Get in touch with them, make a date, tell them you would like to get to know them better, share a secret, invite them to your home once you get to know them, figure out an activity you can share, devote some time to pleasing them as well as getting to know them.

Make sure that you have interesting things to talk about if you want to get to know someone. Sharing intimacies before you get to know someone can scare them off or can be ill-advised until you are sure you can trust them. Be careful about gossip; you don't know where their allegiances lie. (Gossip is treacherous under any circumstances. It makes us all look petty and mean, but it's especially chancy with strangers.)

If difficulties arise, be willing to sort them out rather than ignore them or sulk. Don't expect to be with your new friend at all times. Make sure you have other things to do and other people to be with. Start something new for yourself: Take a course, learn a new skill, join a club. The happier and more interesting and self-sufficient you are, the more attractive you will be to others and the more naturally friendship will flow. Doing new things also gives you an opportunity to meet new people. But friendship never just happens. It requires time and effort and courage and a willingness to put yourself on the line.

The less needy you are, the better you will be at friendship. That's not to say that we don't all need friends; but we also need to be able to use our time alone profitably, so that when we are with someone we care about and who cares about us, we don't cling or suffocate or try to possess but can enjoy the sharing.

This week seek out two new people and just be friendly. You don't necessarily have to have lunch or plan anything, just smile and say a few words. Seek out one person you already know and make a date to do something fun together. Get started. Wear something that makes you feel good about yourself, figure out a couple of conversational topics, put on a cheery face and give it a try. As you feel more confidence, you will appear more confident, and that's at least half the battle. To have a friend, be a friend. You may even want to seek out and be a bit friendly to somebody this week who looks as if they could use a friend. See how it goes.

Every year I make New Year's resolutions and every year they're a burden by February. Any way to avoid the New Year's Resolution Blues?

There is good news and bad news about New Year's resolutions. The good news is that sometimes we really can motivate ourselves to do what is necessary to make our lives happier and healthier; the bad news is that we are usually so unrealistic and overenthusiastic that we don't come close to achieving the objective, and so year after year the resolutions are unresolved and they begin to look like character defects.

The New Year is an obvious time to do a little self-evaluation. It's a memorable time we mark so we can usually remember what we were doing not only last year at this time but for some years in the past. It's also a convenient time to beat ourselves up for all we haven't accomplished during the year that we had hoped to. We feel we've wasted a year, and with the clean slate a new year offers we can make up for lost time. You can see the whole problem in a nutshell.

Instead of piling all of those leftover nasties onto one list, we might be a lot more effective if we made a list of only three resolutions or reminders of things we'd like to accomplish—complete with a sensible time frame and a suitable reward. Instead of just beating ourselves up if we don't accomplish the goal, it's also not a bad idea to attach a specific penalty to failure to accomplish a specific goal. It could be a donation to a least favorite cause, a hated chore, an expensive bet. A suitable reward for accomplishment also makes sense.

If one of those three goals appears every year on your list, why not give some thought to why you haven't accomplished it yet. If nothing changes, nothing changes; and it won't do any good to just put the little dickens at the top of the list for the twentieth straight year. Give it and yourself a rest or figure out a different strategy, don't set yourself up to fail one more time.

Again, remember: if nothing changes, nothing changes. If

it didn't work last year and you haven't done anything different, it's not going to work this year, so rather than beat yourself up, figure out a way to do something different.

A couple of more bewares: The strength to change usually has to come from within. We can't change because someone else wants us to. If your resolutions aren't working, maybe it's because they're not yours, really and truly. Do you want to lose weight or does someone else want you to? The word "should" is a terrific tip-off. "Should" means we've given up control of our own life. We don't say, "I should go get a hot fudge sundae." We say, "I should lose weight." At the moment we use the word "should" we've given up control. "I'm going to lose weight," "I want to lose weight" are statements about self. "I should" is a statement about somebody else and their expectations.

A buddy system can also be remarkably effective. Most of us can use the companionship when we're trying to change and the motivation that comes from sharing or the shame that comes from blowing it. Humiliation can be as strong a motivation as anything else.

Which brings me to the public vs. private dilemma. Do you tell everybody or keep your resolution a secret? If you've told in the past and it hasn't worked, try keeping silent this year. If in the past you've been a tomb, try blabbing or at least telling somebody. Try something new if the old hasn't worked. Don't continue to beat yourself up, since you've probably done that for years and it's obviously not working.

As long as you're going to give yourself a hard time, why not take a few moments and figure out what you've done that warrants praise, at least from yourself, during the last year. Don't you dare tell me that there's nothing. There must be something; just look a little harder, dig a little deeper. What nice things have happened, friendships renewed, projects accomplished, kindnesses given or received? A good feeling or two about yourself may help you to knuckle down to one of those big-three resolutions.

Getting back to the big three, are they specific? Are they

time-oriented? Do you have a graduated plan of attack? Are there rewards along the way? Are you being realistic? Might the order be appropriately changed?

All of us change and grow; resolutions are just the formal and outward acknowledgment that we still have a way to go before we're completely perfect. They're your resolutions and you can do them or not do them as you see fit. If you do decide to do them, it's not so bad to have a six-week checkup sometime in February to remind yourself and re-evaluate your goals, your progress and yourself.

Don't try and change everything at once. You've already said only three things this year, and they don't all have to be big things. If they are going well, you can have New Fiscal Year Resolutions on July 1. Give yourself a break. You can also give yourself a break by including at least one enriching rather than abstaining resolution, one lovely addition to your life, something that will make you feel happy rather than strong and virtuous. The two in tandem may be just what the doctor ordered.

All my friends envy my life, but I'm miserable. Am I crazy or ungrateful or what?

You remind me of one of my first clients, when I was a brand spanking-new therapist. She was a smart, attractive, well-to-do suburban lady who plunked down in my office and said, "I've got a beautiful house, a terrific husband, two gorgeous kids, and I want to kill myself. Do I need Valium?"

She didn't need Valium, but she did need to have a clearer sense of herself not as somebody's wife or somebody's mother but as an individual and a clearer sense of what it was she wanted from her life.

When is the last time you asked yourself what it is that makes you happy? When is the last time you were happy? Not the last time you felt you should be happy but really were? It may have been doing something silly or inconsequential. Once we get into the shoulds, we have lost control over our life. We've given in to somebody else's idea of how to be happy, of what's important.

All of us have to get through this life however it seems appropriate, and it sounds as though you've lost your way or perhaps never really have known it. Our parents try and give us some idea of what they think will make them happy and therefore, I suppose based on some theory of genetic similarity, what will make us happy. With luck, they've at least sorted through for themselves this happiness question rather than passing it along unexamined to us.

As adults our responsibility is to figure out for ourselves what it is that is sensible, what it is we want to do, what it is that will make us happy and get on with it. It is not in another soul's contract to make us happy, nor is it in ours to make anybody else happy. Happiness is an individual responsibility that has to be undertaken personally. Other people can add to or detract from it, but the responsibility rests squarely on our own scrawny little shoulders.

You obviously either haven't asked yourself the question

or haven't asked yourself the question recently enough. And if you feel absolutely confounded by the question, you need some practice.

Don't allow yourself to say, "I don't know." If you don't know, who does, and how will you know if you're on the right track or even going in the right direction? And don't say things like "I want to be rich or healthy." While it may be true, it's much too general a statement to be the least bit helpful. If you want to be rich, how rich? (No, the answer is not "Very rich.") What do you want the money for? Are there ways to accomplish the same thing with less money? For example, if you want to travel, you need less money if you work for a travel agency or work for the airlines or join the armed services.

What are you willing to do to earn the money? How long are you willing to give yourself? What will the consequences of your plan be on other facets of your life? Are the demands in this one area compatible with the goals you've set in other areas? Get going and get specific and use paper and pencil and borrow my magic wand. When you begin to set life goals for yourself, there is no reason to be sensible, at least initially. That's what dreaming is all about.

Don't be bitter or cynical or question your own sanity. Just get a better hold on your value system. What's important to you and how are you going to go about achieving it? You may find yourself doing something completely different from what you're now doing, or you may find yourself doing the same things but appreciating the fruits of your own labor a great deal more.

Sounds like either is a better deal than what you're now doing to yourself, so get on with it. One final word of caution. They're your goals and your values. Other people may or may not support them, believe in them or be supportive of you. Be prepared for the fact that if other people want what you already have and don't value, they're not going to be real cheerful about you giving up what they'd kill for.

Don't let that deter you, but don't be surprised and don't blame them. It's irrelevant. You figure out what makes you happy and let them do the same. Life isn't a Baskin-Robbins where everybody has to like the same flavor. Just make sure you know your own preference.

My best friend and I hang out all the time, and now he's hanging out with a guy who drinks and does drugs and I can't get him back. Should I do drugs too?

There is no doubt in my mind that you are asking me the question to make me say no and give you a lecture about the evils of drugs; and then you can think, Sure, she's just one more adult who doesn't remember how it feels to be a kid and she probably did drugs anyhow when she was my age and besides she doesn't know how important friends are when you're my age. Right? Wrong.

No lecture. You know drugs are poison or you wouldn't be so upset about your friend. Making a distinction between drugs and alcohol is also foolish. They're both poison, and both affect how we see the world and how we act. That's why people do drugs in the first place. Obviously the answer isn't taking drugs, because then you'll get goofy and out of touch with reality too, and it sounds like you're a bit unhappy and maybe a bit jealous right now.

Now to your friend. Maybe this will help you understand why your parents might be concerned about your friends. For a lot of years, until we have our own personality really well defined, sometime around twenty-five or thirty, friends are very important in helping us figure out how to act—not right and wrong, just cool and not cool. You're undoubtedly right that your friend is being influenced by his friend to do drugs and that's why he's dropped you for now. You may look an awful lot like his conscience to him right now, and none of us like being reminded that we're acting like dopes, literally in this case.

However, if you want to, you can get in touch with your friend, not to deliver him a sermon or read him the riot act but to tell him how much you miss him and how distressing it is to see him when he's high. (I'm sure nobody would ever do drugs again if they were forced to watch a videotape of themselves when they were high.) The more specific you can be about what you like about him when he's straight and what you don't like about his behavior when he's high, the less likely it is that you will permanently lose a friend and the more likely that you will be effective.

You can tell him that you're still his friend and look forward to when you can spend more time together. You can also tell him that you're there for him, with no "I told you so's," should he need someone to talk to. He may feel that by experimenting with drugs he's lost all his old friends, so you may really be throwing him a lifeline.

It will take some courage on your part, because he isn't going to want to hear it. Make sure, if you decide to do it, you do it when he's sober and alone. Keep your voice calm and try not to be judgmental about him—just about his behavior. You're probably not going to tell him anything he doesn't already know, but coming from a friend may make it different.

However, maybe not. It may be that he's not ready to hear you yet and he may not ever be ready. You're not responsible for what he does, just what you do; and if you want to help him, see if you can put aside your hurt feelings, your anger and your jealousy and be as calm and well-meaning a friend as you can, even if he doesn't appreciate it. Nagging won't do any good, so give it your best shot—once—and then tell him you'll leave it up to him to get back in touch with you. Remind him that you love him and you'll be there for him and try not to be angry if he ignores you or lashes out at you for being holier than thou.

Friendship isn't always easy, but at least you'll know that you did the best you could.

My friends want me to listen to their troubles, but they get
bored silly when I try and tell them mine. Is this fair?

It's certainly not fair, but it's certainly not uncommon. The simplest basis initially for any relationship is dependency. One person gives and the other takes. It works very well until one or both people get tired. The giver gets tired when he needs something other than gratitude from the taker, and the taker feels suffocated and restless and begins to feel stronger.

I found myself in exactly the same situation shortly after I got my doctorate. I mention the timing only because it was at a time that I felt especially vulnerable as to my helping skills. I don't think I would fall into the same trap today; another trap perhaps, but not that one. I had been introduced to this lovely woman by a mutual friend, and she began calling me several times a day for advice and solace. I was flattered by the attention and the intimacy and her trust in me. This went on for months, during which time she would share her few triumphs and her many sorrows in great and graphic detail. I was thrilled to have such an exciting friend who liked me so much that she was willing to spend all of this time with me, telling me her innermost secrets. After about three months she called one morning at her usual time and conversationally asked how I was. It had been a most unfortunate morning. My husband was ornery, my baby was cranky or vice versa. I said things weren't going so well. This was a radical departure from our usual scenario of her asking me how I was, my telling her fine, then her launching into her latest tale of woe or ecstasy. My admission that things weren't fine caused a silence on her part, most likely stunned, then a quick good-bye. She never called again.

This is undoubtedly an extreme example of your problem, but you have to remember that I was a therapist as well as a needy, naive dummy. It was easy to dismiss her as an unpleasant, exploitive woman, which was probably true. On the other hand, I most certainly helped to create the situation. Her confiding in me made me feel wanted, needed and loved. I felt that she wouldn't leave me, because she needed me; and in a way I bought her friendship with her weakness and my strength. That certainly is not to say that friends don't need each other and help each other, but true friendship, unlike probably any other relationship, is based on balance, reciprocity. There is give and take, not one person giving and the other taking. The giver often feels in control (usually an illusion) and powerful because of the other person's dependency. Need is a great short-term basis for a relationship, but it simply can't hold up in the long run; it is suffocating to the one and exploitive of the other. Think of need in its purest form: the parent and child. Unless the relationship can evolve from that most primitive and basic physical need, the child will leave the parent once he can tie his own shoe or fix his own dinner. A friendship is presumably between adults who can take care of their own needs and choose to share their strengths as well as their weaknesses.

You have helped to create the inequity in your relationships. It is perhaps not too late to change them, but you will have to do it carefully and gently. You may want to remind yourself that you were the one who was profiting most from your friends' neediness. It made you feel important and wise and valuable and, most of all, needed. Shifting the balance will take some kindness, gentleness, patience and courage on your part, and the relationships may not survive the shift; but at the very least you will be in a better position to set up balanced, "fair" relationships in the future. You will have the sense to ask as well as offer and to show your weaknesses as well as your strengths. If you've set yourself up as the giver, when you do ask for something people will either feel betrayed or incredulous or they just won't hear you.

My best friend only has time for me when she's not seeing someone. A new man shows up and she dumps me. Should I dump her this time before she dumps me?

Ain't it the truth. Somehow sisterhood goes out the window with even the most liberated women when a man comes along, and I for one think it stinks. If it's any comfort, she probably treats her non-romantic men friends the same way, but it still is a wrongheaded way of viewing the world. If you think about it, for most women, lovers come and go; friends are what sustain us, and your friend has nutsy priorities.

That's not to say that a new love doesn't take time and energy, but ignoring the cake for the icing means that she's not going to have friends around when she needs them, e.g., when the current relationship ends.

I know this is a silly question, but have you ever told her about your feelings? Could it be that you're so glad to see her and spend time with her when she shakes loose from a man that you haven't explained how it makes you feel? If not, that's certainly the first step.

Unless she's a complete cad, she is probably aware, on some level, of her behavior and compensates by being especially charming and giving and considerate when she's around you so you don't just give her up as a lost cause.

She obviously doesn't possess the reliability to be considered your best friend unless all of your other friends are less reliable and even less charming. It may be this same characteristic that eventually dooms her romantic liaisons. Sooner or later even the most passionate love affair needs to broaden to include friendship if it is to survive.

I have exactly this problem with a woman who would probably be my best friend were she not a carbon copy of your friend. She wants to spend gobs of time with me as long as she's not involved, and when she is I won't hear from her for months at a time. She won't even return phone calls. I've explained to her that it feels lousy from my end; she apologizes and then does it again. What I have finally decided is that I like her well enough to see her when she gets around to me if it's convenient for me and to accept that this is who she is. I don't like it, but I'm not in charge of her life, just my own.

I never count on her, don't consider her in my first tier of friends, just someone more than an acquaintance but less than a true friend. She isn't reliable enough. I miss her, but the real loss is hers, since all of her potential friends view her in the same way. We all love her but understand she has some growing to do before she becomes a grownup. She may or may not make it.

We've been friends for twenty-five years and all of a sudden
she won't speak to me and I don't know what's wrong and I
miss her. What can I do?

It sounds like, unless your friend has had a complete personality change due to a medical condition, you hurt her
feelings. If her personality has changed, she very likely has
exhibited other symptoms including shortness of breath, a
change in her vision, weakness, hallucinations, either visual
or auditory, a change in her eating patterns or her sleep
patterns, a general lassitude, crying jags, suicidal thoughts
or other major changes in the way she acts. If none of these
are exhibited, she's probably all right, just mad or hurt. If
you have noticed any of the other symptoms, it's urgent that
you get her to see a doctor immediately. Assuming there are
no scary physical symptoms, let's look at how you can solve
the puzzle.

It very likely won't do any good to go to her and ask what's
the matter. You've hurt her feelings and she's not going to
volunteer why or she would have already done so, so you
had best comb your memory and figure out what's most
likely. Even if it's something you've said a million times before, she may have decided that she's had enough. Were you
thoughtless or inconsiderate, did you tease her or make fun
of her? Did you interrupt her or talk about her to a friend?
Did you betray a confidence or make an unkind remark about
her husband or kids? After all these years, you know each
other well and you may take each other for granted a bit.

If you can figure out what you did, take her some flowers
and apologize profusely and tell her how much you've
missed her and ask her what you can do to earn her forgive-
ness, but only if you really mean it. If you absolutely have no
idea, do the same thing and tell her that, whatever it was,
you want to know, so you can make it right and have a
chance to show her how important her friendship is to you.

If the thought of expressing these sentiments makes you
squirm, you may need to re-evaluate just how much this

friendship means to you. We all get a little sloppy, and if you feel you would be debasing yourself by being so obsequious to her, you may have had a long-standing acquaintanceship, not a real friendship. Are the two of you honest with one another? Is there give and take, or does one give and the other take? Has there been a recent change in either of your lives that makes one of you a bit more needy than usual? Have either of you taken that into consideration?

Women all long for the closeness that we had with our best friend when we were twelve years old and shared everything. It's probably the first and last time that two people are ever that close. Because we have so much in common in terms of school, family, boys, stage of development, and our personalities are so unformed, we can meld as we can never do again. Many women go through life and through friendships longing for that closeness. It can never be that way again as adults, because our lives change, our personalities become distinct and we become clearly ourselves. Don't lament the loss of that closeness, but understand that adult friendships are based on more individual characteristics. As friends, we don't ignore each other's faults and we don't love each other in spite of them but because of them.

You need to re-evaluate what your friendship is all about, what you might have done to harm it and what you can do to repair it. You can't assume that once you've made an overture she will instantly respond. You need to decide you're going to work at this until things are right between you two again and tell her that. This isn't the time to be prideful or stubborn, but dedicated and tenacious. If you can do it, you may find that you have a different but more resilient friendship than you had before.

*We've been friends since sixth grade. I want more from him,
but I'm afraid he just wants to be friends. Any suggestions?*

Hasn't there ever been somebody in your life you really
liked who obviously had a crush on you and told you about
it? You liked him but didn't feel the same way and politely
told him—but, boy, were you flattered. Right? Why should
this situation be any different? It took enormous courage
from your friend who confessed his passion to risk your
laughter or derision, but it probably made both of you feel
better unless you were a complete nincompoop about it.

Being admired by another person is one of the wonderful
things to happen in this life, bettered only when it is reciprocal. He will be flattered by your attention and affection,
especially when it is based on such a long and knowledgeable
relationship. He's not exactly a flash in the pan. He may even
feel the same about you. However, some words of caution.

While he may be flattered, you may take him by surprise,
so realize you've had a long time to think about this. Go slow.
You may want to give him some warnings by increasing the
physicalness of the relationship. A few more hugs, taking his
arm, a meaningful glance or two. You may even want to
escalate to a kiss somewhere other than his cheek, or his
cheek if kissing hasn't been a part of the relationship so far.
Don't pounce; don't jump his bones. It may scare the daylights out of both of you, and you don't want him to feel that
you've betrayed the friendship or trust the two of you have
established.

Timing is also real important. Is he seeing someone right
now? Are you? Could it be that you think of him as old
reliable when you're not seeing someone? If so, your passion
may diminish when somebody is in your life, which is unfair
to him. Is it really he that you value or just having somebody
to love? If you're very clear about your motives, you can turn
up the heat a bit, but sooner or later you're going to have to
verbalize your feelings.

Before you tell him what you have in mind, you had best

figure it out yourself. Do you want to be lovers? Do you want exclusivity? Are you thinking of this as an experiment or a lifetime commitment? Do you want to go to bed with him or just hug and kiss? You don't have to have answers covering the next twelve years, but the clearer you are about your own motives and goals the less likely you are to be unclear or ambivalent or angry and hurt by his response.

You may be pleasantly surprised to find that he has been thinking along the same lines, but if he hasn't, you don't want to nail him simply because you're feeling a little dumb and vulnerable. That's not fair to him. It's your risk and you have to take responsibility for the awkwardness. Remember he is your friend and you don't want to embarrass either of you and lose the friendship.

It is flattering to be told that you make somebody's heart beat fast, especially after you've known each other for as long as you have. Love affairs coming out of long friendships are often the very best kind, but it would seem to me that you will feel most confident if you decide your primary goal is to preserve the friendship while exploring the possibility of a romantic involvement. Be clear, simple (this is not the time or the place for coy or subtle; you need some information) and brave. You may also want to give him time to mull it over privately, and keep a smile on your face. The worst possible scenario is that he's just not interested and you'll need a bit of time to lick your wounds, but he still values you as a friend and you may need a bit of recovery time. The best case is that he feels as you do and just hadn't gotten up the courage to discuss it. Be gentle, be sweet, be brave and be a bit physical. You have nothing to lose but a bit of face, and between friends that's not much of an issue.

Don't be tempted to be cute in a note or a phone call. This needs to be done face to face.

*I'm recently divorced and I hate the singles scene. Where can
I meet a decent man?*

I'm not sure who it is who is hanging out in all those
singles bars. I've been doing research on the singles scene for
seven or eight years and I have yet to meet even one person
who says that they have met anybody there, let alone that
they hang out there.

The first thing you need to take into consideration is that
it's always tough to re-enter the dating scene. The words
themselves conjure up pictures of zits, sweaty palms and
braces. I don't know anybody who liked it the first time
around when everybody was in the same boat at seventeen,
let alone now. You're not alone.

The second thing you may want to try doing is to think
about a search for new friends and activities rather than for a
mate, a date or even an affair. If you're newly split, you may
even want to think of a vacation from the opposite sex.
You're probably insecure and needy right now, and that is
the worst possible time to look around. Even if you found
exactly the right guy, you would probably scare him away
with the intensity of your need to prove that you're still lovable and desirable. You need time to regain your sense of
equilibrium—even if you were the dumper, not the dumpee
—and to feel comfortable with yourself, with being alone,
before you can successfully negotiate a relationship with
more than the shortest-term potential. In two words of one
syllable: Chill out.

Spend some time getting your life, your body, your apartment, your checkbook, your resume, your family, your cor-
respondence in order. Once you're over the initial "Where
am I, what will become of me?" four A.M. blues, get yourself
off house arrest and figure out some new things to do, new
skills to acquire, new places to visit.

You're much better off looking for new friends in these
new places, practicing being outgoing and charming and
alone without fear. Think of the world (I know this is going

to sound trite, but it's amazingly helpful) as a collection of friends you haven't met yet. People who don't know you can't reject you. Besides, rejection is just somebody else's opinion. You don't like everybody and not everybody is going to like you. Once you like yourself, their opinion will matter a lot less. Until you like yourself, you will only be able to think in terms of possible rejection, which will definitely increase the probability.

The best place to meet a man or anybody else for that matter is where you are doing things you enjoy. Then if you do meet somebody, you've got something in common, something to talk about, a non-sexual, non-threatening way of getting to know one another. If it's something new and unfamiliar, you have an even greater opportunity to ask questions and get to know somebody that way. Besides, it's fun to acquire a new skill. It's a bit tough in the beginning. Attempting something new can make you feel like a dope, but everybody in your class is in the same boat. (I'm sympathetic. I too hate learning and love knowing. Learning makes you feel embarrassed and sweaty and self-conscious. Knowing is fun. You get to apply what you've learned.)

Even if you don't meet the person of your dreams, you're having a good time, meeting some new people, getting out of the house; and who knows, one of your classmates may have a scrumptious brother who's just dying to meet you and doesn't know it yet.

It may be worthwhile at this time to get real specific about what it is you're looking for in a mate. A quick fun shortcut to this procedure that gets you a bit beyond the tall, dark, handsome and decent category is to write a personal ad describing who you are and what you want. Look carefully at the ad and make sure that who you are and what you want are consistent and at least somewhat realistic. You may even want to place your ad. (If you do, make sure to meet any respondents during the day in a public place, and never give your home phone or address in the ad.) The clearer you are about who you are and what you want, the more likely you are to communicate those thoughts to others, consciously or unconsciously. Be honest. What's the point of fooling yourself?

In the meantime enjoy being alone and the independence that allows. Understand that loneliness is part of the human condition. It doesn't mean you're a bad person if you're alone. Life is not a dress rehearsal for Noah's Ark. We really don't have to be paired off. Develop your friendships. And make sure not all of your new activities are isolating. (Movies, all-women aerobic classes and knitting seminars may be a way to get out of the house, but you're going to find them a bit short on men with whom you can strike up conversations.)

The worst that can happen is that you'll be alone the rest of your life. But you're obviously surviving that. It may not be exactly what you've anticipated, but think of all the things you can enjoy alone without needing somebody else's permission or even presence. Stop thinking of yourself as incomplete. Enjoy yourself and you may find someone you really like. The person may even be you.

People are always disappointing me. My mother says I ask too much, but she's not exactly Pollyanna herself. Who's right?

You are. Is that what you wanted me to say? Look, the issue isn't who's right. You have to fashion a life that works for you, and your mom has the same task. It may be that you're unrealistic about how people behave, which means you're more than likely unrealistic about yourself. Are you perfect all the time? Do you expect other people to be perfect? Do you ever let other people down? You haven't been very specific with me, so I'm not sure if one category of people let you down. Is it men or friends or relatives? Are all of your disappointments in one particular area? It's not that you're wrong and they're right or vice versa. If you see a pattern, it may be worth examining, because the likelihood of your changing everybody else's behavior is remote. You can change your own.

That's not to say that you should become cynical and nasty and expect people to do their nastiest to you so you won't be disappointed. You may find that they do their nastiest because you expect it. People have a way of tuning into our expectations; it's called a self-fulfilling prophecy. You may have noticed that while you view your mom as a bit naive, people are relatively gentle with her because of her more positive outlook.

Are you asking more of other people than you're willing to offer them? If so, that's not very realistic. Are you asking things of them without being specific in your demands? If you don't ask, you don't get. Even if you ask, you may not get, but it sure does increase the probability. Unspoken demands are treacherous, the kind that take the form of "If you loved me, you'd know . . ." Are you afraid that people might not go along with your requests if you verbalize them? You may be right, but there's only one way to find out and it's not by keeping them quiet. At least if you know what's going on, you can talk about their unwillingness or their reluctance and negotiate or make better, clearer, less angry and hurt decisions.

Is there a particular area of concern you have that is not commonly shared? I'm a demon about time. I figure it's all I really have of any value. For years I've sold my time (think about what I do for a living before you jump to nasty conclusions), and becoming a broadcaster only added to my impatience about being kept waiting. For my chronically late friends I update times, and for my acquaintances I warn them that I hate to be kept waiting and may possibly disappear after twenty minutes. We can talk about it and negotiate it, they can bribe me with flowers, some get to buy dinner if they're more than fifteen minutes late; the point is that it's my concern, but it needs to be admitted, discussed and dealt with.

Some of my friends are funny about money or unsolicited advice or gossip or politics or religion. Most of us are possessed of some little quirk or idiosyncrasy or hang-up. What can be charming in oneself can be downright infuriating in someone else.

You need to get a good deal more specific about how and why and when and where and who is disappointing you. Make sure that you're not disappointing yourself. Beware of expectations.

You may also want to be sure that somehow you have not entered into a subtle competition with your mom. It's a natural thing to do but not very comfortable or profitable for either of you. You have every right to be as demanding and crotchety and persnickety as you wish. Just make sure that you don't end up able to stand only one person's company —your own.

Women really like bastards. I'm a nice guy and they all think
I'm a wimp. Where can I find bad-guy lessons?

I think the question is more where you can find stop-feel-
ing-sorry-for-yourself lessons. Listen, some women like to be
abused; some men like to be taken for granted. It's a big
world, and with luck the two can find each other and fall
blissfully in hate.

There are some masochistic women who want to be dominated, just like there are some overbearing men, but what
does that have to do with you? How would you feel if the
next woman you met said all men are little boys looking for
their mothers? You'd probably want either to pop her one,
walk away or ask to sit on her lap. "All men" is a chauvinis-
tic, unrealistic, harsh, inaccurate statement. The only thing
all men have in common is a penis. The statement "all
women" is equally offensive and equally untrue, so get the
chip off your shoulder and let's figure out how you can present a more accurate picture of yourself that will attract a
woman more likely to appreciate you for what you are, not
what you're not or what you feel you need to pretend to be.

Most of us want someone we can love and trust and like
and respect. Those qualities have nothing to do with good
guys or bad guys, wimps or bastards. It may be that you're
too passive in relationships; it may be that you're attracted to
strong, powerful women who push you around while wanting to be dominated. There's a lot of that going around these
days as both men and women search for new and different
ways of relating to one another that aren't so dependent on
the traditional me-Tarzan, you-Jane model.

You need to be who you really are in a relationship, your
best, truest self, right from the beginning rather than pretending to be a nice guy that you think she will like or some
half-cocked macho fantasy notion of how you think "real"
men act. The problem may be more that you're acting out a
role than that real women like hateful men.

What are the parts of your personality of which you are

the most proud and feel most comfortable? Most of us are aware of our deficiencies much more acutely than we are of our strengths. And because we are aware of them, in times of stress we lead with them.

If your strengths are along the lines of being a good listener or being a loyal friend or liking the gentler things in life, you are not likely to find Ms. Right in a noisy bar or a disco. You should be hanging out at church socials, libraries and concerts. Otherwise you're playing on alien turf and to your weaknesses, not your strengths. Figure out how to present yourself in the best light in a flattering setting and where the likelihood of meeting kindred souls is highest.

Admittedly there are women who want danger in a relationship, who are happiest off balance. You are going to seem wimpy to those women. There are other women who value serenity and dependability and continuity. That's not to say that you should fall into the trap of being boring or letting a relationship be totally without surprise or passion or fun. It takes some effort to keep even a serene relationship fun and fresh.

Be careful that you're not unconsciously asking your partner to supply all the fireworks. The more mature we are in a relationship, the more likely we are to look for someone who is like us, not our opposite. If she supplies the fireworks and you just ooh and aah, sooner or later she's going to go look for someone with some potential for sparks unless she's awfully young or awfully insecure; but even then, with your support, she will mature and want more sharing in the relationship, so you're in trouble eventually anyway.

I am also willing to admit to you that these days women are a little confused about what we want. On the one hand, we want to be independent and tough and liberated, but there is still a hidden unacknowledged part that wants to be taken care of and dominated. We say we want real men, but when the real man wants his shirts ironed we balk. A little inconsistent and unfair to say the least, but that's our problem, not yours. It's okay for you to gently point out the inconsistencies, but you are only responsible for your behavior. You need to be who you are as clearly and consistently as possible and let us sort our own way through the confusion of emotions and inconsistencies with your help if you wish, without it if you prefer.

Your responsibility is to be a man in whatever way seems right and reasonable and profitable and true to you. If you are, sooner or later you will find a woman who is looking for exactly that. In the meantime, you will be happy with the person who is most important in your life now and forever —yourself.

So no bad-guy lessons for you, just a clearer sense of who you are and how you can be comfortable acting with just a teensy bit of gentleness and a drop of excitement thrown in.

How can I avoid the risk of AIDS and still have a normal sex life?

AIDS (Acquired Immune Deficiency Syndrome) will very likely turn out to be the bubonic plague of the twentieth century. As you know, it is a virus that is probably anaerobic (i.e., it cannot survive exposure to the air) and is transmitted via bodily fluids, usually blood and seminal fluid. The virus seems to need immediate access to the bloodstream, which is why it seems originally to have been limited to the homosexual population, in which anal intercourse is a common practice. It can be passed from men to women, women to men and men to men. It is not clear whether it can be passed from woman to woman. We do know that it can be passed in utero as well as by blood transfusions, by drug users' hypodermic needles and by dental equipment.

There currently exists a test to detect antibodies to the virus. The test covers all but the prior three to six months, since it takes that long for antibodies to form. There is some question as to whether or not the virus may act slowly in some people, taking longer to form antibodies.

At this time about 20 percent of those having a positive antibody test do eventually contract the disease, although the estimates are that eventually the conversion rate will reach 50 percent. A positive antibody test therefore means that you are carrying the live virus and you can transmit it to others, although you may or may not come down with the disease yourself.

At this time, when there is no known cure for AIDS and only a 20 percent chance of contracting the disease, unless you are planning to become pregnant or are stupid enough not to use or require your partner to use a condom during intercourse, the value of the test to you is unclear. Which gets us to your question. What to do about safe sex?

The only truly safe sex is masturbation. Obviously you're not going to get or give anything you don't already have. For a lot of folks masturbation leaves a lot to be desired. The whole idea of casual sex has become a lot less casual. For many single men and women, sex has become a much more serious choice. It may be fun, but is it worth dying for?

The combination of AIDS and herpes has probably caused us to do what we should have done a long time ago, which is to rethink the seriousness of our sexuality. We have to rethink it now on a physical basis. We should have done that years ago on an emotional basis. For most people, both men and women, quality sex may or may not require love, but it is strengthened and deepened by a sense of trust, of sharing oneself as well as one's sexual organs; and trust requires some degree of intimacy and intimacy requires knowledge and disclosure and both require some time. The slam-bam, thank-you-ma'am approach to sex isn't all that much fun for most people and has become just too physically dangerous to consider. I would maintain that it has always been too emotionally dangerous.

For women, throwing off a millennium of conditioning is not done without peril; and for men, the ability to regard sex in one context as a commitment and a sign of loyalty and domesticity and in another context an itch to be scratched is unrealistic from the standpoint of human nature.

Safe sex means that neither your mind nor your body will bear lasting scars from the encounter. If you think about it for a moment, there is no such thing. Caring about somebody means you can get your heart if not your arm broken. The risk was always there. The only way to be completely safe is to be alone, which gets us back to masturbation. The question should be How can I be reasonable in terms of the risks I'm willing to take with my mind and my body in a sexual relationship?

The answer is what it has always been. Get to know somebody. Stay out of bed until you feel comfortable and happy with one another, until you can comfortably talk about going to bed with one another, until you know one another's middle names. Courting really did have its advantages. You got to establish a sense of communality, of shared experiences, of a circle of friends together. You could take the time to get to know one another before you had any sense of commitment to one another. Sex moves things along at a fast clip, unnecessarily fast sometimes. Anticipation can be part of the fun. It's also a lot less troublesome to discuss sexual practices, experiences and condoms with a friend than a stranger.

Which brings us to the question of condoms. For heaven's sake, use 'em. Women should carry them as well as men and probably always should have well before AIDS. Any man who says it's like taking a shower with a raincoat on should politely be requested to take his showers elsewhere. Condoms have to be used at all times to be effective, have to be worn correctly (at least a half-inch reservoir at the head of the penis), need to be checked periodically to make sure they're still in place and should be removed carefully. One size really does fit all.

Finding the appropriate partner is as tricky as it's always been. Looking for the partner at a place that you would enjoy going to without a partner is a good way to start. And avoiding places you don't like also makes sense. Think in terms of shared interests and values when figuring out your happy hunting grounds. This means avoiding bars if you don't drink or discos if you hate to dance.

Dating has taken on either sinister new connotations or a welcome new caution, depending on your perspective. As a psychologist I still think the heart is our most vulnerable organ, and if we are forced to become more thoughtful about our sexuality I think that is all to the good. The horror of AIDS has caused many of us to do what we should have done a long time ago—realistically evaluate the risk of casual sex without intimacy, trust, knowledge and the awful "c" word, commitment. Maybe in the face of this calamitous disease we will all grow up a little and take a bit more responsibility for our sexual behavior.

I always seem to lose my identity in relationships. Am I trying too hard to please?

I think you've put your finger on it. Most of us want to be liked; and when it comes to members of the opposite sex or even the same sex, we sometimes become resonators. We try to figure out what it is someone wants from us and to deliver that to them. It undoubtedly stems from our childhood, when being able to please a grownup was often a matter of survival. We figured out the rules, followed them and were rewarded with gold stars, warm cookies or, most importantly, love.

As we get a little older, we realize that it's not all that hard to figure out what people want from us and even to deliver it in the early stages, but sooner or later we discover what you have so painfully stumbled across. If all we can do is please someone else, we stop being ourselves. We all deserve to be loved for who we really are—not who we pretend to be but who we really are. The trick is that first we have to figure out who that is. During childhood we please other folks; during adolescence we make sure to annoy any adult we can find while trying desperately to please our peers; and then comes adulthood and we're supposed to do our own thing and be our own person. Not so easy, especially for women who feel that they have to please men. Men get caught up in pleasing bosses, but at least most of them feel 1) that they have some potential to someday become boss and therefore be pleased rather than having to do the pleasing, and 2) that at least they can go home and be themselves. Women are never going to be men.

Sometimes when we figure out that we're leading our lives trying to second-guess other people who may or may not know what they want, we get good and angry and decide to please only ourselves. This is just adolescence all over again. The trick is to know who we are, what we want, and to be calm, serene and pleasant about accomplishing it; takes self-knowledge and a lot of practice but causes a lot less wrinkles and headaches not only for us but for everybody around us.

Some of us are pearls, some diamonds. It's not that one is better than the other, just different. First you have to figure out what you are, not what you wish you were, and then make sure you're not guilty of false advertising. If you pretend to be a diamond, you're only going to attract people who like diamonds, and they're not going to be thrilled when they figure out you're a pearl. You're also going to forget how to be a good pearl, and you're never going to attract pearl lovers, because you're so busy pretending to be hard and shiny and bright.

You don't have to be tough, but you have to be who you are. The way to know when you're off track is when you find yourself censoring your thoughts or your comments. This will make you feel tense all the time and feel exhausted (from trying to be someone you're not). Being yourself is not necessarily an aggressive act. At its best it should feel calm and natural, but you're out of the habit. Sometimes the easiest way to get in touch with being yourself is to ask yourself what you want from the other person. Verbalizing it is okay as well. Maybe he or she can do the same thing. You don't like everybody and everybody isn't going to like you; but once you're okay with yourself, you have the time and the basis to go out and find people who genuinely value you and not the person acting as you think they would like.

If being yourself means you don't have any friends after a while, perhaps you need to temper your behavior a teensy bit to find a middle ground. You've spent so much time trying to please, you may be overdoing it slightly. The real trap is that there will never be enough gratitude, because it's not something someone asked of you. They're being who they are and assume that you are doing the same.

Make sure you like you, and I guarantee that you will find another couple of souls hanging around who do too.

I always seem to find men who need me, but what's in it for me?

Good question. The place to start is why you attract these guys in the first place. Odds are you're strong, attractive, independent, self-sufficient and appear liberated. You are able to take care of yourself, you're cool in a crisis, calm under fire, incredibly dependable, unquestionably reliable and a comfort to your friends. You say you want an equal for a mate and are perfectly willing to shoulder at least half of the burdens, financial and otherwise, in the relationship. You seem confident and sure, stylish and poised. At least on the surface.

Everything up to the last sentence is why you attract needy men; the last sentence is your part of the bargain.

For most men a strong woman is still Mom; and women fall into only two categories: those *you* take care of and those who take care of *you*. If you're not in the first category, which you obviously are not, then you must be in the second category, at least in their minds. Hypothetically there may be men who really want a helpmate, someone to share equally, but they're going to be few and far between and most likely very young if they exist at all. Society has not brought men up to think of themselves and their women in equal terms. Women have only recently begun to think of themselves in those terms and mostly because it was getting so claustrophobic not to. Even the most liberated woman occasionally finds herself longing for a flower, a soft word, a romantic notion and a man who takes the sexual initiative and offers to pay at least more than half the time.

Men are attracted to strong women because they're one of the two types they have been taught to recognize. It means less responsibility for them, more being taken care of, a chance to indulge their boyishness. We let them hang around for two reasons.

The first is because we're a little confused ourselves about the distinction between being liberated and sharing and occasionally wanting to be taken care of, so we deny that "weaker" impulse and show 'em our clout. It gives us power and makes us feel wanted and needed, and we convince ourselves that's the same as feeling loved.

There is a second, less palatable reason, which is not very sisterly. Being strong in our society hasn't been equated very long, if at all, with being feminine; so a strong woman is caught in the dilemma of on the one hand wanting to be strong and powerful and on the other hand believing that that makes her less womanly and therefore less desirable. If her man needs her, then maybe he'll stick around and be less tempted by other women who are less strong and less able to take care of his needs; so strong women sometimes find themselves encouraging a male's dependency and then getting angry with him sooner or later for being a wimp. He gets caught in the same trap.

At the beginning he is flattered and thrilled by her ability to take charge and mother him and may then find it stifling or seductive or both. But whatever else Mom is, she's not very sexy; so as you find yourself becoming more and more powerful in the relationship, taking more and more care of him, you may find him less romantic, less interested in sex, less interested in pleasing you and more and more adolescent or even childish in his behavior. Both of you may begin seeing him as the bad little boy, and you're the strong but loving mom. Yech. It will bind him to you but not forever, since he very likely already has a mom; and most of us outgrow the need for that kind of nurturing eventually, even if we think we won't. Besides, as you pointed out, what's in it for you? The answer is of course a temporary power, a sense of being needed and wanted and very important.

But even with our children we need to teach them to walk and then walk away. Unless you want to find yourself being continually left, you might try picking men rather than letting them pick you. Show them your needy side as well as your strong side, and show it early on so they haven't already begun to perceive you as the one who will do all the giving. You will lose some of the control in the relationship, but you will gain a potential mate rather than a foster child.

That is not to say that you can't be loving and giving and occasionally nurturing, but only if it's reciprocated. It's not that all men are beasts who only want to be taken care of, or their mothers are all monsters who spoiled them and gave them an inflated picture of their own importance, it's that society is changing and you can get sucked in just as easily as somebody with a penis. Don't take the easy shortcut to a relationship. Allow yourself to be yourself and to show your strengths and your weaknesses, and he may do the same. Especially if you set it up that way from the beginning.

I really like giving in a relationship, but I feel like I'm getting taken advantage of. Do I have to change?

Of course you do. Martyrdom is a pain in the neck to live with. It's terrific that you like giving, but your giving can be overpowering and a way of controlling the other person in a kind of cotton-candy web. Sweet, sticky and treacherous. That's not to say that you have to instantly turn into a selfish, uncaring rat, but it does mean that you need to be clearer about your own motives and ways of giving. Are you giving because it makes you happy to do it or because you expect gratitude or giving back in kind? Give whatever you can with no strings attached because it makes you happy to offer it. If it's accepted, you're ahead of the game. You feel good, the other person feels good. If they don't accept it, you at least did what felt sensible and right to you. You're happy, it is their choice to accept or not, so presumably they're happy too. It doesn't get much better than that. Unless they decide to reciprocate or be grateful, but that's just gravy. Both of you were happy before that, assuming that you gave only what makes you happy to give.

If you're giving with thoughts of gratitude or reciprocity, especially if you're giving without making those assumptions explicit, you're a pain in the neck, angry and resentful all the time. A gift is a gift. If you want something in return, it's a barter arrangement or a contract. Nothing wrong with either of those, but they're sure not gifts.

I agree that it's nice to be in a give-and-take relationship, but those are not usually achieved through mind reading. If you want something, ask for it. Don't assume the other person can read your mind or that if they really loved you they'd know. If you want, ask. You may or may not get it, but you'll at least know where you stand. Discuss it and run a lot better chance of getting what you want. It also gives you the added opportunity of assessing whether it's really what you want. The only behavior you can control is your own. If you give expecting something in return, make it clear that those are your expectations and also make it clear that you will stop giving if you don't get what you want. But again, that's barter, not bestowal.

If you plan to change your behavior, to give less, don't just do it without explaining what you're doing. It will make the other person, at the very least, resentful. After all, you're the one who taught them to expect this from you: unconditional giving. You don't have to be angry or nasty, just firm and clear about the facts. This is not the time for self-justification or self-serving kudos. You're not Saint Theresa or Saint Matthew. You were just a little unclear about your own motives, and now that you've clarified them you want to share that clarity.

By all means continue to offer that which makes you happy to offer unconditionally. For that which you want and expect some response, be explicit and specific. You will know very quickly whether the new deal will work or if one-sided is all this relationship can ever be. If so, decide whether you value it enough to continue or go on to the next. But for heaven's sake, use what you've learned this time so you don't do the whole thing again, which it seems has been your pattern in the past.

When my boyfriend and I disagree, I just cringe. He yells and always gets his own way. How can I get him to stop yelling?

Before we start discussing your boyfriend, please keep firmly and uppermost in your mind that the only behavior you can control is your own. Your boyfriend may have come from a family where the only way to be heard was to holler. He may feel that it's manly to holler; he may feel that he'll get an ulcer if he keeps it all inside or that that's the way people show emotion or win arguments or let off steam. Most importantly, you've taught him that it will work in an argument with you.

When we're arguing, most of us lose sight of the point of an argument, which is not to win but to exchange information. When he yells and you cringe, no new information is actually exchanged. You shut down, he gets carried away. Nothing very constructive gets done. He views you as a wimp, you view him as a tyrant. Not good for either of you.

The first thing you have to realize is that he's not your father and you're not a little girl and his anger won't kill you. It may not be very pleasant to be yelled at, but it can't do you any lasting damage. Your cringing may. You may be doing it because you're reluctant to bring things up, to discuss problems, to air your feelings. That is poison for a relationship.

You can ask him to stop hollering, you can bribe him, fine him, walk away from him, but sooner or later the problem is going to come down to not what he is willing to do but what you're willing to do.

You have to stop cringing and start talking. If he tries to overpower you, you can ask him just to wait a moment, not to interrupt, to be patient. You may want to write down some of your points so you're organized. Arguing well and effectively is a skill like any other. Some people are just naturally better at it, and everybody can use the practice. You may want to ask him if you can go first, but even if he goes first just wait him out and then calmly present your point.

Even if he acts like Genghis Khan, you may as well practice with him; he may be a perfectly nice guy that you've taught to roll all over you. If you can deal with him, especially after you've reinforced his tendency to bully, you can deal with anybody. If you don't value your own opinion, neither will he.

If you want his help in arguing a bit more quietly, figure out an appropriate bribe that will work better than a punishment anyway. Help him understand what's in it for him if he's a little calmer in his approach.

He yells because it works. Once it doesn't work anymore, once he can't control you with the volume of his reply, the two of you have a shot at real communication. Even if he won't stop, either the two of you will have more productive screaming matches or you will move on to quieter pastures. The important change won't come from him but from you. Once he knows hollering isn't an effective way to muzzle you anymore and that you will speak up, you will have a whole new relationship, which you can then decide is valuable or not. Once you can stand up for yourself, you can choose with whom to stand.

He never calls, but he seems glad to hear from me. Should I call him?

Any relationship can work as long as both people are approximately equal in degree of commitment. If both of you want to date around or both of you choose exclusivity, the relationship is balanced and relatively stable. Trouble begins when one person is more committed than the other. In this case, it sounds like you are a good deal more committed than he is. There are two possibilities: Either he has to become more committed or you have to pull back a bit. Since the only behavior you can control is your own, you either need to convince him that it is in his best interest to change his behavior or you have to chill out a bit.

I assume that you've explained to him that you would appreciate it if he took more of an initiative, and I assume from the tone of your question that he has agreed to and maybe does for a time or two and then falls back into his old pattern. If you haven't talked to him about it, do so, for heaven's sake. He can't read your mind.

It is now time to evaluate in your own mind what you want from this relationship. If you want companionship, you've got it. He's glad to hear from you. If you want equality, you've got a problem. You do all the calling, but it may be that he balances by doing something else more. Perhaps he does the paying or planning for sex. Relationships don't have to be fifty-fifty in all areas on an everyday basis. If you're getting what you want from the relationship, you may not want to complain, but obviously you have to know what it is that you want. If you want eagerness from him, it's best to explain that to him.

If you want him to call, explain to him that that's what you want. You can ask him why he doesn't call, but that will most likely make him feel defensive and he will just say he doesn't know. You can tell him you'll call him less and only when he has called you. Why he's not taking more initiative is not clear. He may not care as much as you do, he may be seeing other people, he may be preoccupied at work, he may be spoiled, he may be passive and he may not like telephones. Why he's not calling is not as important to you right now as the fact that he's just not doing it.

You still have to decide whether you value the relationship enough as it now stands to continue it as is. Talk with him about it or change your behavior. If you think the situation is only going to make you angrier and angrier, you may as well give it a shot while you still have something left to gain. If you would prefer a more active involvement from him, talk with him about it, but don't threaten. If you would rather have it this way than nothing at all, be wonderful and sweet and don't challenge him. You may get more, but since you value what you already have, enjoy it. If the relationship in its present form isn't satisfactory to you, explain that to him, call less, get involved doing other things with other people (less is more) and see where this one goes.

You're in the worst possible situation now. You don't like his behavior. You haven't talked with him about it, yet you're accepting it. You can either change your behavior or your attitude. Things as they are now are guaranteed to make you maximally unhappy. Think about what you want, then decide.

This may not seem too important to you, but I really like this guy, and he chews with his mouth open. Should I marry him?

Unless you plan to sit side by side at all meals for the rest of your life, you do have a problem. Bad table manners are probably responsible for more arguments than anything but money, and that probably includes sex. Our table manners we learn at mother's knee and are somehow reflective of lifestyle, upbringing, breeding and general ability to get along in life. One of the historical ways to tell the difference between a prince and a pauper was to sit them down with knife and fork.

It may be that your friend's lousy manners seem to you a harbinger of more ominous things to come, and hence your sence of foreboding. It may be that you're just plain nauseated.

I would suggest that you take him quietly aside and explain your dilemma to him: that you have a particular aversion to slightly chewed food ever since you had a run-in with a garbage disposal, and while you realize that it's a bit extreme on your part, it really is troublesome. Make sure you reiterate how much you value him in other areas and how charming he is in general (be specific).

You will learn more about him by his reaction to your criticism than you know now. Expect him to be a bit hurt initially but if he lashes out at you, huffs away or worst of all doesn't make a concerted attempt to change, you've got a bigger problem than his table manners.

It will take some guts on your part to bring it up, some tact to minimize the hurt to his feelings, but if he's really a man with whom you can do business, he'll appreciate your concern and your courage and realize that it is in his best interest to hear your comments. If it's troublesome for you, it's a problem for anybody else with whom he sups. He can't go through life being oblivious to the impression he's making, and you can't go through marriage with a brown paper sack over either his head or yours.

Also be prepared to have him bring up some little nasty about your behavior that annoys him. You may even want to invite him to do so. If you can't be honest with one another in a kind and loving way, your relationship is already in trouble.

If you're just looking for an excuse to dump him, do yourself and him a favor and dump him. If you love him and are seriously contemplating a lifetime commitment, tell him to keep his mouth closed, at least while he's eating. Be gentle and do it now.

We've been dating for seven years and we're trying to decide
whether to get married or not. What do you think?

What are the two of you waiting for? Unless both of you
are junior high school sweethearts, presumably you are both
adults, have dated other people, have some sense of what
you are looking for in a mate, have discussed children,
money, politics, career strategies and whether you like sleep-
ing with the window open or closed.

If you are each other's first loves, it may be a good idea for
both of you to take a couple of months and date other people
just to make sure. If neither of you has ever been close to
another person of the opposite sex, it's hard to gauge your
attraction to each other. You haven't told me whether or not
you've been seeing each other exclusively for the past seven
years or sort of bounced back to one another between other
unsuccessful liaisons. You also haven't told me whether
you've living together or not or whether you're sexual with
one another.

There is no doubt that living together is different from
marriage. It really is a different level of commitment, to at
least one and usually both partners. If it weren't, the question of marriage would never arise. Often in these modern
days women feel that it is tacky and old-fashioned to push
for marriage, even if they really would prefer to be married.
Occasionally the man feels the tug, more often the woman,
but she refuses to admit it, because she feels the man
wouldn't marry her anyway.

It is time for both of you to be honest. Regardless of
whether either or both of you have been married before, each
of you has an idea of what marriage is, either from previous
experience, watching your parents or friends or living in the
twentieth century. Your marriage can be as similar or dissim-
ilar to all the others as the two of you decide, but it's awfully
hard to evaluate whether either or both of you want a marriage until both of you decide exactly what you mean by the
term, and I do mean exactly. This discussion should include

any and all assumptions, fantasies, fears, preconceived notions, horror stories, previous experiences, folk tales and grandmothers' admonitions that either of you can conjure up. One or the other of you may be dragging your feet because of some real or imagined misgivings. This is not the time to ignore them or run from them. For heaven's sakes, you've known and presumably loved each other for years. Hopefully you trust one another enough to talk with one another.

If you don't feel passionately about one another, you may want to rethink this whole deal. Marriage is tough, and passion can supply a motivation to work things out that can sometimes be lacking in the middle of an argument when both of you are sure you're right or the baby has just thrown up for the twelfth time in two days or the dog has chewed up a hundred-dollar bill that you left on the table. There is one and only one reason to get married: You really want to spend the rest of your life with this person, up to and including abandoning all other sexual relationships. If you're just good friends, why not just stay good friends. If you want to have a baby, think about a puppy for a while. Marriage is tough stuff and should not be entered into lightly or because it seems like time or everyone else is doing it or your mother is getting edgy. Marriage may mean a lot of different things to a lot of people; but everybody agrees divorce is the pits, sometimes necessary, but the pits nonetheless.

Each of you needs to make up separate, private, specific, comprehensive lists of all the reasons to get married and all the reasons not: what marriage means to you, what each of you is willing to give and what each of you expects to get back.

As long as you have such a long history together, you might also include how you think marriage will change what you've already got. If either or both of you are uncertain, maybe you both should wait.

However this really is the time to be painfully honest with yourself as well as each other about what you really want, not what you think he or she wants or what you think it's okay to say. If you're thinking of throwing your lot in with one another permanently, you owe it to yourself and to each other to do the tough work of knowing what your true feelings are and having the courage to communicate them.

Nobody can take away from either of you what you've already had. The question is: Is there enough to warrant the next quantum leap? Assuming that marriage will change things for the better—either the situation or the individual—is a futile and painful assumption. Given who each of you is today, can either or both of you see spending the rest of your lives together? If yes, you may want to go for it. If not, do both of yourselves a favor and call and cancel the caterer. It will save a lot of tears, recriminations and legal fees in the long run.

It's time to do some tough, precise analysis. However it works out, both of you will know that you made the decision with your heads as well as your hearts and other miscellaneous organs.

She wants to have kids. I've had a vasectomy. Should we get married?

There are a lot of issues in life that are negotiable, but having a child is not one of them. You either do or you don't. Does your fiancée know that you've had a vasectomy? Does she know why you've had a vasectomy? Do you? One of the reasons men have vasectomies is because they don't want to father any or any more children. How does this fit in with your fiancée's wishes?

Assuming that everything will change once you're married is one of those assumptions that make only lawyers happy. The two of you need to discuss why each feels the way you feel about kids and see if there is anything that can change your minds. My fear is that you feel that sooner or later you can talk her out of her wish, knowing that biology prevents your capitulation.

Obviously the two of you could decide to adopt or she could be artificially inseminated, but those solutions are still begging the issue of whether or not you really want to take on the responsibility of fatherhood. This must be resolved before you can go forward. As painful as the discussion is today, at least the two of you can agree to disagree and walk away from each other with your dignity intact and with no bloodshed, or you can agree to get a golden retriever. Several years from now it won't be that simple or that easy; lawyers have a habit of complicating life.

The two of you may decide that you will love one another until the day you both breathe your last rattly little breath, but you may not be able to put together a life because of your disagreement over this issue. Please, please have the courage to be honest with each other and face this issue now.

You can both babysit a friend's child and see if either of you changes your mind. You can visit a newborn nursery. You can investigate the remote possibility of vasectomy reversal. Just don't assume that this problem will take care of itself. As her biological clock keeps ticking, it is likely that her sense of urgency will increase not decrease, and she will not thank you for not being totally honest with her now.

Lots of people have decided that parenting isn't for them; your fiancée doesn't sound like one of them. If she feels that her life will not be complete without a child, you will never be able to fill that void. Agree to love each other always, cherish the time you've had together and both of you get on with your lives.

I know it's awfully quick, but we met three days ago and are thinking of getting married this weekend. Is there such a thing as love at first sight?

There is certainly lust with potential. We humans rely greatly on our visual sense. Nothing wrong with that, but we may need to process some other information for a long-term commitment.

We live in a country that is obsessed with the idea of efficiency. We want it and we want it now; fast food, fast times, fast cars, fast love. Perhaps the most important part of love in the long run is trust, and trust takes time. No shortcuts.

Most of the things we call love at first sight—sweaty palms, preoccupied thoughts, queasy stomach, hearing bells, cold chills—are not only not love and not only lust but lust tinged with fear, an overactive sympathetic nervous system.

I'm not trying to take the wind out of your sails, and when everything turns out fine somewhere down the road it's lovely and romantic to call this love at first sight; but if you're really thinking of marriage, what's your hurry? Wouldn't it be fun to get to know one another just a teensy bit better? Think of all the times in the past you've been absolutely sure that this was *it*, the *right* one, and it wasn't—at least six weeks down the road. I know this is different, but wouldn't it be wonderful to find out together.

The more you know about one another the less likely there will be an overwhelming number of unpleasant surprises next week or month or year. Lust can hurry past an awful lot of things that might more appropriately be dealt with at leisure. There may be such a thing as love at first sight, but there probably isn't trust at first sight or friendship at first sight or knowledge at first sight. Think of all the things you haven't told him; might there be things he hasn't told you? I'm sure you're soul mates and think this is truly a match that's meant to be, but think of all the fun you'll have discovering who each of you really is when you're not on your best behavior.

Statistically, in about one-third of all marriages that have lasted twenty-five years or more at least one of the partners felt that it was love at first sight. Not a bad batting average, except that we don't know in how many marriages that lasted less than a year the partners felt the same thing.

You're undoubtedly on the right track, and the fact that both of you have had such an overwhelming, positive, reciprocal reaction to one another means that both of you will probably try a little harder to make things work. That doesn't mean ignoring the bumpy spots but being committed to smoothing them out.

I think you should savor what you have, assume that if you're meant to be you'll be together and it will all be made known to you in the fullness of time. Love each other to pieces and realize that only the very young and those who have allowed themselves to become cynical while wanting to believe traffic in love at first sight. Enjoy and give it a bit more time. Okay. I know, I know, I sound like your mother and the Wicked Witch of the North combined. I just don't want either of you to be embittered and unhappy a couple of years down the line. Enjoy the really fun possibility of getting to know each other with no strings attached, no promises, no commitments, just wonderful feelings.

He won't give me his home phone number. Do you think he's married?

Yes.

SUMMARY
FRIENDS

In this life spouses and lovers come and go, as do kids, jobs, neighbors and even family members. What can sustain us through all the trials and tribulations, celebrations and successes are our friendships. Our friends love us not in spite of our shortcomings and blemishes but because of them. It is the one place we can go to be not who we'd like to be or wish we were or who someone else wants us to be but who we really are. We can revel in our successes and rightfully expect sympathy and succor for our pain for the simple reason that we are quite willing and able to offer the same back if and when the situation arises. What is more, we expect the situation to arise, because unlike relationships based on power or need or birth, friendships are voluntary, often the result of adult decisions, and most importantly equal and reciprocal or at least as much so as any human institution yet devised. We don't have to be perfect or even our best selves as long as we are willing to offer the same latitude.

We get into friendships with our heads as well as our hearts. Sex is seldom a complicating factor, since it precedes the friendship, follows it or destroys it. Power is left behind, as is the need to control or contrive. It takes time and energy, commitment and trust, and is worth every dribble of each, since true friendships can be sustained over time, through literally thick and thin, through marriages and death, ups and downs, sickness and health and all the other times that other relationships sometimes let us down. While there is eventually stability in a relationship that offers reciprocity, friendships are tricky to get off the ground because of that same equality. Power is much easier in the beginning but harder to sustain over time as a basis for a relationship; friendships are more difficult in the beginning but easier to sustain over time.

Why, if they're so valuable, are they so hard to come by and so often abused? Women have been taught to value intimacy, especially in same-sex relationships, and often enjoy unbelievable fun and closeness with another person when both are about twelve or thirteen. Oh, the bliss of another soul with whom you can share everything. Unfortunately that bliss is a product of the age and hard to replicate later in life. If this reality isn't understood, a woman may go through life hoping for the effortless melding of two souls that she first experienced as a twelve-year-old. It will never be that way again and may very well subvert later friendships if she expects that same ease. Adult friendships take time to cultivate; they take nurturing and care and a willingness to *be* as well as *have* a friend.

Most men are untroubled by the remembrance of a pre-teen friendship; or if one occurred, it is often viewed as having happened in their pre-male days. Once hormones hit, they see themselves as needing to assume the strong, silent male model where intimacy and feelings are something to be denied as unquestionably feminine, weak and softening. Right. Except that people need to talk about what's troubling them—not baseball scores or the stock market. One of the ways we gauge our normalcy is by confiding our deepest fears to someone who still likes us and who is willing to show their concern.

Friendships take time, and in an increasingly busy world too many people find themselves making excuses to the people who are most willing to forgive them their busyness. We make time for work and for kids because they are a responsibility, for spouses because they can cause severe problems if ignored, even for haircuts and clothes shopping and business lunches and doctor's appointments, and we commiserate with our friends about how much we miss them and how we just don't seem to have the time.

Make the time. Friends are what will sustain us. If you find yourself saying as I did, "Gee I'd really love to see you, I miss you, but I have all this company coming," listen to yourself and clean up your act. People who use your house as a hotel are not friends. Say no to acquaintances and yes to friends and you will find your life happier, easier and more serene.

If I haven't convinced you to do it for your head, maybe I can convince you to treasure and nurture friendships for your body. I was part of a group that sponsored a program in California several years ago that tried to educate the public that Friends are Good Medicine. People who have friendships live longer, happier, healthier lives. I am personally convinced that it is one of the reasons that women outlive men; women have people to talk with who really listen— each other. Leaving that burden of isolation behind can make a huge difference to our hearts as well as heads, mentally and physically.

Dealing with someone with whom we can interact without pretense or illusion or the necessity to expect perfection from ourselves or them can be downright relaxing. Our hair as well as our guard can be let down.

SUMMARY
LOVERS

Ah, bodies. That gets us to the tricky part of friendships—lovers. If the two are unrelated in your mind, go back and reread the first part of this section. Until we like ourselves, friendship is an impossibility, since friendship is based on reciprocity and disclosure, being and showing who we really are. If love relationships are less than friendship, they're doomed or at least unhealthy and should be doomed. Sex is powerful and interesting and important and treacherous. We ought not to move too quickly past the underpinnings that allow us to know someone, to show who we are and see how the two meld.

If we are confident about who we really are, then where to meet somebody, how to act, when to call, when to trust become if not foregone conclusions at least familiar issues, since we've already dealt with them within ourselves and within our friendships; and if we won't put up with a certain behavior from our friends, we certainly shouldn't put up with it in a lover for the sake of sex. That's not to say we should delude ourselves into looking for some imaginary Prince or Princess Charming, an unrealistic perfect dream of a mate who will make us feel better about our less than perfect self, but we should have realistic expectations about considerate behavior.

If it is difficult to learn to accept ourselves as we really are and friendship is the proving ground, love relationships, if we're not careful, can be the disproving ground. We have all been conditioned for so long to think of the opposite sex as the enemy, and if we have the power to exploit them and if we are powerless to try and please them, then the idea of equality gets trampled in the dust, all political rhetoric to the contrary.

If we choose friendships on the basis of similarities in our own personalities, we seem perversely to choose lovers on the basis that opposites attract and then annoy. I guess it's not too surprising when we understand that for most of us love objects are members of the opposite sex. Once we set out with that in mind, why not take it to the limit? Why not indeed? Love relationships need to be as affirming and sustaining as friendships. The reason they are not is because of the opposites, and the reason we accept that difference goes back to sex. If that is the problem with love relationships— Why won't he talk? Why does she bully me? Why won't he help out more? Why does she only take from me? Why isn't she more sexually responsive?—the solution is obviously to treat lovers more like friends or at least be friends first so we don't get seduced by the differences and then annoyed and testy down the road. Traditionally we seem to have believed that the less we know about a person, the sexier they are, and our intimate relationships pay the price. Sex with strangers is dangerous; sex with friends could be long-lasting, sustaining and even sexier, although we may need to redefine the whole notion of "sexy" for both men and women.

If we can understand how and why friendships work and don't work, we have a shot at understanding how to make love relationships work. Friendships are as individual as the parties involved and for many in our somewhat disjointed world can and do serve the function of voluntary family: people who nurture and support us. If family is where you go and they have to let you in, friendship is where you go and they want to let you in, not because we're perfect but because we're human, flawed, lovable and loving. Sometimes you don't even have to go; they might come to you. And lovers who are friends first might not only come but give you a backrub in the bargain. The only trick to any of this is that you have to know who you are, what you want, how to negotiate and be patient and flexible. A tall order but usually more than worth it. Besides, knowing ourselves is probably the business of adult life anyway. Friends and lovers are the reward.

PART III

MARRIAGE

INTRODUCTION
MARRIAGE

It's hard to tell these days whether marriage is back in style or not. The statistics are being disputed by both the pessimists and the optimists. Reality is undoubtedly somewhere in between and next to irrelevant. Who cares about the statistics? You and I care about our marriage, our parents' marriage, our next-door neighbors', our sister's and/or our married lover's.

The optimists trot off to the altar, cry at weddings and affirm that a good marriage is what life's all about. And who can argue? The idea of a soul mate with whom you can share your thoughts, your bed, your kids, your hot fudge sundae, the Sunday morning newspaper, your heartaches and promotions as well as your body and soul . . . well, how bad can that be?

The pessimists point out that they too cry at weddings, but for very different reasons. They suggest that the pro-marriage group are all divorce lawyers and point to the statistics on adultery, which are going up (or at least were before the publicity surrounding AIDS), the divorce statistics, the number of people in marriage counseling and the most chilling statement: "Name somebody you know who has a good marriage who has been married for more than five years and has kids."

The problem with marriage is a combination of outdated expectations and changing social conditions. The whole idea of modern marriage is out of touch with its origins. Marriage originally was an economic vehicle to allow for the care of dependent women and children. It evolved into a political instrument to cement alliances. When women became a form of barter and offspring kept countries from going to war with one another, it became important to structure the exchange of both women and their progeny, which meant setting up

some rules for sexual behavior. As long as tribes are no-
madic, the paternity of children isn't crucial. Once you're
talking about city-states, knowing the identity of the father
becomes much more important. Hence marriage defines who
takes care of the helpless, who has access to the women
sexually, and the bloodlines of the kids.

It is most likely that marriage as we understand it didn't
even come about until the sixth century or so. That isn't to
say that men and women didn't mate and that kids weren't
born, but that the rules in terms of at least women's assumed
fidelity, of sexuality confined to marriage and focusing exclusively between men and women only became crucial when
knowing who your daddy was became important for political
reasons. Before that the connection between sex and procreation was less important. Fidelity also had a different weight
if you remember that nearly half of all women died in child-
birth and the average life expectancy around the sixth century was less than forty years. Puberty occurred later, so the
life span of the average marriage probably varied from a few
years until the first child was born and the woman lived or
died, and fifteen to twenty years, when both parents died.
As a woman had more and more children, her probability of
surviving was still only fifty-fifty per child. The point is that
marriages lasted for a much shorter period of time, and it is
unlikely that either partner thought in terms of being happy.
So much for origins.

Today puberty starts in the early teens, life expectancy is
in the mid to upper seventies and both men and women
expect to be happy. Half of all marriages end in divorce;
children can be born without the mother having a husband
or to a man and woman who are learning the advantages and
disadvantages of taking care of themselves. Add to this the
reality that more and more children are having children (25
percent of all live births in this country occur to girls under
the age of nineteen). It is small wonder that marriage as an
institution seems to be foundering.

The bad news about all of this is that both men and women

are confused about how it's supposed to work. The good news is that there are certainly a number of options. The idea of being happy with your mate is a relatively recent and unconventional one. Marriage wasn't supposed to make people happy. It was necessary and political and important, not romantic or even necessarily voluntary. But let's face it, there was always one man and one woman, and people need to talk and be hugged and have the demons held at bay. There were probably wonderful, warm marriages in the caves and some even floating around today. It's just that today they're both more expected and harder to find, a dangerous combination.

Only two people in the world can determine what your marriage will be: you and your spouse. Other people can hint or write books or talk about their marriage or give you lots of pointers and shoulds and rules, but it is still true that nobody knows what goes on behind closed doors and your marriage is nobody's business but your own, not even your kids' and certainly not your parents' or in-laws'. It is a mythical creature that has only to serve the needs and desires and expectations of both of you. However, since one of you most likely grew up male and one grew up female, you may find that you have significantly different views, philosophies, experiences, expectations and tastes in ice cream.

When people talk about the difficulties of marriage, they're not talking about balancing the checkbook, although money is a major source, in fact *the* major source, of conflict in a marriage. They're talking about being willing to be honest enough with yourself and clear enough about what you're feeling and thinking to tell someone and trust that they won't use that information against you.

The old-fashioned rules are serving fewer women, although the female urge to marry seems to have intensified, not abated. Unfortunately the rules and conditions under which women are willing to live have altered substantially, and sometimes females fail to communicate their expectations to their besotted grooms. A recent survey suggests that the vast majority of men are happy with their marriages and a nearly equally vast majority of their wives are not. This isn't too surprising, since men's view of marriage is probably relatively unchanged: Women bear kids, clean the house, take care of the social obligations, fix the meals and provide safe sex. A woman, instead of being content with a good provider, a good father, an acceptable escort, wants a sensitive, sexy, smart, funny, caring, talkative guy who is not threatened by her independence, her salary, her friends or her newly discovered aggressive sexuality. No wonder things are a bit muddled nowadays.

Whatever else is true, marriage will survive, but not necessarily as we know it today. Men and women can complement each other, it's the neatest and most efficient and certainly most fun way to have kids and it shares the task of addressing Christmas cards. It has never been more true that the two of you get to decide just what it is you want from each other, what you're willing to offer and how and why and when the negotiations will occur. Marriage has always been what went on behind closed doors, it's just that now the room behind the closed doors is bigger and more varied, with more options.

The questons and answers in this sequence provide a cross section of the pleasures and pains of this most uniquely human of all social institutions. There is no doubt that marriage is complicated, challenging, terrifying, changing and, when it works, the best of societal institutions. Who could resist the possibility of coming home on a cold winter's night to a warm face, a warm fire, a warm bed, a warm heart and an eager ear. No matter who gets home first, who made the fire or the bed or the stew or the first move, it's what most of us are looking for, regardless of the reasons we find a tear on our cheek at the wedding.

QUESTIONS
MARRIAGE

1. *I just found out my best man has been having an affair with my bride-to-be. We're supposed to get married this Saturday. Should I call it off?*

2. *We've been married only three months and already he seems to be losing interest. Help! Any books or underwear you can suggest?*

3. *Both sets of parents live fairly close and both want us for the holidays. She thinks we should go to her family's. My mom is alone this year for the first time. I know she doesn't like my mom, but I think she's being callous and unreasonable. Don't you agree?*

4. *He's a spendthrift and I'm a hoarder, so all we do is fight about money. We love each other, but this is getting ridiculous. Would a banker help?*

5. *I've been trying to give up smoking for years. My husband smokes, so it's doubly difficult. Do you have a foolproof method?*

6. *We fight all the time. Our sex life is lousy. Will counseling help?*

7. *He won't talk to me. He's always been the uncommunicative type. His whole family is that way. It's like he has no feelings. How can I make him talk to me?*

8. *He wants me to listen to his problems, but when it comes to listening to mine he's not interested. He says all I do is bitch. How can I make him more sympathetic?*

9. We've been married for four years and I love my husband, but I'm just not in love with him. I feel restless and I'm thinking of an affair or a divorce. Which is easier?

10. I love my wife, but our sex life is really boring. I'd like her to be a bit more adventuresome. Do you think I should just have an affair?

11. I've heard of the seven-year itch and the mid-life crisis, but what is the hardest year of marriage?

12. I think he's having an affair. Should I confront him?

13. My wife is insanely jealous. It's become ridiculous. She accuses me of having an affair with the postmistress, who is ninety and bald. Is there a cure for this sickness?

14. I've just finished an affair. I feel terribly guilty. How should I tell my wife?

15. Whenever we have a fight, she withholds sex. Is there such a thing as marital rape?

16. Our marriage is the pits, but I'm afraid to be alone. Besides, he owes me. What should I do?

17. We're staying together for the sake of the kids. Is an affair legal?

18. My daughter-in-law hates me. No matter what I do, she's cold and distant. I've tried my best for my son's sake. What's wrong with her?

19. He's married, but I love him. He says he wants the kids to finish high school before he leaves her, so it won't upset the kids' routine. Is he jobbing me?

20. *I can't decide between my wife, my mistress and my girl-*
    friend. I love all three and they all need me. I don't want to
    hurt anybody. What do I do?

I just found out my best man has been having an affair with my bride-to-be. We're supposed to get married this Saturday. Should I call it off?

It is not unusual for the bride to develop cold feet, but warming them on the best man's back is more than a little tacky. I am curious as to how you found out about the affair. Did your bride tell you as a way of testing you or trying to call off the wedding? Did your best man tell you in a fit of envy? Did a well-meaning friend feel that you shouldn't be the last to know? Did an old girlfriend start a vicious rumor? While it is often difficult to determine motivation, you might do well to consider the source. Assuming for a moment that you are absolutely sure of your information, the question is What now?

You and your fiancée need to have a serious non-judgmental discussion about the readiness that each of you feels to forsake all others. If fidelity is important to either of you, now is the time to reaffirm that commitment to one another and to monogamy. If this affair has been going on a long time, I would question whether she has made the choice to cling only to you. If it is a recent one of short duration, I would question her judgment not so much in having a final fling (after all, rightly or wrongly, that is the symbolic function of the bachelor party) but in her choice of flingee. It seems a choice which, in addition to its convenience factor, is designed to wound and to be found out.

Maybe the two of you are not quite ready to commit to one another. Maybe you have overlooked the differences in your value systems. Please don't be tempted to just let it go. Marriage doesn't change basic personality structure or worldviews. Both of you are probably on better behavior now than you will be after you're married. It's embarrassing to postpone a wedding, but it's a hell of a lot cheaper than getting lawyers involved in a divorce. The two of you have to sort this out, and the pressure of a wedding only days away may tempt either or both of you to sweep not only this problem but others under the rug. Marriage is for a long time. The hours you invest now in sorting out the meaning of her behavior will be time well spent even though it will undoubtedly be painful. It may be that the two of you can go on from this with a stronger belief in one another and a firmer foundation for your marriage. It may be that this event will have so undermined your trust in her that you will be unable to resurrect a trusting basis for your relationship. It's important that both of you discover which is the case, and it may take more than the time available before the wedding. I would at least postpone the wedding to give you both time to decide whether or not you want to get married.

We've been married only three months and already he seems to be losing interest. Help! Any books or underwear you can suggest?

Oh, my dear, I'm afraid you've just run into one of the nastier differences between men and women in their view of marriage. To most men courtship is serious business where the possibility of rejection looms daily. Once they're married, they figure all that they really have to do is relax, enjoy having a spouse, make a reasonable living, be nice to the kids, occasionally bring home flowers, not forget birthdays, and everything will be relatively terrific. For a man the hard part is often over once the woman says I do.

For a woman the opposite is generally true. For most women sex is much better once you trust somebody, and for a lot of women the question of a man's commitment is always looming in the backround, hovering over the bed. Will he call? Will he respect me? Will he be faithful? Once he says I do, she figures he is capable of commitment, really does love her and she can now relax and enjoy sex. At least sexually, men and women are often moving in exactly the opposite direction during the honeymoon if not by the reception.

This certainly doesn't mean that you have to give up all hope of an active sex life with your brand-new husband, but it does mean that you can't take for granted the fact that now that you're married the sex will be great and plentiful.

The first thing the two of you have to do is to talk about it. Notice the word "talk," not nag, not lecture. Talk. He is very likely going to tell you that he's worried about work, car payments, finding a bigger house, planning for kids. He's not lying. He's got one task out of the way—you're married —now he can focus more attention on things he neglected while he was pursuing the business of courting you. He's not an insensitive bum; he's been socialized to think in terms of goals and the hunt and a job completed.

Once you've told him how much you're learning to enjoy sex with him and how much you're looking forward to seeing him and playing with him all day long, you'd best look at your own bed behavior. Do you let him take most of the initiative? Are you passive because you were inexperienced, afraid, fearful that he wouldn't respect you? He was pursuing you. He was making you feel special. It may be time to return the favor without overwhelming him. It's very sexy to feel that somebody wants you. Remember? It's something men find sexy too. This is an opportunity to use your new-found self-confidence and comfort in his love, to demonstrate how much you love him too.

It is not true that his job has ended and yours has just begun. You don't need new underwear, although if you're tempted, go ahead; it can't hurt unless he's overwhelmed by your sudden turnabout. You don't even need a book, although a little experimentation might be fun for both of you. What both of you need to do is understand what the other one is feeling and why and what each of you can offer for what you'd like to receive.

For instance, it may be that he likes making love first thing in the morning and you're a night person. How about alternating? How about you taking the initiative every other night? How about some backrubs? How about notes in his briefcase? How about meeting him at the door smelling like something other than furniture polish or a long bus ride? The two of you are just starting out. Obviously you love each other, but one of you grew up male and the other grew up female and the difference in expectations is going to come up over and over again. If you can get in the habit of talking about them now, you'll have a much better, longer, happier, not to mention sexier, marriage.

Both sets of parents live fairly close and both want us for the holidays. She thinks we should go to her family's. My mom is alone this year for the first time. I know she doesn't like my mom, but I think she's being callous and unreasonable. Don't you agree?

I suspect this problem has been going on for a long time and this is just the year it's chosen to roost. It sounds like neither of you has worked out the "where do we spend holiday and weekend" blues. With both parents living so close, you have been able to finesse it. Finesse time is over.

Let's look at the general problem first and then the specifics of this year. In our society, girls are encouraged to be and remain closer to their families than boys (remember, the bride is given away by her family, the boy is assumed to have split years ago). It is viewed as appropriate and right for girls to keep in touch and spend time at home even after they are married. While boys' families may miss them, most have been accustomed to the idea of male independence for years. This is usually acceptable until one of two events occurs: either the birth of a grandchild or the death of one of the man's parents.

The problem can be circumvented before either of these eventualities if a plan is worked out so that neither partner nor family feels deprived. Then when the pressure is really on, an equitable system will already be in place and can be modified temporarily if necessary, since everybody feels they were getting a fair shake before. With both families living close by, holidays are not nearly as complicated and can be negotiated by Christmas Eve or Christmas Day, every other Thanksgiving, a Thanksgiving/Easter trade-off, Fourth of July and Labor Day, and so on. One year you can give one family first choice and the next year the other set of in-laws. It is even okay to establish your own family traditions in terms of staying home, which is usually easier if the families live far away from both of you and far away from one another. Ironically, at the logical time to establish your own family tradition, i.e., the birth of a child, it is most likely that the demands will increase to spend holidays with your parents or your spouse's. Weekends can be apportioned in a similar way when families are in close proximity—the first Sunday of the month at your folks', the third at hers, or once every other month at each. Even though it seems like a pain in the neck, scheduling usually is a way to avert hurt feelings, nagging and fights about either set of parents.

As I said, if the two of you had started out this way, you wouldn't be in today's pickle. Even if both sets of parents were feeling a bit slighted, both sets knew they had access to both of you and they would see you at a specific time. The panic factor is greatly reduced in their minds and the claustrophobia in yours.

What's changed here is your mom's status. She's lonely and sad and needy. Your wife is afraid that she'll never see her folks again, that your mother will reassert her prior claim on your attention and affections, and not only will her family lose out but so will she. You may view it as a temporary change, but odds are that neither your mom nor your wife is looking at it that way.

Okay, so what do you do now? Sit down with your wife and work out a holiday/weekend schedule that will reassure her and her folks (and you as well) that everybody gets time together and time apart. You don't even have to stress your mom's special needs right now if your schedule shows your willingness to be fair to your wife's needs and her parents'. It's also an excellent time for your wife and your mother to forge new bonds if you stay out of the way a bit and don't push your mom on your wife or make her feel guilty for being a bit threatened by your mother's new dependency (which may also feel a bit scary to you).

We can't put our families up for adoption just because they're needy. Scheduling allows for balance, planning, reassurance, fairness and non-family time as well. The schedule doesn't have to be locked in concrete, but it will give everybody the sense that they're important, their needs will be attended to, and the two of you will also have some time together without feeling guilty. Be gentle, be specific and don't expect your wife to be on your mom's side any more than you're on her mom's side.

You will avoid an obvious and treacherous pitfall if each of you can avoid competitively bad-mouthing the other's parents while trying to work out the schedule.

Most of us aren't that crazy about our parents, but we'll defend them to the death if our spouses dare to criticize. So keep to the point of scheduling without dealing in personalities. Be fair, be consistent and be thankful there aren't more long holiday weekends.

He's a spendthrift and I'm a hoarder, so all we do is fight about money. We love each other, but this is getting ridiculous. Would a banker help?

I'm convinced that opposites attract and then irritate. One likes it hot, the other wants the window open in Nome, Alaska, in December. One is a night owl, the other loves waking up with the birds. It's possible that the two of you had very different views of money before marriage which have now been emphasized by who makes the money in your family and who spends it.

In the traditional American family of our parents' and grandparents' generation, the man made the money and the cute little wife with bubbles for brains was accused of squandering it on fripperies. The male took an affectionate and tolerant view underscored by his pride in being able to earn the wherewithal for her to spend childishly. Barf!

Money is power. In a corporation there would no more be one department that would bring in money and then have no say-so in disbursement than a department that spent money without reference to income. Somebody is in charge and oversees both departments. As long as one person brings the money in and the other spends, there will be a war. How money is spent is a policy decision, and both people need to participate in that decision.

The two of you need to sit down and figure out how much is coming in and how much is going out. If you're lucky and very unusual, you have more coming in than going out. If this is the case, both of you should have some percentage of discretionary income over which the other has no say-so. If you want to hoard, hoard; if he wants to spend, let him use the money any way he sees fit. There should also, after the bills are paid and the individual caches divided up, be some joint money that the two of you monitor for a trip or a house or a baby or retirement. You notice I suggested first you pay bills; second, each of you have some play money; and third, you have some long-term money. This can be further divided into savings, recreation, luxuries, and so forth. The reason I suggested the order I did is that, if you are like most of us, the third category may not exist after all the bills are paid. The second category, no matter how small, can mean the difference between a tolerable but tight life-style and a desolate ongoing battle about money. Adults need some money they can call their own, no matter how little. Money for which they don't have to account or agree or ask.

How we view money has to do with how we were raised, our ability to earn it, our own self-worth (do I deserve this watch?) and probably even our sex.

I put a husband through graduate school, was going to school full-time and working full-time, and I can distinctly remember feeling furious at my husband when he went out for a fancy lunch with some of his friends and I wouldn't buy myself a good lunch because I was the only one benefiting. (It was okay to buy a special treat for dinner, because that was for *both* of us—read him.) Once I realized the source of my anger, I decided it was my problem, not his, and that we both needed some money, even if it was a couple of dollars a week, to do with as we wished. It was, literally, not the other one's business. It certainly eased the tension.

If it's any comfort to you, the number-one, -two and -three major causes of the breakup of marriages are money. It can be incredibly destructive because it is the exercise of power. It's not a matter of who's right or who's wrong but that you can agree to disagree. Pay the bills if you can, make sure each of you has a tiny hoard to do with as you wish, and see if you can't figure out a compromise for long-term goals and short-term pleasures.

It might also help you to feel less insecure about money if you feel a bit more independent, which may mean a job or acquiring some marketable skills if you don't already possess them. Your insecurity about money may have something to do with feeling passive and childlike and under somebody else's control. If that's the case, investigate your feelings about your dad as a provider. If you already have a job and/

or marketable skills, is there a part of you that doesn't trust your husband's earning ability or him? Why are you so uncertain about your financial future, or is it your future in general?

Try talking about money together; and if it seems to you to be just a matter of dollars and cents, try the three-tiered budget of bills, private, and long-term money I've described. If it still seems a question of money to you both, perhaps a banker or money manager could help. My guess is that either the two of you can sort it out together or it doesn't have much to do with money in the first place.

I've been trying to give up smoking for years. My husband smokes, so it's doubly difficult. Do you have a foolproof method?

Up until a few years ago as a therapist the whole issue of smoking was somewhat of a lost cause. Both my parents smoke. I have never smoked and none of my five brothers or sisters do; we are all adamant, intolerant non-smokers. When clients asked me to help them, I pointed out that I had absolutely nothing to offer them other than my undying support and unwillingness to let them smoke during our sessions. That is until that magical day when Wayne Dyer came on my program and told a story about a patient who had been referred to him as a chronic nail biter. She had been to see all the best therapists and had come to him out of desperation, hoping he could offer something no one else had. Her fingernails at this point were bloody nubs; she wore gloves to conceal them, but nevertheless during the interview relentlessly brought her fingers to her mouth and chewed on her nails through the gloves.

As she and Wayne delved into the intricacies of her past therapeutic failures, Wayne, being increasingly disturbed by her incessant nail biting, calmly said, "Don't put your fingers in your mouth." The discussion would resume, as would the nail biting. Wayne is not known for his patience and found himself even actually hollering at the top of his lungs, *"Don't put your fingers in your mouth!"* The woman asked if it wasn't possible that she would regress or substitute some other form of oral gratification. Wayne, by now at wits end, just kept repeating, "Just don't put your fingers in your mouth!" Client cured, case closed.

The same afternoon Wayne had shared this story, a favorite client of mine who had been seeing me for several years came in and announced she wanted to give up smoking and wanted me to help her. I told her that had she come to me with her request a day earlier, I would have had to admit my inadequacy in this area and send her to Smokenders or a hypnotist or some other variation on the theme. However, I now had an idea. I told her the fingernail story, concluding with the statement, "Just don't put the cigarettes in your mouth." She too asked about oral gratification, overly simplistic solutions, regression, hidden Freudian meanings. I cheerfully just said, "Don't put the cigarettes in your mouth." She said, "What about buying them or cutting down or tapering off or withdrawal?" I said, "Just don't put the cigarettes in your mouth."

She said she wanted to think about it. I told her it made no difference to me whether she quit smoking or not, but since this was the day she had chosen to make her request, I had just offered her my best shot and it seemed to me it was now or not at all. She furiously threw her pack of cigarettes at me and never smoked again. She was ready.

When you're ready, you're ready, and until then it won't make any difference what you do. Once you decide, you can stick M & M's up your nose and it will work. Just don't put the cigarettes in your mouth.

Admittedly if you and your husband decide to quit together, you can reinforce one another just as you're now doing as smokers. But your mouth is your mouth—his is his —just don't put the cigarettes in your mouth.

We fight all the time. Our sex life is lousy. Will counseling help?

In this country, we often get married for the wrong reasons: because everybody else is doing it, because we want to have a baby, because we want a date for New Year's Eve, because our mom's on our case, because we're tired of being alone. We should get married if we have decided that there is one person with whom we want to spend the bulk of our time, share the majority of our secrets, who adds to our happiness but respects our independence and for whom we are willing to forsake all others, at least sexually. Marriage is easy to get into and tough to exit. Which brings a lot of people to where you are today—in an unhappy, desolate war zone. Before either or both of you even decide whether you need a counselor, both of you need to find out whether either or both of you have any wish to remain together.

What is each of you willing to offer the other, and what do you want in return? Do you have any mutual interests other than bickering or the kids. Do you like each other? Do you enjoy spending time together? Is there even the faintest spark of love remaining? Would you miss each other at all? Do you remember why you got married in the first place?

Believe it or not, there may be some hope in the fact that you fight; at least you're not simply ignoring one another. It is much harder to resurrect a union out of apathy than anger.

Are the two of you blaming each other for disappointments in your own lives that have nothing to do with the marriage? Life isn't easy all the time, and like marriage it requires compromise and work and it is constantly changing.

The two of you might want to sit down independently and write up a list of what each wants from the other and what you would be willing to give in return. Don't say things like "More consideration" or "Be nicer." It's very important to be specific. It's much more helpful to say, "I would like him to stay in the kitchen when I'm cleaning up after dinner," than "He ignores me and takes me for granted."

Be as specific in terms of what you're willing to offer him. Maybe your "lousy" sex life is a place to start. Are you loving and giving and occasionally innovative with one another, or is one or the other of you using sex as a weapon to be brandished or withheld or expecting it to work like crazy glue to hold things together when nothing else is working?

Each marriage is an individual creation. Yours doesn't have to be like anybody else's as long as it works for the two of you. It's like a unicorn, an imaginary creature that exists in both of your minds. Yours obviously isn't working. The question is Does either of you feel enough motivation to make it work rather than fighting?

If neither of you is willing to work at it, get a good divorce lawyer and a counselor to help the two of you maintain some dignity as you dissolve it. If both of you want to put in some work, start with the lists. You may even want to investigate a "Marriage Encounter" weekend. They are often sponsored by local churches and synagogues even though they're usually non-sectarian. As the name suggests, the idea is to get marriage partners back in touch with their positive feelings about one another. It won't heal your wounds, but it might go some distance in reminding you why you want them to be healed.

If only one of you wants to work on the marriage, that one should figure out an appropriate bribe to induce the other to at least try for a specific length of time. At that point a counselor may be of some value so the interested partner doesn't have to take all the responsibility. If the two of you are expecting the counselor to save your marriage, you may as well save your money. The only ones who can save your marriage are the two of you, and then only if you both decide to work at it and cherish it because you cherish one another. If both of you want to make it work it usually will, but the two of you will be the ones to make it work, not the church, not the in-laws, not society and certainly not the counselor. Day-to-day intimacy is hard work, and we expect a great deal more out of our marriages than anybody ever has for the entire period of human history.

A good marriage is the best of all human institutions; a bad one may very well be the worst. You're lonely without at least the privacy and opportunity of being alone. Both of you have some soul-searching to do and some hard questions to examine. But for heaven's sake stop the bickering, the blaming and the threats. Fish or cut bait and get on with it.

He won't talk to me. He's always been the uncommunicative type. His whole family is that way. It's like he has no feelings. How can I make him talk to me?

Men and women treat their emotions differently. Men hide from them, view them as weaknesses, loss of control. Women parade them, admire them and cherish them. Once you understand this, you understand a lot more about your husband's reluctance to talk about what you want him to talk about. He probably doesn't want to talk about work, since that's what he does all day. He will be even less willing to talk about it if he doesn't like it or it isn't going well or he's feeling underpaid and overworked. Men feel that they are what they do to earn a living. So it's either a case of overkill —"I can't talk about it twenty-four hours a day"—or embarrassment.

First, make sure you're not asking him to be the only adult in your life. Women friends can absorb some of your need for conversation and communication. Second, make sure you're not talking exclusively with him about "women-type" things—emotions, angers, hurts. Many men would probably be willing to talk to their wives more if they could pick the subject. What they feel is that wives don't want to talk, they want to complain or they want their husbands to talk about things that don't make any sense to them, like feelings. For instance, he might be willing to talk with you about sports if you promise not to make dumb comments. He may even have tried, but you may not have been interested.

Most men today feel caught in a bind. They try to make a good living, keep gambling and drinking and carousing to a discreet minimum, but they don't understand this sensitivity stuff, either in bed or out. Talking about feelings is wimp stuff, and being sensitive means you're less than a man. My exaggeration is slightly farfetched but only slightly, to make a point.

Understand that by your own description you're asking your husband to change the habits of a lifetime. His family doesn't talk; he doesn't talk. That's not to say that you have to give up on him, but you are going to have to be realistic and patient.

It is also important that you have things to discuss with him that are of some interest to him. I'm not suggesting that you revert to being a teenager who talks about things that interest him to ensnare him; but back when you were courting one another you probably mentioned something other than dreary household problems or money complaints or mother-in-law horror stories. In other words, if you're more interesting to listen to, he may be more willing to listen. I know that's still not the problem, but it's a step in the right direction.

Most men consider discussions of personalities as gossip. They may even be right. Discussion of people we neither know nor like is boring to most of us.

If he gets in the habit of listening, not just tolerating or spacing out while you yammer away, he may be more willing to contribute in kind. I know you still want him to share feelings, but both of you have to start someplace.

Timing is also important. He may want to talk right after he gets home, or after dinner, or in bed, or over breakfast. It may be that the times he is most relaxed are those when you are most harried. Try to negotiate a time that is initially most convenient for him. After all, you're asking him to change his behavior, so best make it as easy as possible for him.

Make a deal with him that you will try and talk to him in a way that is interesting and easy for him and you'll let him join in if and when he's ready. Don't force him, but explain to him what you're trying to do and that you understand that you're asking a favor from him—one that is difficult for him and valuable to you.

It's also not such a bad idea to figure out some new activities that the two of you can launch together—take a class, begin a new sport, a club, a new project. It should be something that is new to both of you and has potential interest to both of you. If possible, you may want to lean it in his direction a bit, to get him used to the idea of sharing. Instead of harping at him, tell him how much you value his companionship and input and how you miss the old days when you were courting.

Don't blame him for doing what he's always done. You can't make him talk to you, but you can be more interesting to listen to, less strident in your demands and gentle in opening up new avenues of joint exploration. It will require more time and effort than just getting angry with him for not being more like a woman, but it could also be a lot more fun for both of you.

He wants me to listen to his problems, but when it comes to listening to mine he's not interested. He says all I do is bitch. How can I make him more sympathetic?

We have a double standard when it comes to complaining. If men do it, they're opening up; if women do it, they're bitching. Part of the problem lies in how men and women view communication; part in the different value we place on men and women; part in the different ways men and women problem-solve; and part in the way men and women have been taught (or not taught) to organize their thoughts for presentation. And then there's the matter of timing. Let's go through the issues one at a time and see if the problem lies in presentation rather than lack of sympathy.

When and how do the two of you complain to one another? How does each respond to suggestions from the other, or does either offer suggestions? What do you complain about? How often do you complain about the same things?

If the two of you are like most couples, he complains about work and you complain about home, the kids or the people at work. By and large men have been taught to view work as important and people problems as distractions. It's an inaccurate but commonly held view. Women, on the other hand, view people as the real issue and work problems as mere reflections of people problems—more accurate than not, but still lacking in a perspective that allows for problem solving. Both of you may view his problems as more important because they have to do with the "outside" world, which is unfamiliar and dangerous and tied to a paycheck. (Even if the woman works, she may diminish her problems in both their eyes by making them people problems, taking about them second, presenting them in a disorganized, emotional, ditsy fashion and bringing the same issue up repeatedly.)

Men also often feel that problems should be borne silently and alone and either endured or quickly solved and dispensed with. Women tend to chew on them for a while, savoring the complexity and the flavor and even the familiarity. Men feel problems should be listed logically, dealt with summarily, and then on to the next.

Having said all this, how do you make him listen? To start with, you have to view your problems as important. If you don't, he won't. Prepare an agenda, yes, written, so the problem is logically presented, organized and complete. Decide ahead of time with him when the two of you can talk about both sets of problems, so you will have the time and both of you will have the inclination. You may want to alternate who goes first in these discussions, and there should probably be time limits that aren't too rigidly enforced but are respected by both of you. Both of you should be encouraged to ask questions at the end of a brief presentation, and both of you should decide ahead of time whether you are inviting suggestions or just want a sympathetic ear. A sympathetic ear should be used sparingly. Most of us are flattered to be asked our opinion, but we get bored fairly quickly with being used as a tape recorder or mute audience.

However, if either of you solicits the other's opinion and ignores preferred advice repeatedly, it's a real turn-off. Practically this means that if you ask for advice you either have to take it, take it partially or stop bringing the problem to your spouse's attention. Most of us get miffed if we're constantly ignored when we're trying to be helpful and sympathetic and solicitous.

If this sounds unduly formal to you, you've got to realize that in the work world if problems are ever even admitted to they're handled in a "businesslike" manner. It's a bit of a defeat even to admit that there is a problem, let alone one that you haven't solved, so anything less than an orderly presentation is viewed as the mark of a complete goof, and nobody listens to goofs. We turn them off and tune them out.

You may find that the procedure will help you not only define and clarify some of your concerns but also allow you to solve some of your own problems. Once you get the hang of it, neither of you will need to be so formal; and when things are orderly, concise and presented to be interesting and accessible, you may find yourselves much more interested in each other, to say nothing of the other's problems.

If you still find that he's not interested in hearing your problems, maybe he's not interested in you, or at least not in you as anything other than an audience. If that's the case, you've got another problem, but by then you'll be able to be orderly and clear about that problem too. Don't assume he's unsympathetic until you're sure that you wouldn't bore the daylights out of yourself if you were the listener rather than the speaker. (Actually taping yourself isn't a terrible idea. If he's boring, you might even suggest that both of you might tape and then listen to yourselves.)

The idea isn't to turn either of you into a champion debater but to understand that complaining aloud can be good communication and creative problem solving if either of you can even figure out the real problem. Once you can clarify the problem in your mind and in your presentation, you may find a very sympathetic listener.

We've been married for four years and I love my husband, but I'm just not in love with him. I feel restless and I'm thinking of an affair or a divorce. Which is easier?

We have a terrible tendency in this society to confuse lust with love and lust with terror. Those sweaty palms, rapidly beating heart and anxiety about whether or not he'll call aren't love, not even lust. They indicate fear, insecurity and social conditioning. I'm the last person in the world to try and convince you to lead a life without passion, but passion and the fun and juice of brand-new sex aren't the same thing. Love isn't even the excitement of bridal showers and a fancy wedding and being everybody's favorite honeymoon couple. That's a heady combination of Madison Avenue, show biz and self-absorption—fun maybe, but not love.

So what is love? Love is probably most of all trust. Not very exciting maybe, but true. It's trust, compatibility, acceptance, a willingness to give as well as get, warmth, fun, shared interests and goals. It's caring about somebody not in spite of their glitches and failings but because of them. A little liking isn't such a bad idea either.

It's obvious that the honeymoon is over, and I'm not even suggesting that you have a marriage that is worth continuing; but what I am suggesting is that you're on the wrong track when you talk about loving but not being in love with someone. It's a great slogan for selling soft drinks but doesn't have much to do with real life.

Is it possible you're looking to your husband for all the excitement and fun you need in life? If so, you're going to have an exhausted husband and a frustrated self. You've got to supply your own excitement. Learn, if you don't already know how, to make yourself happy. A husband can be a friend and a lover and a confidant, but he shouldn't be the only friend in your life. You need to have other interests (no, not love interests) in your life. You need to feel interesting and independent and useful apart from your marriage. When was the last time you did something neat or fun or unusual for yourself, something you could share with your husband? Are you bored, and could that be the cause of your restlessness?

I suggest that you do things that make you happy: Make some new friends, learn a new skill, get a new job, do something for yourself. If then you still feel restless and unhappy, ask yourself whether your marriage is worth working on. Could you be a bit sexier, more giving, more inventive?

Affairs don't save marriages; they complicate lives, because you're either going to have to lie or hurt your husband and you're probably going to be using the other man. Not very nice.

The idea that someone else can make you happy is more often than not a dangerous, misleading, inaccurate assumption. You make yourself happy, and then you can decide what to do about your marriage.

Divorce isn't fun. It's sometimes necessary, but it's usually expensive emotionally as well as financially. And for heaven's sake don't even think about getting pregnant. Babies aren't patches for an ailing marriage.

It's also important that you rethink the word "easy" in your life. Easy is a shortcut. The easiest short-term solution is always to cut and run—have an affair, get a divorce—but it's seldom the best long-term solution. It's time for you to realize that you're a grownup, not a child whose every whim must immediately be satisfied or you'll take your marbles and go home or have a temper tantrum or hold your breath till you turn blue.

You're an adult, and adults sometimes have to work for what they want—to trade off short-term discomfort for the achievement of long-term goals. What do you want for yourself? Can you be specific enough to figure out a strategy to achieve your goals? Once you can, your marriage may or may or may not play a part, but until you've done that kind of analysis you'll never even have a clue. You'll find yourself bouncing from man to man, whim to whim, and sooner or later you'll believe that men are no damned good, that you're crazy, that life stinks or that you're doomed to be miserable your whole life or all of the above. None of the above are most likely true, but a happy life and a good marriage both take work, planning, courage, time and a specific set of goals, combined with a little flexibility, a bit of common sense—and a sense of humor doesn't hurt.

Stop being a brat and figure out what you can do for yourself and then decide what to do about your marriage.

I love my wife, but our sex life is really boring. I'd like her to be a bit more adventuresome. Do you think I should just have an affair?

Whoa, sonny. Who's kidding whom? If you want to have an affair, admit to yourself you want to have an affair and don't use your wife as an excuse. The last thing in the world that will make your wife more trusting and loving in bed is your infidelity, so be honest.

If you're looking to me to give you permission to have an affair, forget it. You're not a child, you don't need anyone's permission, much less mine, and if you have an affair to jazz up your marriage, I think you're a damned fool. An affair means at least two and more likely three people are going to get hurt, at least one is going to get used, at least one and more likely two are going to be lied to, and the only person to benefit even potentially is you.

Now, if you're really looking to spruce up your sex life, you may want to focus outside the bedroom. I'm not necessarily suggesting sex on the kitchen table, although it may not be such a bad idea as long as you're on the bottom, but a little affection outside of the bedroom, a little conversation, a show of interest in your wife as a woman, an individual, a thinking, feeling organism may be an investment that could pay off in juicy dividends. Most of us are more responsive in bed when we think we're loved and appreciated and valued. Feeling loved makes most of us feel more loving.

You courted her once, and think what fun it was for both of you. And lest you think I've lost sight of the issue here, she will be more trusting if you're more loving and affectionate with her. Do you have some specific practices that you'd like to try? Have you told her? Is there something that she would like? Is a trade-off possible? How many alternatives can you suggest? Has your repertoire become a bit limited? If your wife trusts you, feels secure in your love and accepted, even cherished by you, she is much more likely to feel relaxed in bed and allow you to be a bit more adventuresome

—perhaps even let herself go a bit. If she trusts that you won't hurt or mislead her in any way, you may find a bedrock of comfort on which to build.

Many women feel that liking sex or becoming too aggressive will make their men think less of them, treat them like tarts and therefore be less protective and respectful of them. If you think about it, her fears may be justified. How would you feel if your wife all of a sudden turned into an insatiable tigress in bed? If you're grinning widely, you're probably not taking this question very seriously. What if you've had a hard day at work or are worried about how to meet the mortgage this month or whether your car will make it through another winter?

It may be that you like thinking of yourself as the aggressor and in control even if you don't feel that way outside the house. Are you really willing to give up that role? Maybe you're willing to compromise it a bit. You may need to share some of your feelings with your wife rather than various body organs.

Alex Comfort's *The Joy of Sex* is a good Sears, Roebuck catalogue of sexual options for the two of you once you've paved the way for some *discussion* on alternatives—not rape, not demands, but some soft coaxing and cuddling and contemplation. If you're a more loving lover—not acrobat, not ringmaster, but lover—you may find that she's not only more adventuresome but more loving, more fun, sexier and happier. You might find yourself all of the above as well.

I've heard of the seven-year itch and the mid-life crisis, but what is the hardest year of marriage?

The hardest year of marriage is the one you're in.

The first year is tough because of all the adjustments made to living with a stranger, no matter how long you've known each other and even if you've lived together. Marriage, as you've undoubtedly discovered, is different. Changing jobs or homes, moving away from parents, moving closer to parents, the birth of a baby, the loss of a parent, the acquisition of a pet, a physical illness, a loss of weight, a weight gain, a drinking problem, a resolved drinking problem, all take their toll of a marriage, since a marriage is the emotional and legal and financial creation that exists between the two of you.

Any change in either of your lives will affect your marriage; and while the change may be good for either or both of you in the long run, it very well may cause some tension between the two of you, and your relationship may suffer at least temporarily because of it. The difference between a temporary rift and a permanent chasm probably depends more on your commitment to one another and the flexibility you've built into your relationship than on the problem itself.

You've already survived all the past years; the future ones are currently irrelevant; they haven't yet occurred. The only one you have to get through is the current one. A ten-year milepost can be a problem or a comfort; a fifteen-year mid-life crisis can be a cause for celebration or consternation.

This can be a simple but very helpful thought to remember when Aunt Mathilda starts telling you about the birth of her child and Uncle Harold's drinking problem, or your mother-in-law tells you she knew by the end of the first year, or your sister splits just before her seventh anniversary. Your marriage is yours and nobody else's, so nobody else can tell you how to run it or save it or enhance it. They can tell you what worked and didn't work for them and that may be of some interest, but it's still your marriage and your timetable and your expectations and your spouse. Quizzes in magazines are fun and sometimes helpful, but comparing your marriage to anyone else's is an exercise in futility. Society offers an overall view of how marriage is supposed to work; TV simplifies it. Religious organizations set rules, states define the legal principles, mothers-in-law, comedians, sisters, all have a perspective.

If your marriage works, don't worry about what anybody thinks of it but you. If it doesn't, it doesn't make any difference what other people think anyway. You can't stay together for the sake of the neighbors. Once you try to measure up to somebody else's notion of how a marriage is supposed to be, you've lost your sense of individuality, or privacy, of control over your own life and, most importantly, the idea that a marriage is an abstract, fragile union for the benefit of the two of you. If it works for the two of you, you're home free; and if it doesn't, you both need to figure out why and what you can do about it.

In the waning days of my marriage, my then husband pointed out that we had the best marriage of anybody we knew. He was right and it still stunk. It has to work for both of you or it doesn't work at all.

I think he's having an affair. Should I confront him?

Before we ask any question in this life, we had best be very sure that we're willing to hear any answer it might elicit. Would you be asking him about the affair to be reassured? Do you want him to lie? Do you think he'll tell the truth? Are you looking for a reason to leave him? Before you ask him, ask yourself what a yes answer would mean. A no answer. Let's go through the possibilities.

He says he's not having an affair. He's insulted at the question. He wants to know the basis of your suspicions. He calls you paranoid and jealous and crazy and says you need help. Have you collected any usable or helpful information from this confrontation? Have you made matters between the two of you better or worse? Do you know anything you didn't know before this messy little encounter? Have you given him permission to have an affair, since you already distrust him?

He admits he's having an affair. What do you do now? Do you leave him? Have an affair? Tell the kids? (Don't even think of doing that.) Demand that he choose? What if he chooses her (or him)? What if he says it's over? Do you believe him? What if he says it doesn't mean anything? Do you feel better or worse?

If you're getting the idea that asking him isn't such a hot idea, you're right. At least at this stage.

Let's first look at you and your marriage. Do you love this guy? Why do you think he's having an affair? Most importantly, do you want the marriage to continue? If you love him and want the marriage, it may make more sense to fight fire with fire and become sexier and more alluring and more fun. It's easy to become lazy about showing someone that we love them. Remember how it was when you were dating and in the early days of your marriage? (If it's still the early days of your marriage, either he's a scoundrel or you're dreadfully insecure.) Pour on the heat and see if he responds. Don't assume anything, just work on your marriage. If there is someone else, maybe you can erase her by your ardor and love. If not, you'll likely force him to choose sooner or later and you will at least have given your marriage your best shot. I'm not suggesting that the only reason people stray is boring sex or lack of attention, but it's a major cause. If the two of them are meant to be together, it's going to hurt, but will it hurt any more just because you've really tried to rekindle the flame?

And there is the possibility that you're wrong. If you honestly feel that you have to know, you can try and ask him as gently and straightforwardly as possible, but the real issues are your feelings and your marriage and your options, not his answer—even if you could count on that answer being true.

If you can find the courage to work on the marriage rather than confront him, I think you'll win in the long run. If you're just looking for an excuse to have an affair or leave the marriage, be honest with yourself and don't manipulate him. If you're going to assume anything, assume something that makes you happy, not miserable.

My wife is insanely jealous. It's become ridiculous. She ac-
cuses me of having an affair with the postmistress, who is
ninety and bald. Is there a cure for this sickness?

I'm afraid you've really put your finger on the problem. Extreme jealousy is indeed a sickness. Jealousy says much more about the person who's expressing those feelings than it does about your behavior. Jealousy is a statement of insecurity and inadequacy, and since it has to do with her and her lack of self-worth there is nothing that you will be able to say or do to reassure her.

On the other hand it is important that your behavior is truly blameless. This doesn't mean that you can't smile at the postmistress or comment on a blouse. It does mean that constant references to other women and their attractiveness or nasty little digs about how poorly your wife measures up are in poor taste, mean and just plain rude.

The problem about jealousy is that initially it can feel flattering and reassuring that someone feels intensely and possessively about us, but it is a long-term trap. If your wife has always been jealous, she needs some help and the sooner the better. If this is a recent occurrence, the two of you might be able to figure out the trigger. Are you working later? Is a new baby making her feel tired? Is her health deteriorating? Has she experienced a recent loss in some other area of her life? Has one of her friends' husband run off with the carwash attendant?

Please also be painfully honest with yourself and make sure that her suspicions are indeed groundless. Is it possible that you might be deriving some sly satisfaction from them?

Are you having an affair? Are you thinking about having an affair? Are you distracted from her? If you are truly blameless in all this and her jealousy is of long duration, there is nothing you can do to assuage the problem. It is deep within her, and she will have to decide to tackle it or not with some professional help. This does not mean that you can justify any naughty behavior on your own part by saying, As long as she's going to blame me, I might as well enjoy myself. You're responsible for your behavior, she's responsible for hers. It is not accidental that jealousy is referred to as the green-eyed monster. It can truly be monstrous.

I've just finished an affair. I feel terribly guilty. How should I tell my wife?

Don't you dare tell your wife. You're the person who enjoyed the affair. Your wife derived absolutely no benefit and she shouldn't have to bear any pain. Your need to confess is utterly selfish. You want her to forgive you or punish you so you can lessen your own guilt. You had the affair, you carry the consequences. Telling your wife is cowardly, manipulative, self-indulgent and mean. If you want out of your marriage, leave; but have the guts to do it on your own, not manipulate her into tossing you out.

If you want your marriage to survive, work on it, but for heaven's sake keep your mouth closed. If you need to confess to someone, find a priest, but don't kid yourself that you're doing the honorable thing by fessing up.

Whenever we have a fight, she withholds sex. Is there such a thing as marital rape?

You better believe it. Rape occurs when any sexual act follows the word "no." Period. We are our bodies, and nobody has the right to encroach on that sovereign space unless they're changing our diapers. I cannot stress too strongly that you do not own your wife's body (nor does she own yours).

Somehow it seems that the two of you have forgotten what marriage is all about, not to mention love, making love and sex. It is not unusual or uncommon or even necessarily bad for two people to disagree with one another. After all, you were raised in different families with different rules, regulations, values. You're not even the same sex, so to expect the two of you to agree on everything is ridiculous. It sounds like the two of you are lousy at airing disagreements and resolving them, so there's a lot of hostility, unresolved anger and boring here-we-go-again fights.

If I had to guess, I would guess that you tend to dominate your wife verbally as well as physically, and she may feel the only way to get your attention is to pout sexually. It's not a terrifically good way to make her point, but it does succeed in getting your attention.

Maybe the two of you could agree to disagree more profitably. Set time limits on the amount of time each of you talks, make sure that both of you do talk, penalize one another by fines when either of you says, "You always" or "You never," or makes nasty references to the other's mother. It might also be a good idea to try and get a handle on the kinds of things that touch off fights. Are you arguing about specifics or the same old generalities? Is there anything short of complete surrender that one can do to please the other? Does either of you want to resolve arguments or just win?

Marriage is whatever the two of you want it to be. Hopefully the two of you don't want it to be an arm-wrestling contest, even though it seems to have evolved to that point. Do either of you remember why you got married or how you once felt about one another? Do you remember when you made love instead of had sex? When sex was the closest the two of you could feel to one another, not a salve for hurt feelings or wounded pride or imagined or real insults?

If neither of you can remember the good times or foresee any good times down the road, maybe it's time to re-evaluate whether it's worth the trouble, because it's always a bit troublesome to live with another human being, and we decide to do it because there is more value than hassle. If you are angry enough at your wife seriously to consider raping her, maybe it's time seriously to consider leaving her and finding some peace for both of you apart.

If you exaggerated your anger, maybe it's time to let some of that anger go and channel your frustration in more appropriate directions. Rape is a crime of violence, not sex; and if the two of you have gotten to the point where violence is the language of your relationship, it's time to get some help to redefine it or get out before somebody gets hurt.

Our marriage is the pits, but I'm afraid to be alone. Besides,
he owes me. What should I do?

My dear, you *are* alone. The reality of life is that we enter
it alone and we leave it alone. The question is whether or not
we can take an edge off that state at any time between the
first event and the last, and it doesn't sound as though your
marriage is doing the trick.

I was at a Christmas night party several years ago. Christmas night, not eve. Everybody was there with their families,
spouses, kids, the works. There was one single friend there
who had recently been divorced by a man she still loved. Our
incredibly tacky hostess came up and asked the woman if she
wasn't feeling particularly lonely, to which she responded
that she had never felt as lonely since the divorce as she had
during the marriage. Points for my friend, slaps for my hostess.

You see the point. Living with someone you can't stand is
the ultimate loneliness. We go home to escape the boss or
the crazies in the subway or the uncaring strangers, and if
home is a hassle as opposed to a refuge, what's the point?

When you say you're afraid to be alone and then in the
next sentence suggest that he owes you, it may be that you're
afraid to have to support yourself financially. If that is your
only concern, that's why lawyers were invented. If your concern is more deep-seated, perhaps it's time to ask yourself
whether he doesn't offer some other kinds of support as
well? If your answer is an emphatic no, then call your lawyer,
think about a job or another place to live or both. If there is
the merest shadow of a suspicion in your mind that he is
offering you something of value to you personally, then it
might be a good idea to begin to build on that and see if it
can't be the beginning of a path back to one another.

You have to make your own way through this world, but
he is neither the problem nor the solution. You have to decide what you want, from him, from your life, from your
bank account.

If the debt you feel he has incurred has to do with time or emotions, you need to analyze what you have gotten out of the relationship during the same period of time. If the answer is nothing, then for heaven's sake get out before you waste any more time; if you have gotten something of value, cherish it and build on it. If you've gotten something but nothing remains, decide whether it can be resurrected or if it's time to cut your losses.

You are staying because you choose to, not because you have to. He's responsible for his life, you're responsible for yours. That marriage is as much yours as his. Feeling that someone owes you is not pretty for either party.

You need to stop blaming, assess what you want, how to get it and get on with it.

We're staying together for the sake of the kids. Is an affair legal?

Trust me, nobody stays together for the sake of the kids. People stay together because they're afraid to be alone, because it's cheaper to support one household than two, because they're afraid of losing contact or status or money or friends, and sometimes because they really care for one another. People who say they are staying together for the sake of the kids are kidding themseves. Kids aren't stupid, and they are almost always aware of tension in the household, of the whispers and fights and phone conversations and lies. Kids care about their own world and their own security.

The roles of spouse and parent are separate. It may be most efficient when both roles are combined under the same roof, but they're not the same, nor do they require the same characteristics. Many people actually become better parents when they are forced to consider that role independent of living arrangements and actually spend more meaningful time with their children.

Neither of you is really staying together for the kids, and to pretend that you are uses them as chess pieces and more importantly allows both of you to ignore your real feelings, so nothing will get resolved. By pretending to consider the children's welfare above your own, both of you are allowing for holier-than-thou games. Righteous indignation is a lousy basis for any kind of sane negotiation.

You and your spouse have to sit down and be honest with yourselves first and then with each other about what each of you wants and what each of you is willing to offer in return. If you can't do it, then a therapist may be able to facilitate either the list-making or the discussion. It's tough to be honest with yourself, let alone share those thoughts and feelings with someone you may no longer trust or like, let alone love.

Because you do have children in common, you will always have a bond with one another, no matter how tenuous, so the more honest (not brutal, just honest) you can be now, the better your long-term prospects for calm, unbloody, dignified interaction and *that* is for the sake of the kids as well as one another. Self-respect is a hard thing to buy back.

As for the affair, no-fault divorce has made affairs less dangerous if both of you can agree and a great deal more dangerous if you can't. The point is an affair is only going to complicate matters now. If it's only for sex and/or reassurance, you're running a high legal risk. Making your current spouse angry and humiliated won't serve you very well in either the long or short run, and it may jeopardize visitation rights and custody issues, not to mention your kids' feelings about you. If you just happen to run into the perfect mate while you're still married, you will complicate any future you might have together, not to mention all the legal, emotional and child-centered issues already mentioned.

It is perfectly understandable that you are tempted to lash out at your spouse while simultaneously reaffirming your own desirability, but if you can possibly withstand the temptation, it will pay off handsomely. I know I sound like your mother, but trust me on this one. Tend to the business at hand first. You'll feel better about yourself, and those kids about whom you are so worried are going to need time and reassurance whether you're all in the same household or not.

Work on your marriage or junk it, but don't lie to yourself or to each other about why you're together. Presumably your marriage came before the kids, and in theory it can withstand their departure; but it is a separate issue from them. It's between the two of you.

My daughter-in-law hates me. No matter what I do, she's cold and distant. I've tried my best for my son's sake. What's wrong with her?

How did you get along with your mother-in-law, especially when you were a young bride? If you're like most of us, you were a bit intimidated, a bit threatened, especially if your husband suggested that his mom was a better cook, house-keeper, mother, spouse than you. We live in a country where Mom does most of the nurturing, and since boys historically have been more valued than girls, boys get an especially good deal. A difficult situation for a new bride who is feeling insecure and incompetent to begin with. A tug of war for the affections and loyalty of son/husband is not unusual, just uncomfortable.

You say you've tried your best, but did you oppose his choice? Were you pleasant to her when they were dating? Were you open and friendly to her when she was newly introduced? It doesn't sound to me that you're all that crazy about her either. Are you nice to her for her sake rather than your son's?

You're the grownup in this situation. Have you gone out of your way to make her feel welcome and at ease? Helped her out in family situations without being overbearing or pushy? Not offered unsolicited advice?

Presumably you both love the same man, but you don't want him on your hands forever; and if you do, you're offer-ing a distorted life-style for him, which at the very least isn't very good parenting.

Ask yourself what you would have wished from your mother-in-law. Or if you were lucky enough to have gotten a peach of a one, what did she do that made you so comfort-able?

You might invite your daughter-in-law out for a grown-up-lady lunch (your treat) and charm her a bit. If you've been a witch, you might want to set the record straight by admitting that you've been hard on her and offer to clear the air and apologize (wholeheartedly) and ask her how you can make amends. Humble pie is not inappropriate for lunch. It may be that her distance results from fear of you or reaction to knowing that you don't like or approve of her, or she may be intimidated or hurt by your lack of acceptance.

Try and be gracious and give her a bit of time to readjust to the new charming you. If she still doesn't like you, that's okay. You didn't pick one another, but your son picked her; and if you make him choose between the two of you, you're very likely to lose. Even if he decides to dump her, he's not going to opt for you as a wife, and he very well may blame you for poisoning the marriage whether or not it is your fault.

Besides, you may like the next one even less. Be charming, be fair and keep your mouth closed about how she should treat him; and above all, remember how it felt when your mother-in-law criticized you or seemed to be competing for your husband's time, attention, loyalty or love.

He's married, but I love him. He says he wants the kids to finish high school before he leaves her, so it won't upset the kids' routine. Is he jobbing me?

Yes. On the other hand, he may very well be jobbing himself. Women who date married men should not wear mascara. You're going to be sitting next to the phone a lot, alone on holidays, waiting for him to show up, wondering if something has happened to him, because no one would think or maybe even know to call you.

Supposedly there is a man shortage these days, but unless you're just in it for the sex, and it doesn't sound like you are, married men should instantly flash a picture of a skull and crossbones to your heart, brain and any other appropriate organ. For most of us sex is best when all of our body parts are involved and we tend to get more involved over time. Married men can offer you nothing but lies. They are going to tell you how much they love you and want you and need you and how it's never been like this for them before. They will swear with tears in their eyes that they never believed someone like you could exist and yet they have been looking for you their whole life. They may even believe some part of this, which isn't hard, since they are in the lovely position of having their cake and eating it too. They can promise you anything because there is a wife at home who is prohibiting them from loving you in the way you deserve. She of course is an unfeeling bitch who only wants his money. When you point out that you are willing to work or that you can live on less money, the kids come into play. One woman against another in the sympathy sweepstakes may balance out fairly evenly (unless she suddenly comes down with cancer or becomes suicidal), but kids are another story.

You now get to play Wicked Witch of the West. If you are kind and understanding (which is of course what he loves about you most and sets you head and shoulder above *her*), then you patiently wait until the kids get their braces off, graduate high school, college, get married, get divorced and apply for Social Security. If you decide to be pushy, you're the bitch, unfeeling and selfish, and you either lose him or your self-respect or your membership pin in the Mistress as Saint Club.

If you've suddenly figured out that you can't win in this situation, you've just figured out what you probably should have thought about when this whole thing got started.

Let's give him the benefit of the doubt and assume that he really believes what he's telling you. Accept his time frame and get on with your life. He's not the one sitting by the phone or alone on birthdays or holidays or New Year's Eve. He may feel some pain, but he's got another life. If the two of you are meant to be, you'll be together, rickety perhaps in rocking chairs, but together nonetheless; and you'll have a relatively clean slate, so you won't have to feel guilty about his marriage or his kids. If he's jobbing you, you only have to feel dumb about the time lost so far, not all the time to come.

It won't be easy to let go of him or the fantasy that the two of you will be together; but the way you've got it set up, he'll never have to choose unless his wife hears about you and throws him out. (Don't even think about calling and telling her anonymously. She may or may not believe you, but he'll never forgive you.)

Tell him you understand how important his kids are and you feel you have to allow him time to be a good father and, if and when he ever feels that he is ready, to give you a call. In the meantime you plan to continue to become the wonderful woman he thinks you are. You can even tell him you need his help to stay away, but don't count on it. If you think he's been seductive so far, you ain't seen nothing yet. He will be relentless. You've rejected him; he's got nothing to lose by pursuing you, so make sure you're serious before you even attempt the split. But I would really encourage you to think seriously about dumping him.

He's wasting your time, and when all is said and done, time is all any of us have in this life. Get mad and get out.

Spend time with friends, exercise, get out of the house, don't get involved with anybody immediately, but do get uninvolved with him. If the two of you are meant to be, he'll get his act together and come and find the wonderful, independent, blameless you. If not, you don't need to feel like any more of a dope than you already do.

You don't have to hate him or argue with him or confront him. Just end it.

P.S. If this has happened to you more than once, you may need to talk with someone about a difficulty with commitment, going for the unobtainable, disliking men, difficult relationship with your own dad, and so on.

P.P.S. If none of this has convinced you, ask yourself if this man would cheat on one wife, what makes you think he wouldn't cheat on you if you were the wife.

I can't decide between my wife, my mistress and my girl-friend. I love all three and they all need me. I don't want to hurt anybody. What do I do?

You, sir, are a scoundrel. What you do is go find the nearest mirror, look yourself in the eye and ask yourself what has happened to you that you are willing to torment three women whose only crime is to love you and then to have the effrontery to suggest that you are acting in their best interest. What nerve! Either you hate women or you hate yourself and you're an unprincipled, undisciplined child. You cheat on everyone and lie to everyone, including yourself. If you find the restrictions of fidelity overwhelming, then do not marry or involve yourself in committed or seemingly committed relationships.

You deserve to be loved for who you are, not who you pretend to be; and it sounds like your entire life is based on pretense. I suspect you are unwilling to let anyone know who you really are, since you don't like yourself. As anyone gets close to you, you move away; but because you are terrified of being alone, you pour on the charm if they move away from you emotionally. Sex is probably not even much fun for you except as a challenge, a game in which you feel free to continue to break the rules.

You are a hurt, rebellious little boy who feels unloved and unloving and angry and abandoned all the time, so you vent your frustration on anyone you can charm into your web. I suspect that you had a terrible, intense relationship with your mother, and I would encourage you to seek professional help immediately before you can do any more harm to yourself or to those innocent others in your life.

Growing up loathing yourself to the extent that your self-delusions imply is a terrible waste. If you are willing to do some serious, painful work, you may be able to salvage what sounds like a truly tragic and empty life. I wish you courage and speed.

SUMMARY
MARRIAGE

If nothing else, this section on marriage should give you the idea that on the one hand most people want pretty much the same thing in a marriage—companionship, some excitement, appreciation, occasional hugs as well as pats on the back—and on the other hand that there is a wide variety of possibilities and problems in meeting those seemingly simple, universal and straightforward needs. If you're getting the feeling that one of the major problems in a marriage is the communication of those universal and simple but not necessarily easy conditions, you're right.

To begin with, it's obvious that most of us get married for the silliest and most flimsy of reasons and expect the commitment, no matter how unreasonable, illogical or instantaneous, to hold up for a lifetime. It is obvious that sometimes it doesn't hold up through the wedding reception.

Not only does a marriage need to be entered into seriously as well as romantically, but some of the same practices that work well in a business setting could take a lot of the worry out of being close. For example, no business would try to meet various departmental needs without scheduling, yet many marriage partners frantically try to juggle historical, real or imagined responsibilities, historical commitments to parents with new ones to spouse and job and children, without setting up a fair, logical, specific, easily identifiable system. No wonder holidays strike fear in the hearts of newlyweds and glee to those of travel agents, Alka Seltzer representatives and telephone operators. The expense of not working out a clear, definable system can be measured by MasterCard, Maalox and mother-in-law jokes.

Stressful situations are often made worse when money becomes an issue and it almost always does sooner or later in a marriage, no matter how much or how little is made or who's doing the making. Money is the most common cause of disagreement in a marriage and the single greatest cause of divorce. It's not only dollars and sense, but the inability to deal with what money represents: power. If couples can discuss money quietly and pleasantly, they can probably even discuss in-laws and whose side of the family contributed genetically to Johnny's crooked teeth and straight smile.

The problem is that most people come to a marriage with absolutely no idea how to resolve conflict, perhaps because they never admitted to any conflicts during the courtship. Both were on their best behavior and quite willing to kiss and make up over even the most important issues. Pretending to be the perfect companion-lover is hard but justifiable work during courtship if permanency is to follow and the courtship doesn't go on too long. A problem arises if courtship is successful—marriage is supposed to last forever and nobody and no relationship is perfect. Whoops. Once married, some of those trivial, cute little disagreements don't seem so sweet anymore, especially when they've just come up for the twelfth time and a solution is no nearer to hand. Bickering can become a way of life when two people have forgotten why they wanted to be together in the first place. Sex can become the whitewash that hides all the pain or the battleground. When the same old words are used, when nothing is resolved and only hurt is inflicted, telling people they need to communicate is true but irrelevant. Both partners have to be willing to be honest, specific and kind, not an easy order when trust has become problematical.

When one partner never talks and the other never stops, the problem becomes even more serious. When they seem to be speaking different languages and neither listens and one only wants to win or lose but mostly have it over, solutions are seldom found and gentleness is at a premium.

Unless new things are said or old concerns are voiced in new terms, very little is accomplished. Communication requires motivation, insight, time and willingness. When both want to hear as well as be heard, bridges can be built, but both have to be willing to find a new way, not win or turn off or tune out or walk away.

In some marriages, the excitement of a fight is preferable to the apathy and anger and bitterness that take over when one or the other partner decides he or she is unloved or unappreciated. Somehow we are taught to believe that the passion and the excitement and romance will not only last forever but will effortlessly last forever; and when that doesn't happen, we are often quick to play word games about the difference between loving and being in love, about commitment and fidelity and self. Marriage is damned hard work; it is the melding of two separate and distinct souls who have to maintain their own individuality and sovereignty while somehow merging into a viable, flexible unit that can not only accommodate who each of them is at this moment but who both of them were, who they will become, and miscellaneous third parties that may come on the scene from time to time like children, in-laws, bosses, teachers, relatives, temptations and next-door neighbors. Pretty tall order but often worth the effort. The problem is that most folks haven't figured out either the problem or the solution.

We are so unwilling to look at our own lives that we find it easier to demand, often unconsciously, that our partners make us happy, make up for what we feel we are lacking, for what we're not or haven't become. We're not perfect, but we want and need our partner to be. Quite obviously the basis for a happy marriage is two independent, secure people who feel competent and confident apart and therefore choose to be together rather than need to be together. Is it any wonder that so many marriages get in such trouble when we ask our partner to fix what's wrong in our own lives? The responsibility for all of us to make our lives work rests firmly on our own scrawny little shoulders. A marriage can't make you happy, it can only make you happier.

Nowhere is that dependence more evident or more shattering than in the bedroom, where we are not only physically naked but emotionally so as well. And if we're not both, what's the point of sex, let alone intimacy?

The fairy tales always end with a kiss that awakens, a romantic wedding, and then everybody goes to live happily ever after without any information on how it feels to live with somebody who has a completely different worldview, a different biological clock and the strangest bathrooom habits. (Why can't they be taught to put the toilet seat down after they've used it in the middle of the night? Does testosterone kill those specific brain cells, and should a telethon be organized? How many poor souls are the victim of testosterone poisoning?) Our sex education in this country is for the birds. Television convinces us either that nice people just hint dirty all the time, kiss a lot and then close doors or are always having affairs. Women who enjoy sex are usually dead by the last commercial, and men who seem to flaunt their sexuality are usually rich and powerful unless they're drug dealers too, and then they're dead by the last commercial too, often in the arms of the above-mentioned woman. Great sex education.

It's not terribly surprising that since most people marry for the sexiest and silliest of reasons, a lot of the concerns of both partners get played out in the bedroom without any hope of understanding or resolution, let alone orgasm. It probably also goes a long way toward explaining why so many men and women often decide that the cure for an ailing marriage is an affair. That's sort of like saying that the cure for cancer is heart disease. Distracting, yes; curative, of course not.

If we can't talk about what we want and need and value outside the bedroom, it's not too surprising to find out that communication between the sheets isn't terrific either. Not coincidentally, women who can at least make some attempt to express dissatisfaction at the breakfast table are often mute in bed, while their husbands barricade themselves behind the sports section at breakfast but can be pretty explicit about their needs in bed. The problem is that oral sex isn't a substitute for talking, and talking isn't a substitute for oral sex. Both parties have to be able to admit to the problem rather than camouflaging their need for affection, attention and affirmation in traditional but inappropriate and inaccurate ways.

For both partners it often seems easier to focus on an affair than a marriage whether you are the one straying or being left. An outside party is seldom the issue, often the symptom of a problem with the capacity to divert from the real issue, the viability of the marriage.

The good news and the bad news about marriage is that it's so day-to-day. That means it can get stale and repetitious and boring and taxing and irritating; and if home is where we go to escape the rigors of daily life, where do we go to escape the treacheries of a marriage gone sour? A bad marriage can undermine us in a way that a bad job or a lemon of a car or a relentless neighbor never can. Day-to-day intimacy that is abrasive can erode our very sense of worthiness as a human being.

On the other hand, a good marriage offers all that a bad marriage poisons for the same reason: its constancy and ordinariness. A sense of acceptance, of serenity, of belonging, of cherishing and being cherished, of rootedness, can enhance our lives to a magical extent. A good marriage is much less magic and luck than it is hard work, perseverance and self-knowledge, not to mention patience, passion, pride and the willingness to negotiate, to lose a battle to win a war, cooperation rather than competition and oh, lest I forget, love. Like is nice as well as cheerfulness, some time out, a long-range perspective and a day-to-day recognition that nobody's perfect, not your spouse, not you, and certainly nobody else's marriage.

At its best, it truly is the best; at its worst, it can ruin your life if you let it. Here more than anywhere else you can only control and be responsible for your own behavior, and if I hear even one of you muttering about accept them now and change them after you're married, I'm personally going to come to your engagement party and strangle you.

PART IV
KIDS

INTRODUCTION
KIDS

We are a country that believes in its kids. We believe that they are our future, our salvation and our legacy. To say we live in a youth-oriented culture is to mislead by blandness. We center our marriages to a ridiculous extent around them; most women assume their lives would be incomplete without children. Record and movie companies plan their projects around them. Television gears to their mentality. Grocery stores plan their aisles around their eye level, rock stars curry their favor, cereal manufacturers their patronage. Kids set styles, trends and slang vocabulary. They terrorize our elderly, and their concerns dominate our tax rolls. There has probably never been a culture so devoted to the propagation and the pleasure of kids. Yet despite all of this attention, perhaps paradoxically because of all this attention, things aren't quite right. Teenage pregnancy, drug use, illiteracy, lawlessness, violence and suicide are national epidemics.

Kids can make your life terrific or hellish. Everybody seems to want them and nobody seems to know how to raise them. In an infamous survey several years ago a newspaper columnist asked her readers to tell her, if they had it to do all over again, would they have children. Nearly three-quarters hollered a resounding no. We are a country that has been seduced by the Gerber baby, the smiling, happy, perfect infant who demands nothing and smiles lovingly, always happy, dry, well fed, pleasant and beautiful. The discrepancy between that image and the reality of any normal infant or child leads parents to regret their procreation and kids their existence. This section on kids isn't meant to be used as birth-control propaganda but as reality testing, giving you some idea of normal problems between parents and kids at various ages if you don't have children, some comfort in the fact that nobody has perfect kids if you have some of your own, and an idea of what's to come if you're just starting out to raise your own little charmers.

Kids are neither good nor bad; they're just miniature individuals with distinct personalities, good days and bad days, interesting little pings and dings and tempers and skills. It is also worthwhile to note that we only become perfect children when we become parents. A worthwhile perspective on raising your kids might very well be gleaned from your parents. Don't ask if you were a perfect child. Of course you were. Inquire tastefully about toilet training, lying, smoking, getting up in the morning, helping around the house, getting along with your little brother, picking your nose, shoplifting and Aunt Hilda's favorite porcelain doll. Don't forget brussels sprouts as long as you're at it. The intelligence gleaned in this fashion is not only helpful to have but also to share. The worst part about being a kid is that nobody listens to you and you're small and weak. A grownup talking to you as though you're a person and even sharing stories about how it felt to be going to a first dance or first grade or a first dentist can be very comforting to both of you. Not the "When I was your age . . ." story that makes everybody's eyes roll back in their head, but real stories of the pain and humiliation and fear that are part of childhood.

Just as our parents before us, most of us do the best we can with what we've got at the time, but we were raised imperfectly, we are imperfect, we have imperfect kids and we will raise them imperfectly.

My worst nightmare as a parent, other than the obvious—pregnancy, debauchery, robbery, San Quentin, drugs, prehistoric men with huge sex organs and low foreheads as my daughter's prom date—is that I will make the same mistakes with my kid that were made with me and that my grandparents made with their kids. At that point it will seem genetic, chromosomal, inescapable destiny. My only real prayer is that I will make different mistakes with my kid, so they can be sorted out, corrected, forgiven, understood and at least not passed on.

As parents, we need to pass along what we have learned, who we are and why we do and say what we do and say. In order to tell our kids, we need to know for ourselves. Probably fewer of us should be parents than are; we should wait longer and think more. It is hard to imagine two tasks with less in common than making a child and raising a child. The Gerber baby is the ultimate seduction. Babies don't love you, you love them. They don't give back for a long time, if ever. The best way to be a good parent is to be a happy, healthy, non-needy individual who is consistent, thoughtful, content, communicative and sane. Or at least has the potential to achieve all of the above.

If you lined a hundred adults up in a room and asked them what made them feel most insecure about themselves, many would say sex but would really feel worse about their ability to be parents. There are very few of us who are crazy about the way we were raised. Most of us feel that we would have turned out much better if we had only picked better parents. When it comes to raising our own kids, we either unconsciously replicate what we have experienced, our own upbringing, or in some futile emotional gesture decide to compensate and do exactly the opposite—terrific, the unthinking emotional approach: life as extremes. It seems like our adolescence revisited, that time when nothing went right and we knew we could no longer accept the rules and security of the past but were absolutely unclear and confused about the rules we could adopt for ourselves. Blind acceptance or fierce emotional rebellion. It didn't work that well then, and it won't work any better now.

As parents, most of us love our kids and want to do right by them and haven't the foggiest notion of how to do it. The only reassuring thing is that nobody really knows.

It is also worthwhile to remember that we can raise our kids to be successful children or successful adults but probably not both. Af first blush we all would opt for making our kid a perfect kid: obedient, respectful, neat, cheerful, docile, quiet. However, those characteristics have very little to do with the factors that make a successful adult: independence, self-reliance, innovative thinking, courage, ingenuity, inner strength, resilience, a strong sense of self. People don't instantly change because they're twenty-one from one pattern of behavior to another. And while fashioning a child who will be a successful adult is a pain in the neck while you're a parent, it's probably the way to go; be prepared to be asked why a lot and be prepared to be able to answer why as well. Not only will you have a better child/adult but a better relationship and a clearer life. Incidentally, "Because I'm the parent, that's why" must be used sparingly at times when the end of your rope has not only been reached but is unraveling.

Raising kids is probably as much about unlearning as it is about learning. Whenever you hear yourself uttering words that you detested as a kid, you've just switched over to automatic pilot and need to become disengaged. Parenting requires a lot of patience, concentration and, most of all, consistency. If you do the same wrong thing every time, at least your kid will come to expect it of you and count on it; and I or one of my colleagues can help them sift it through one of these days by saying, "Look your parents are who they are; they made mistakes, but so will you. Who are you and what can you do now?"

Just as you felt overwhelmed by all the rules, the sense that no matter what you did it was never enough, so does your kid. Your rules need to be few, simple, enforceable, obvious and consistent. The more thought you've given to them, the less defensive you'll feel when your kid says, "Why?" You'll know. That's not to say that you can plan your parenting completely. The little urchins can always come up with a surprise or two, or what's a childhood for. If your parenting is consistent, the surprises will be less upsetting, cataclysmic and traumatic, perhaps even occasionally amusing or touching. I keep telling you we give our kids roots and wings, and the hard part isn't the wings. We have to be prepared to teach them to walk and then walk away.

If it seems to you I'm suggesting that that's the best way to be able to deal with our kids and to know ourselves, you're on the right road. Being a good parent is mostly about being a happy individual and having the courage to remember how it felt to be a kid. From those two factors, consistency, compassion, kindness, gentleness, strength, firmness, honesty, the willingness to admit to mistakes or ignorance or fear, and a generosity that allows us to love without expecting anything in return all naturally flow. It's not an easy job to be a parent but then it's not an easy job to be a kid. With any luck at all, almost all of us survive both.

Society would function better if people were forced to think about why they wanted a child, or more appropriately wanted to spend the next eighteen or twenty or forty years raising a child. Not trying to hold a marriage together or impress an uncle or follow the crowd. It might not be such a bad idea to teach better contraception, since one out of every three births is unplanned in this country (a very conservative estimate in my experience).

I don't think all this introspection would lead to a childless society but one populated by fewer parents, fewer kids and happier people. There is no doubt that the family unit is here to stay and for some resoundingly positive reasons.

This section deals with some of the most commonly asked questions about parenting. Some of the questions are as old as humans trying to send tiny replicas out into a cold cruel world, whether filled with carnivores or corporate types. Some are as current as today's headlines, which seems appropriate, since part of parenting is as old as human history; but the times and the family structure and the expectations of society, they are a-changing. Which is also why many of us are so insecure about our parenting. Not only might society condemn us, but so, very likely, will our kids.

On the other hand, if reading this section can make you a more thoughtful parent, more consistent, less demanding of yourself or your child, more attuned to the changes in our world, you may feel a little less squeamish about yourself, your kids and your parental report card. There is no such thing as the perfect parent or the perfect kid, just we humans trying to perpetuate ourselves and make the world a little better, a bit more civilized, healthier, more peaceful than it was when we were kids. This section is about how to do it with a minimum of wear and tear and a maximum of pleasure, secure in the knowledge that it's not just us or our kids, but that little of it is fatal.

QUESTIONS
KIDS

1. I grew up in a competitive household and it seems to have become chromosomal or contagious or something. When my sister and I get together, I always feel like my kid isn't measuring up, and he's only seven months. How can I get off this treadmill?

2. I want to send my son to nursery school this fall. He was toilet trained, but all of a sudden he's having accidents. Two kids in diapers is making me crazy. Can I send him to nursery school untrained?

3. My kid is only five but he's so bristly. Nothing I do to punish him even touches him. Will spanking do him any good?

4. My kid dawdles so much in the morning that she's always late to school. I'm ready to kill her. I'm late, she's late and the house is in an uproar. Suggestions?

5. I just got married, and my husband's seven-year-old daughter hates me. Do I have to take abuse from her just because I married her dad?

6. My ex has visiting privileges, but the kids don't want to go with him. Should I make them?

7. My kids live with my ex. They have no supervision and they are running wild. Can I go to court and get custody?

8. How and when should I tell my kid about sex?

9. My kid lies all the time. What's an appropriate punishment, and do you think he'll turn into a serial killer?

10. *My kid has no friends. How can I make him some?*

11. *My kid is the class clown; his grades are deplorable. I ground him, but nothing works. Would military school do the trick?*

12. *My kid is coming home from school with all sorts of goodies. I don't think they're his, but I don't want to accuse him. How common is stealing with kids, and if I don't punish him, are banks next?*

13. *My kids just ignore me. I'm tired of being the maid for all of them, not to mention my husband. Are strikes legal for mothers?*

14. *My kids treat me like a doormat. It's all give and no take. Any suggestions?*

15. *I just read my daughter's diary and I found out she's having sex. Do I confront her and admit I'm a snoop or just ignore the whole thing and pretend I don't know what's going on?*

16. *My kid comes home drunk a lot. When I criticize him, he says his father and I drink, but we just hide it better. Is there any way to make him see that it's different when you're sixteen?*

17. *My son wants to have an end-of-school party with beer, but he's under age. He wants us to supply the beer and then disappear. I want him to be happy, but I'm a little nervous about his party plans. Do I have to follow his suggestions?*

18. *My child is seeing a therapist, but I feel I should know what's going on, since I'm paying. Where is the line between confidentiality and ripping off a parent?*

19. My son just told me he has a homosexual lover. He's seven-teen. Two years ago I took him to a psychiatrist because he thought he was gay. His father hates homosexuals. I've offered to take him to a psychiatrist again and he says no. What do I do now?

20. My son is almost old enough to get his learner's permit. I'm scared silly, but all his friends are learning to drive. I don't even like the thought of his being with them, but it seems like it's either them or him. Do you think he'd buy the idea of a chauffeur, except that I don't want to do that either. What now?

21. My eighteen-year-old son has been living with his mother since we divorced seven years ago. He is sullen to me, doesn't come to visit, never answers my letters or phone calls. He has decided he wants to go to Harvard and expects me to foot the bill. What do you think?

22. My daughter is a college freshman and she wants to go to Europe this summer. She's saved her own money, but it's so dangerous these days. Is there any way to convince her that terrorists are dangerous, not romantic?

23. I think my kid is doing drugs. Do I call the police?

24. My thirty-year-old daughter is still living at home. She's sullen and nasty, and I think she's using drugs. Her father says if I throw her out she'll turn to prostitution; I say at least she'd be paying her own way. Who's right?

25. My son never calls. How can I make him keep in touch?

26. My daughter is making so many mistakes with her child. When I offer my suggestions, she's downright rude. How can I make her listen? It's for her own good.

27. *I gave my child up for adoption when I was sixteen. Now I'd like to see how she's doing. Should I go search for her or leave well enough alone?*

I grew up in a competitive household and it seems to have become chromosomal or contagious or something. When my sister and I get together, I always feel like my kid isn't measuring up, and he's only seven months. How can I get off this treadmill?

Good question, good analogy, good insight. I know exactly where you're coming from, since I came from the same place. I'm the oldest of six kids and we grew up competitive—for parents' time, recognition, best TV seat, largest scoop of ice cream, but mostly for parental attention. Everybody needs to feel special, and for small kids it all boils down to Mom and Dad. When there are that many kids and that few parents, competition is inevitable unless some very skilled parenting is brought to bear.

You understand how it feels, but it does sound like you are still a part of the game. Have you compared your kid's birth weight? Walking skills? Newest tricks? Sure you have. It's normal to want to brag. It's not even unusual to feel some sense of pride in your wee one's accomplishments even at seven months; but competition means somebody has to win and somebody has to lose, and if it's our kids we're talking about, the battle can become fierce and deadly.

What each of us learns to feel is pride in our own accomplishments, a well-developed sense of self, a real joy in the accomplishments of others, a sense that somebody else's win is not our loss—and that comes from a sense that whatever we are is okay and different from what anybody else is.

You are going to have a much easier time resisting the temptation to compare your child to your sister's if you feel warm about your sister and comfortable about yourself. You're not going to be able to keep from being competitive about your kid until you can keep from being competitive about yourself.

What are the similarities between you and your sister? Can you be comfortable about the fact that you both are interested in the same things and might share that enjoyment? Is it easier for you to start with the differences between the two of you and relish those differences without feeling any value judgment, that one is better than the other?

Until you can feel comfortable with your sister, you're going to have a hard time not comparing your kids, and it's real important not to do so—for their sake as well as yours. This whole thing really does rest on your feelings though, since it sounds like you're already defensive about your kid, especially if he's the younger of the kids. You and he will always be playing catch-up. Not only will you not be able to share in your niece or nephew's accomplishments but you will find yourself gloating over their misfortunes if you're not careful. Yech.

There's only one way to get off the treadmill and that's to decide to do so. Wear a rubber band around your wrist (not so tight that it turns your fingers purple) and snap it every time you think a competitive thought about your sister or her child or your child. Make yourself verbalize compliments to both of them, so you get in the habit of thinking warm, generous thoughts. You may find that you like the person you've become, the kind of person who can be warm and sharing. We can influence our own behavior by changing the words we use and the thoughts we think. Your sister may be a bit suspicious to start or doubt your motivation and/or sincerity, but give it time, lots of time. You're responsible for your behavior, not hers.

You might be raising not only a healthier, more secure child but a healthier, more secure you.

I want to send my son to nursery school this fall. He was toilet trained, but all of a sudden he's having accidents. Two kids in diapers is making me crazy. Can I send him to nursery school untrained?

I may not be at the top of your good-guy list for this one. Some nursery schools will take untrained kids, although for many, trained is one criterion for admission; but whether you can find one that will take him or not, I would encourage you not to send him right now. I know you're up to your elbows in paper products, but that's why Pampers were invented. I understand they've just come out with a lace-trimmed one so the bride can match her gown.

Sooner or later your kid will stop wetting his pants, and sooner or later off he will go to school and then football practice and then physics lab and then down the aisle with the bride we previously mentioned. And no, I'm not admonishing you that he will be grown up before you know it and that you'll miss the little tyke. No one ever misses the smell of urine wafting through the house. What I'm telling you is your older son needs time at home with you now, even though it's inconvenient. His bladder is telling you what he can't say in so many words. He's feeling threatened and unhappy and jealous and scared and powerless. He's got a brand-new rival who's taking Mommy away from him and Mommy is cranky and mad at him all the time and he needs to be comforted. You're not a bad mom; he's a hurting kid. Any kid feels displaced when a new sibling comes along. (Putting a sign on the outside of the front door saying "Say hi to Jimmy first" really works.) At a time when you're feeling most frazzled, your older son needs some quiet time alone with you.

It's a time to take the extra effort and involve him in helping you care for the new baby. He may get a gold star on his forehead every time he helps like a big boy, but he will cling to or even return to childish things because he's not dumb. He realizes how much attention the *baby* is getting right now.

This is definitely not the time to toilet-train him or wean him or get him to give up his crib, even if you have to buy a bit more furniture. He may go back to his blankie, his teddy or his bottle, wanting a light on in his room at night, a story at bedtime, getting up in the middle of the night, being afraid of the dark, being unwilling even to go to bed at night.

He isn't crazy; he's jealous, manipulative, threatened and feisty and, most of all, a kid.

If you send him to nursery school right now, he will feel even more rejected and will likely act up in school, be a disciplinary problem or sulk, continue to wet his pants, even soil himself if necessary, be cranky at home, develop headaches and stomachaches, nightmares and hysteria. He's fighting back the only way he knows how.

See if you can't integrate him into your busy schedule right now. Let him help with the baby, give him special rewards for being the big boy, get your husband involved, hire a babysitter so the two of you can escape the baby occasionally (time with you and his dad, just the three of you, is also important), get yourself out of the house *alone* every once in a while, and dinners at McDonald's may buy you some slack. (Time with just you and your husband together is almost as important to him as it is to you. A firm parental marriage can be very comforting to a kid in turmoil.)

Your kid isn't ready to leave you right now, and his fantasies about what you and his new sibling are doing at home will make him unable to concentrate at school, an unwilling playmate, an unloving older brother and a generally unhappy pain in the neck. Take a deep breath, grit your teeth, stock up on Pampers and hug the little monster. He'll get back on track, maybe even toilet-train his sibling when he's ready, and grow up healthy, happy, content and secure, eventually.

My kid is only five but he's so bristly. Nothing I do to punish him even touches him. Will spanking do him any good?

As parents, we have to decide early on whether we want to invest our time and effort raising successful kids or successful adults. Successful kids are obedient, well dressed, compliant, polite; they do as they're told and follow the rules. Successful adults are self-reliant, innovative, often unconventional, impatient and self-motivated. Not only do the two criteria have little in common, but they're nearly mutually exclusive.

Fortunately, in your case you don't have to make a decision. Your son has made it for you. The good news is that with a little guidance and fine tuning he will very likely be a successful adult if you can keep him on this side of antisocial. The bad news is that he's going to be a real challenge to raise. He's his own person and will be surprisingly unaffected by tactics that have worked on other kids. Punishment, especially physical, will make him more stubborn, and he will not show remorse. He'll tough it out. The way to get through to this kid is to allow him to help make decisions and take events, goals and ramifications on himself. If you don't push him into a position based solely on stubbornness, he'll usually do the right thing; and even when he doesn't, he'll know it. If he has time to think about issues and decide for himself, he will very likely be surprisingly reasonable, even at five. Inside that bristly little shell is a very self-contained unit that will decide for himself. It is most likely that even at his tender age he already *knows* what's right because he's thought it out.

If you think about it, parenting isn't about making your kid *do* the right thing, although that's nice, but about making sure he *knows* the right thing to do.

With a change in your perspective, this kid could be downright fun to raise if you see him as a shrunken adult rather than a snarly kid. Think midget. This does not mean that he doesn't need to be taught, rewarded and occasionally punished; but his punishments will be most effective if they are reflective rather than physical. For example, this is a kid who will probably benefit more from time sitting in the corner than spanking. (Nobody ever benefits from spanking. It is a morally indefensible act that most of us resort to sooner or later, infrequently. Do we really want our kids growing up thinking might makes right? If so, we shouldn't be surprised when they bash us when they get bigger and stronger and we are weaker and dependent.)

He is also a kid who will profit from being able to determine his own rewards as well as punishments. He will have a surprisingly accurate and innovative view of what will work with him if you allow him to tell you. You may as well start now soliciting his opinion. This doesn't mean that you become his buddy—you're still in charge—but finding out what is going on in his mind will be incredibly helpful. If you start asking him what he thinks, maybe by the time he's a teenager you won't be faced with the "I don't knows" with such regularity.

Asking him what he thinks is fair will most likely elicit an astonishingly adult, reasoned response even though you may have to prod a bit initially. "I'm giving you an opportunity to be treated like a big kid and to help me decide what's fair. I want you to help me on this."

You may find that you have a lot less bristle around the house. A final word on bristly self-contained kids. These kids often need hugs even more than the kids who can ask for them, and while they seem resistant to punishment they will often melt in the face of praise. These are the kids who need legitimate pats on the back and hugs even more than the rest of us. Positive reinforcement, physical contact and praise can keep your self-contained youngster from moving outside the normal bounds of rules. Not only will he not become antisocial but you may find yourself raising a charming, happy kid. And if it's not so obvious on the outside, perhaps it is on the inside. If something isn't working at five, it most likely won't work at six either. This kid needs gentling, not spanking.

My kid dawdles so much in the morning that she's always late to school. I'm ready to kill her. I'm late, she's late and the house is in an uproar. Suggestions?

The place to start with your daughter is a recognition on your part that one of the major significant differences between adults and children is in their perception of time. Kids have too much of it and it always hangs heavy and adults never have enough of it. As adults we are busy and harried. Kids can hardly wait for time to pass so that it will be Christmas, vacation, my birthday or I'll be a grownup like you and then I can push you around.

As parents, when we are trying to convince our kids we move more quickly, we have to remember that there is absolutely no inherent internal reason for them to do so. You're busy, but this can feel like a lot of pressure to your kid and lead to a sense of stress that can escalate into panic and make your kid even slower. Not only that, but there may be a perfectly good reason for them to drag their cute little heels: It makes us absolutely crazy. Two for the price of one. They win by doing things their way and making us lose our cool, a nearly irresistible temptation for any kid worth his Reeboks.

Looking at the specific situation with your daughter, it may be that you have to find a compromise between your needs and her internal natural rhythm.

Maybe you could get her up earlier in the morning or buy her her own special grown-up alarm clock so she can get herself up. She may need to go to bed earlier or substitute Tiger's Milk (milk, a protein supplement, a raw egg and flavoring) that can be gulped down rather than a breakfast that takes longer to fix and longer to eat. If you fixed lunches the night before or organized lunch money or wardrobe the night before together, not only might mornings be calmer but she might feel less need to get your attention in this exasperating way.

You two have lots of options once you decide that she is

not interested in adjusting to your time schedule unless there's something in it for her. She doesn't want to hurry and she does want your attention even if it means being yelled at.

Kids are smart. They know that physical ailments are very effective ways of getting both attention and care. At this point both of you may have noticed that stomachaches are a mutual concern. How can you tell the real ones from the fake ones that are one more part of the morning hassle—and what if you misdiagnose? Hypochondriac forever or a ruptured appendix?

If it's any comfort to you, nearly 90 percent of all visits to a pediatrician's office by children concern either tummy aches or sore throats, and it's nearly as hard for a physician to diagnose without lab tests as it is for a mommy. The growing pains that are commonly felt in the long bones, arms and legs probably occur too in internal organs that are also getting ready to take care of adult needs. Stress also causes stomachaches in kids as well as adults, and appendixes really do burst. My daughter and I worked out a system for dealing with her early-morning upsets. If she was throwing up, running a fever, having diarrhea or bleeding, she stayed home from school. If she felt punk without any of the above, she went, not because I didn't believe her but because none of us can expect to feel chipper every day. We muddle on through and do a less than exemplary job, but muddle we do. If any of these dramatic symptoms occurred at school, she was to report immediately to the school nurse. Otherwise we all have to get on with it. This took her tummy and throat out of the realms of speculation or diagnosis for both of us, allowed her to understand that perfection is no more a part of the physical world than the emotional world and reaffirmed the fact that I loved her and believed her, but both of us had our work to do.

If your child's tummy problems continue after a calm discussion some evening, you need to take the tyke to a pediatrician for diagnosis; but a discussion of school and kids at school and the teacher and her feelings about school is not inappropriate. A hypochondriacal tummy ache hurts just as much as a pre-ulcerous condition or a bout of the flu. The trigger is just different. The issue is twofold: first, the reality of the feelings, which must be granted but evaluated by you, but mostly by her; and, second, the cause of the pain, real or imagined, which also needs evaluation by both of you.

Assuming that you suspect your child really may be hurting and you have determined that she can stay home from school, do make sure it's not play time, or you will help her to develop into a hypochondriac. If she's sick enough to stay home with a tummy ache, she's sick enough to stay in bed, eat lightly and sleep it off. No TV, no stories, no fun and games. Staying home should be recuperative and boring, with equal emphasis. If home is fun and school is hard, which would you rather do?

A child who wants to stay home is either sick, unhappy about what is going on at school or wanting to partake of what is going on at home. You, as Mom, with a little help from your daughter get to figure it out. Calmly and reasonably and clearly.

And speaking of which, back to your initial problem about her foot-dragging in the morning. Might things work out better between the two of you if *you* got up a bit earlier? Are you so harried that an atmosphere of chaos is what greets her first thing in the morning and triggers her sluggishness as a defense? If you created a calmer atmosphere, might she be less tempted to be so pokey and might you be better able to handle her?

Make sure that she's not playing off your ambivalence about being a mom and having things to do outside of the house. You can change the situation by changing your own behavior, tuning in to her motivation a bit and bribing the little dickens. You two need to sit down and discuss all of this quietly some Sunday afternoon with lots of time for questions and suggestions and discussion, institute it the following Monday morning and expect a few setbacks. Both of you might slip back into the old habits, but a calm morning as a cheerful start to the day is pretty seductive once the two of you get the hang of it and will probably develop its own momentum once you get it started. In the meantime, make sure you're giving your kid plenty of time and attention after school and before bedtime and an occasional hug in the morning. For a kid, warm feelings in the heart are even more crucial to a good start for the day than warm feelings in the tummy. Substitute hugs for oatmeal.

I just got married, and my husband's seven-year-old daughter hates me. Do I have to take abuse from her just because I married her dad?

Of course she hates you, and if you were in her position you'd hate you too. You not only dashed her childish fantasy that her mom and dad would get back together (irrespective of the terms or length or conditions of their parting up to and including death, she is only seven after all), but in her mind you've stolen her dad from *her*. Every seven-year-old female worth her pigtails harbors virulent, graphic, intense fantasies of what her life with Dad would be like if she could only get rid of Mom. The fantasy came true, and then you came along and spoiled it.

Even if the two of you were terrific friends during the courtship, both yours and hers, now that it's for real it's all different. Not knowing anything about the circumstances of her dad's marriage, separation, and singlehood, it's hard to know whether any of her concerns are well founded. At this point, they're irrelevant anyway. If her dad was silly enough to suddenly spring your marriage on her, both of you owe her an apology. Not a nice way to treat people we love.

The good news is she's only seven; the bad news is that "leftover children" from the man's first marriage are the major cause of the breakup of the second marriage. This is not meant to scare you but to help you realize that you do have a problem that can't be ignored or finessed.

If you can remember back to being seven, you will have a huge advantage working for you with this little charmer. You're older, wiser, more experienced; and she hasn't the foggiest notion of what it is to be a grownup. Use the advantage by remembering how it felt to be a child and bring your adult head and heart to bear.

She's hurt and afraid and confused. She needs to know that her dad still loves her, that you're not trying to be her mother. For heaven's sakes, don't try to be; she already has a mom, and if you're going to get the title you'll have to earn it and she'll have to bestow it. You're her dad's wife, period, at least for now. And you're not going to be the wicked stepmother she's heard about in bedtime stories and from her friends at school and from Grandmother.

You can try to be an auntie or a big sister or a friendly neighbor. It doesn't mean you need to be a doormat any more than you need to be in the other relationships mentioned; but discipline, at least for the foreseeable future, should probably be via Dad. That doesn't mean you tattle or threaten "Wait till your father comes home." You take care of your concerns yourself, but day-to-day discipline can't fall on your shoulders now.

Bribery is a potent weapon. One of the reasons we get up in the morning when we feel like staying in bed is that we get paid for going to work. That's a fancy name for bribery. Your life and hers will be much happier if you can help her see what's in it for her if she does what you want her to do. Your wants should be very limited and straightforward and no more than you would demand of a favorite niece. The rewards should be tangible and appropriate and swift. Saying, "You're making your daddy unhappy," is ridiculous, abstract, manipulative and mean-spirited and will get you both into an argument of who's making him unhappier. She will most likely win, even if she loses. There is no winning an argument with a seven-year-old. If you win you're a bully, and if you lose you're a fool, so don't argue.

Her grades will fall in school, she may start stealing, she will undoubtedly lie, but she's not evil incarnate; she's an unhappy kid who feels she's losing her dad. Let them have time together, don't be jealous or competitive, be supportive of her when you can and wait it out. She won't be seven forever, and if you play it right you may be around for her adolescence. By then you may even be friends. You are going to start a subtle, serious, sneaky campaign to win this little cherub over. And on those days when you feel that you'd like to take a meat cleaver to her cute little head, remind yourself that you both suffer from the same problem—you love her dad and feel shadowed by her mom. If you can be patient, kind, understanding and keep her dad from feeling he has to choose and keep her from feeling any more acutely that you're her rival, you may find yourself with a happy marriage, a grateful husband and a very good friend when she's old enough to appreciate the fact that you didn't try to become her mother, just her friend, at a very troubled time in her life when she felt the world had caved in on her.

What you need is patience, courage and a sympathetic friend on whom you can unload. A smile on your face and a sense of humor and a good memory for what it felt like to be seven won't hurt either.

*My ex has visiting privileges, but the kids don't want to go
with him. Should I make them?*

How would you feel if the roles were reversed? I know, I
know, you think it's impossible, but trust me, it isn't. Kids
feel that they have to be loyal to the parent they're with, even
if they've just threatened to run away to the other parent.
Their feelings are a mix of loyalty, of not wanting to hurt
your feelings, fear that they will lose one or both of you,
wanting to please you and a genuine confusion about what's
going on, no matter what their age. When you throw in a
child's inborn tendency to manipulate, the result is what
you're seeing when it's time for them to go to your ex. If it's
any comfort, which it probably isn't, they very likely pull the
same number on your ex for the same reason. Plus, for the
kids it's as hard to leave a parent as it is for you to let them
go. They feel even more powerless than you do, less able to
control their lives and make things come out right.

If your kids are young, it's important to reassure them
about when they can come back (a watch or a special calendar
for long visits is a grown-up exciting way for them to understand the concept), how much your ex misses them, what
fun they're going to have and what a good time they've had
in the past. A special toy or blanket or other talisman can
help a young child make the transition from place to place,
especially if an overnight stay is involved. A young child
should also feel that he or she can call you and get in touch
if they want to, although don't be surprised or disappointed
if they don't. Once with the other parent they are often fine
until it's time to leave, and then the whole process is reversed.

As children get older, say ten and above, it is more important that they negotiate with the absent parent about visits.
Teenagers want and need to spend a lot of time with their
friends and at work and doing schoolwork. But even with
older kids it's important to emphasize how important visits
are to both sides in terms of keeping in touch and not hurting

feelings. As kids get older, they can negotiate on their own, but don't be supportive of their abandoning the other parent unless you feel something is terribly wrong in the relationship, and I do mean terribly. Remember, you're not exactly impartial, nor your ex's greatest supporter. If a young child seems genuinely fearful of the visit—not of leaving you, but going to the other parent—and has no difficulty leaving for school or being left with a babysitter or going off with friends, you need to investigate carefully the source of the fear without "leading the witness." Don't put ideas or words into your kid's mind, but you do owe it to the child and yourself to make sure that the child is safe with your ex. Obviously in most cases the child will be, and simple avoidance is attributable to one of the factors we have already discussed. But don't write genuine fear off too readily.

It's important that you don't view this whole thing as a popularity contest that you are currently winning. Kids need to have access to both parents if at all possible, and your firmness will go a long way toward dispelling the notion in your child's mind that it is necessary to pick one parent.

This is also an excellent opportunity to encourage your kids to talk to their parent about what they want to do and how they want to spend time together. Don't get caught in the middle carrying messages. If they can tell you, they can tell your ex and should.

Just as transitions are hard for adults they're hard for kids, and leave-taking feels awful, hence your child's reluctance. Don't read more or less into it than is warranted. Be firm and gentle, supportive and understanding. And think how it would feel if the roles were reversed and how you would want your ex to respond.

My kids live with my ex. They have no supervision and they
are running wild. Can I go to court and get custody?

Look, if you liked your ex, the two of you would still be together, so it's crucial to figure your feelings about this person into the equation. First take a deep breath and think specifically about what is really going on with your kids. Have their grades dropped? Are they any more anti-social than they used to be to anyone but you? Are they getting in trouble with the law? Are there any more teacher complaints than there used to be?

Assuming for a moment that something irresponsible is going on at the other house, you need to be specific about what it is and what you can do about it. These two factors are also going to be influenced by the age and sex of your kids. If your kids are less than ten or twelve and the same sex as you are, depending on the state in which you live you have a shot at custody provided 1) you can substantiate your claims, 2) the kids don't hate you, 3) you have a good lawyer and 4) you can prove that you can provide a better or at least more supervised environment personally. This doesn't mean day care or a babysitter or an after-school program or a grandmother. If you're working, your hours had best coincide with the kids' so you can show that you're home when they are, and you'd best not have a live-in lover. A new spouse is okay providing he or she doesn't bring kids along and your kids can have their own rooms.

If any of the above doesn't apply, you may want to rethink your position at least from a legal standpoint. Add to the mix the fact that in most states the opinion of the child is taken into consideration, and in most states, after the age of twelve or so, especially if the kid is verbal, they get to choose. If your ex really gives them no supervision, they are most likely to opt for Disneyland rather than Stalag 17, at least in their minds. That's the bad news; however, after the initial gnashing of teeth, pulling of hair, tears, feelings of rejection, rage, jealousy and rivalry, there really is some good news.

Childhood isn't forever; and even if you feel your ex is an irresponsible boob, most kids have a sense of right and wrong by the time they're five or so; and if they don't, there's probably not much you or anybody else can do about it. I'm not saying that kids don't do better with supervision, because I think they do; but you can still be a factor in their lives even if you're not on the premises. If you can keep from bad-mouthing your ex when you talk to them or being constantly critical, they will listen to you even if they don't appear to be doing so at the time. Call 'em, keep in touch, write, visit, remain interested and concerned—and they often grow up. There is even the possibility that they will appreciate you not creating a tug-of-war for their attention or presence or affections. You may lose out on part of their childhood, but you may gain adult friends. I know, it isn't what you had in mind and it hurts like crazy, but really, what are your options?

If you feel they are being abused, mistreated or generally neglected, you have no choice but to try and gain custody; but be very honest in your appraisal or you may find yourself at the losing end of a legal battle, a legal bill and a bunch of beady little eyes that belong to your kids.

You do gain some measure of personal freedom. You can turn into the sweet, generous "auntie or uncle" parent if you can remember to keep your temper down and your sense of humor up.

Divorce is hard on kids and it's hard on adults. The parent who has primary custody of the kids gets to see them but also has to discipline them, and sometimes that parent feels the kids' usually spoken if not yelled threat: "I don't have to be here, I could go live with ————."

You don't have the day-to-day pleasure of seeing your kids grow, but you also don't have the day-to-day irritation of the hassles, the whining, the sullenness, the lies, the worry, the crankiness. You get to have a "date" with them. Make sure the dates aren't too superficial or judgmental and you may find, when you least expect it (or want it), that at least one or more of the little darlings has opted to come and live with you for a while. When this happens, make sure not to gloat or pump the kid for information about your ex or lambaste the kid for his tardiness or previous lousy judgment. If you can keep the kids from feeling they have to choose, you and they will be the better for it.

It may be the only time since the divorce that you will feel a tingle of sympathy for your ex. Don't be alarmed. It will pass.

How and when should I tell my kid about sex?

Most of us wait much too long to tell our kids about sex. We're not so much worried about them as ourselves. The best policy is to tell them consistently and clearly long before they need to know. Having come from a household where sex was never discussed and my own mother's response to *the movie* in fifth grade was an embarrassed "Are they going to show Minnie Mouse menstruating?" I decided to tell my own daughter what's what from the age of three on. We used to take baths together and I would explain our genitals and the difference between ours and Daddy's and the basics about how babies are made. I did this not because she wanted to know details but because it came up naturally, and who's going to get embarrassed talking to a three-year-old. It's when hormones hit them upside the head that it becomes hard on you and hard on them. This is a good time to reinforce the idea that our bodies are our own and nobody has a right to touch them without our permission. *Nobody.* It is also okay to talk about masturbation—that bodies are meant to feel good, but we only touch ourselves in private places in private, so other people won't be upset. There are lots of other things we do in private, not because they're bad but because they're private. It may also make some sense to point out that we don't put strange things in our ears or our mouths or private places either, because we might hurt ourselves.

As the child gets older and the questions begin, you have already laid the groundwork for a frank, informative discussion because you're really not telling your child anything new. It's just that he or she is better able and more ready to absorb it. It is appropriate to pass values along even though it's important to realize that most likely you didn't absorb all your parents' values, nor will your child absorb all of yours.

The only thing I would specifically caution against is confusing sex and love. If more parents were honest about the difference, teenage pregnancy might decrease substantially.

Sex may be best when you both love and lust after a person. But it's possible to feel love without sex and sex without love. If we don't differentiate, the first time an adolescent feels the hots for somebody they will convince themselves they're in love.

Which brings us to another sticky wicket. Regardless of your feelings about premarital sex, to tell our kids about sex without telling them about responsible sex and safe sex is irresponsible and not good parenting.

Responsible sex means being careful enough about your own feelings that you're not using or harming another person just because you feel horny. It's being a little bit careful because all of us feel vulnerable when it comes to sex, boys and girls, men and women. Safe sex means that you protect yourself and your partner from unwanted pregnancy and venereal disease. These days that means at least a condom and a spermicide, and any fellow who says it lessens his pleasure should be encouraged to take his sensitive feelings elsewhere. Sexually active females of any age who are not married should be encouraged to carry condoms "just in case." Sex is still a choice, and abstinence is still good birth control. But "no" is not always the answer, and for those "yes" times your offspring should be prepared and have thought out consequences well ahead of time. Like the sign says, a teenager getting pregnant is like being grounded for eighteen years.

If it's any comfort, a few years back my daughter asked me what I thought the right age was for sex for the first time. I told her forty. She said, "Really, Mom?" I said, "Really." I don't think she should have a date before I do. (I was kidding, sort of. . . .)

Kids are having sex earlier and earlier. I'm not sure it's such a hot idea, but very few kids ask for their parents' or any other adult's permission. We need to give them the information to protect themselves and our moral values, and understand that they will evolve their own standards and behavior, as in other things. The fact that sex is difficult for most adults to talk about is not a good or compelling reason to put off talking with our kids about their bodies, themselves and some of our own feelings now and when we were their age. It's human and important and just a little tough, but putting it off till a better time very likely means that your child will be unprepared, at the very least informationally. They really don't know as much as you think they do on the one hand and are getting constantly bombarded on the other hand by sexy ads, soap operas, hormones, peers who lie and a society that uses sex to sell toothpaste and then treats it like a dirty joke. If you don't tell them, and soon, who will?

My kid lies all the time. What's an appropriate punishment, and do you think he'll turn into a serial killer?

Kids lie for the same reason that adults do—to deal with the discrepancy between who they are and what they wish to be. The problem about being a kid is that you're very seldom content with what you are, because any kid worth his Clearasil understands that the powerful position is that of adult, not kid.

If it's any comfort to you, most kids, probably even all kids, lie, and few of them grow up to be serial killers. (In fact the only childhood trait so far discovered that serial killers have in common is that they all seem to torture animals as youngsters.)

There are several factors to examine in your charmer's behavior: age, frequency of lying, number of lies, subject matter, attitude when caught. Let's look at them one by one.

Psychologist Jean Piaget says that kids aren't really very good at discriminating reality from fantasy until six or so, which means it's hard to call a kid a liar much before that. A parent of a very young child doesn't have to buy into the child's fantasy, but helping the youngster to differentiate what he or she wishes was true and what is actually true is good practice for both parent and child. Punishment need not be an issue at this point.

Once school starts, the stakes go up and continue to do so through high school, college and even professional schools. Kids lie to parents about what goes on in school and to teachers about what goes on at home and to their friends about both. As allegiance shifts from family to peer group, truth is often squashed in the middle.

To further compound the problem, some kids are naturally talented liars, which means they're going to get away with it better and more often, which means they're going to do it more. Often those kids are born to particularly trusting parents, as is the nearly laughable case with me and my daughter. When I first began in broadcasting, the station photographer took us both out to dinner. As we were talking, he remarked, "If you're going to stay in this business, you're going to have to learn to lie," to which my daughter replied, "My mom doesn't lie; she's terrible at it. I, on the other hand, am terrific." My whole parenting career passed in front of my eyes. Her candor about her lack of candor helped me to evolve the system I would strongly suggest to you.

If you're sure that your cherub has done something wrong, punish him and tell him why. If you're *sure*. Don't ask, just explain and punish. If you're not sure, tell him that next time it happens he'll be punished, and be specific about crime and punishment. The point of all of this is *don't ask*. Any kid, and most adults, when confronted will lie, and then the problem becomes When if ever do you trust him, what if you in fact punish him wrongly even once?

If there seems to be a pattern to your son's lying, maybe it's an area in which he's feeling too much pressure for his own good, or needs some help or some redefinition of goals. If it's happening all the time, he may be confusing fantasy and reality, especially if the tendency has come on suddenly. He may need to be professionally evaluated.

If being caught seems to cause him no discomfort, you either have a budding sociopath on your hands or you've threatened a meaningless punishment once too often or you're punishing him for such minor infractions that he feels no matter what he does he's going to get it anyhow. If the first is true, and it's unlikely that it is, you need to find him some professional help immediately. If the punishments are empty threats, it's time to involve him in helping to determine both punishments and rewards, even though he will undoubtedly be resistant at first ("I don't know what's fair, do what you want to do"). If the third case is true, give him some slack. The way we learn is by making mistakes. You're not constantly being called to task and neither should he be.

If your son is a teenager, the problem is simultaneously more frightening and more common. Teenagers have more mobility, pressures, options and hormones. Not to mention drugs. On the other hand, if you haven't instilled a value system in a teenager, it's probably too late. It usually works best to try and help teenagers make their own rules, with your guidance, of course, including appropriate rewards and punishments. And get them a job and pray like crazy.

We live in a society that puts very little value on the truth, yet we expect our kids to clutch it to their scrawny little bosoms like a cherished teddy bear after overhearing us tell the boss we're sick when we're not, the IRS less than the truth and our mother-in-law that her meat loaf is tasty. It is important to instill a sense of morality in our kids and an ability to discriminate truth from fiction. Blaming them for not always strictly adhering is a bit unrealistic.

My kid has no friends. How can I make him some?

The first question to ask yourself is whether this is your kid's problem or your problem. Is it bothering him or you? Let's assume for the moment that he has come to you lamenting the fact that all the other kids in the neighborhood have friends and he doesn't. If he hasn't come to you, you can broach the subject gently, but lots of kids take a while to develop social skills and don't need to have lots of other kids around. Make sure you're not responding to your own loneliness either now or when you were a child.

Are there helpful comments you can offer him about his own behavior? Is he bossy? Or too shy? Or too impatient? Does he share? You don't have to lambast him, but you can explain to him the best way to have a friend is to be a friend. Get him thinking about it by asking him what the person he'd most like to be friends with is like, why he likes him. Maybe because he's a good listener or tells jokes or is very trustworthy. You can help your child to realize that friendship takes work, and real friends, not merely acquaintances, are hard to come by in this life. As adults, three or four or five really good friends are a lot.

Making friends is like any other skill; it takes some time and some effort and some practice. Unfortunately when we're feeling our most lonely is when we are least likely to reach out to someone. We want them to come and find us. Just as adults can't allow themselves to be on house arrest when they're lonely, neither can kids.

One good way to begin to make the effort of friendship is to look around and see if there's not a newer kid on the block or somebody who looks lonelier than even your kid feels, maybe even the class dork. Most kids decide they want the most popular kid in school to like them, which is a bit unrealistic to start.

Your son might invite this classmate over after school or have a modest party or organize a small group or even one other kid to go to a school event. Even packing an extra cookie at lunchtime might work, although bribery isn't a terrific way to build self-confidence.

At one point I realized just after we moved to California that my kid didn't have any friends and I didn't seem to have a bunch either. We were clinging to each other, which is sort of nice but not real helpful to either of us in the long run. She needed to practice making friends and I needed some grown-up company. She was resistant to subtle overtures about needing kids her own age to play with by flattering me into thinking I was much more fun. It worked until I realized that of course I was more fun; I was a grownup, and this wasn't helping either of us. I finally resorted to threatening her with Girl Scouts if she didn't put some genuine effort into making some friends. (Before I get sued by the Girl Scouts, I might add that I was a G.S. Poster Girl, president of the local chapter, candidate for international exchange and a troop leader through college. I think they're terrific; it's just that lonely kids don't necessarily think so.)

We talked about the same things you're going to share with your son, and presto, she found somebody with whom to go trick or treating. Once she had made the effort and built some confidence, she was well on her way, as is the case with most kids, who think that friendship is both easy and given to only the most popular. It gets back to the idea of perfection and loser very quickly. If I have friends, nobody will know I'm not really perfect, but since I know I'm not perfect, I'll never have friends.

If you can remember being the new kid in school or trying to make friends or feeling picked on, your son will be spellbound and very likely reassured right after he's told you, "These days it's different." It isn't. It's still hard to find people who will like us and accept us for who we are, not who we would like to be or who we pretend to be.

If you can help him learn this skill, you will have helped him obtain a very special gift that will see him through a lifetime, not to mention bolstering his confidence and his sense of self-worth.

If he still seems unsure about how to proceed, try a little role playing where he can approach somebody at school or call on the phone. Emphasize to him that putting in some effort is the crucial factor, letting people know him and know that he's interested in them usually does the trick, especially when combined with a group activity.

And both of you should try to make an effort to remember these days—you for a few years from now when he wants to stay out all night with his disreputable friends; him, once his social life is cooking, when you can remind him to be kind to whomever has replaced him at the bottom of the totem pole.

My kid is the class clown; his grades are deplorable. I ground him, but nothing works. Would military school do the trick?

All kids would rather be praised than punished, but they would rather be punished than ignored. Your kid has figured out a way to get attention. It may be that he has older brothers or sisters who are good in school, athletic or unbearably attractive, so he's staked out the funny turf.

You already know that grounding him won't work. He needs to feel important at school, so grounding him at home is too removed, remote and generally irrelevant. Military school may make him stop clowning around or it may not, but if it does, it may be at the cost of his spirit, unless it's something he wants to try.

Before we get into strategies, it is probably worthwhile to remember that we can raise either successful children or successful adults; and while your kid may be a current pain in the neck to you and his teachers, he has demonstrated a sense of humor, an ability to think through alternatives, a sense of what will work with his peers and a certain amount of inventiveness. All of these characteristics often appear in very successful adults. These characteristics also mean your son isn't dumb. What would happen if you sat him down and explained that you think he is clever but it isn't going to feel so funny to him if he has to repeat his grade next year and be left behind all of his friends. That while you have been thinking about sending him away to a stricter environment, you would really like to hear his thinking about the possibility of him clowning after school and working a bit harder or at least not being disruptive during class. I wouldn't make grades a part of the initial deal, just no cutting up or talking during class. In the meantime, I would definitely have him tested for hearing impairment and dyslexia to make sure that he can read correctly. If he can't do the work because of a physical impairment, his clowning may be a cover-up. Assuming he is not physically disadvantaged, what about getting him into a drama club or having him take mime lessons or work with a Cub or Boy Scout troop that entertains at hospitals. Your kid has the ability to entertain, it's just misplaced. By including him in some decision making, you are acknowledging him, empowering him and giving him a chance to get some recognition for doing something constructive rather than irritating. He is clearly outgoing and needful of attention.

If these groups aren't readily available, it may be that, with his personality, he could start a group. The clue to all of this is his involvement and his ability to see that there is a time for clowning and a time for studying; and even if he's very good at one and not so hot at the other, timing is crucial for both. My favorite way of explaining this to kids is that dirt is just matter out of place, hair in the butter or butter in the hair. Neither is bad, it's just timing and placement that make the difference.

Your son, just like the rest of us, has to feel good about himself in order to shoulder the responsibilities of his life and find the discipline to avoid constant destructive goofing-off. The days when your word was law have come and gone. Obviously the approval of his friends is more important right now, but you can help him find their approval, keep them close (he loses contact if they go on to the next grade and he doesn't) and feel good about himself in more areas of his life.

Again I would emphasize that it's not crucial that his grades come up this term, just that he stop being a distraction in class to the other kids. It's important that he does not feel overwhelmed and panicky, because if he feels that way he will revert to clowning, which very likely evolved originally as a response to his nervousness, to not knowing the right answer or not having his homework done. As he feels better about himself and finds more appropriate and productive outlets for his sense of humor and playfulness, you may find yourself with a much happier, more resilient, even talented kid. If not, think Jerry Lewis.

My kid is coming home from school with all sorts of goodies. I don't think they're his, but I don't want to accuse him. How common is stealing with kids, and if I don't punish him, are banks next?

People steal for three basic reasons. They steal because they want the goody; they're feeling ripped off and they're acting out that feeling that the world isn't doing right by them, so they'll just take what they want; or they're doing it for attention. Since kids are people-in-training, the three basics apply.

If your kid is bringing home comic books or new sneakers or fancy sunglasses or a new computer, it's likely he's doing it because he wants it. If this is the case, it's important to suggest to him that he takes no goodies to school and therefore brings no goodies home. If he doesn't already have one, he needs either an allowance or a job to enable him to buy his own goodies. You don't have to accuse him of stealing; just explain that you're uncomfortable with his trading efforts and to cut it out so other parents don't object. You might even be able to institute a series of chores which will enable him to earn the money that will then be matched by you.

A second way of understanding your son's behavior is noting to whom he shows his booty. If he shows it to no one, he probably wants it for its own sake. If he shows it to his friends, it may be that he wants his friends' approval, being a big deal in class. If he's showing the stuff to you, he's most likely asking for help.

If he's showing it to you, ignore what he's stealing and focus on why. Does he have an older brother or sister who gets a lot of attention for good grades or sports? Does he have a new sibling who's getting attention for being cute and helpless? If this is the case, he needs reinforcement from you about what he does well, including gold stars on the forehead, pats on the back or help with a purchase. Any kid hates to be criticized but would rather be criticized than ignored. He's figured out a way to get your attention, and unfortunately punishing him will only emphasize the attention. That's not to say that you should either condone or ignore his stealing, but the emphasis has to be shifted from negative to positive so that he is not stealing to get attention. You don't need your kid to be the first kid in the neighborhood to be in the slammer.

It is not unusual for kids to steal; however it's not something you want to encourage as a way to glean attention. When adults do it, they're either crooks or kleptomaniacs. When kids do it, they need to be redirected, caught and made to understand that it's not acceptable behavior. The issue isn't blame but redirection.

My kids just ignore me. I'm tired of being the maid for all of them, not to mention my husband. Are strikes legal for mothers?

Unless your kids are teenagers, they ignore parents if they figure that whatever is being said will be said again. If you always tell your kids to pick up their room three times, the only time they will pay any attention is the third time. If you threaten but never carry out your threats, you're also teaching them to ignore you. You have to figure out a way to make your words count. The best way is to say what you mean once, loud and clear, and then keep still. Call your kids for dinner—once. If they're not there when you sit down to eat, clear their places. Don't let them near the fridge until the next morning. No bread and water, no nothing until breakfast. I guarantee they'll get the point fairly soon. You don't have to be angry, just authoritative. Nagging is the best way in the world to be ignored. Why listen this time when you'll have twelve more opportunities?

Henry Kissinger used to tell a story about Richard Nixon and his Irish setter, King Timahoe. Apparently the dog had a habit of scratching at the carpet in the Oval Office. Nixon would yell at the dog; the dog would keep scratching; Nixon would yell again, the dog would scratch again. Finally, Nixon yelled, the dog scratched, Nixon opened up the bottom drawer of his desk and threw the dog a bone. "Congratulations," said Kissinger, "you've just taught the dog to scratch three times and you'll throw him a bone."

If kids understand that any laundry not in the hamper won't be washed, the idea of wearing a smelly shirt or wrinkled clothing may succeed where all the yelling in the world doesn't. And if the state of their clothes doesn't bother them, why should it bother you? (Their friends can also offer a terrific incentive when they won't sit with your offensive little cherub at lunch.)

It seems that a lot of your complaint centers around a messy house. I personally believe that everybody is entitled to a messy private place as long as no food is brought in, so the Health Board doesn't get involved, and the offending room has a door. Most kids will clean up if a friend is coming over, and as long as you can shut their door when your friends come over, who cares? Tit for tat works well for keeping public areas picked up and neat; e.g., if you want cookies for your class on Wednesday, a ride to the movies, a friend for dinner, I will be better able to find the time if I'm not picking up your barbells from in front of the TV. (I once pointed out to my daughter that it was not worth endangering life and limb to come in and kiss her good night after breaking a toe on a cleverly constructed Mom trap. A path through the debris was hastily dug by her so that she could be safely tucked in. Obviously, she was not a teenager at the time.)

It seems that you may have trained your family to treat you like the scullery maid. It's a pain in the neck to teach a three-year-old to dry dishes. They're clumsy and slow. But it's impossible to teach a fifteen-year-old that they should be doing it when you've been doing it for them for the last fifteen years. Getting kids and spouses involved early may seem a bother at the time, but it pays handsome dividends later and, more importantly, keeps us from the role of Wicked Nag of the West later on.

Bribery is a perfectly good motivator. It's just the fine art of helping someone to understand what's in it for him if he does exactly what you want him to do. Punishment is much less effective a motivator than reward.

Money isn't a bad motivation for messy kids, early on. I don't think kids should get money for everything they do around the house, but if allowances are started early, kids get a sense of responsibility as well as pocket money and can be fined for lack of helping out. If worst comes to worst, you can use their allowance to pay the next-door neighbor to do their work, which at least cuts down the wear and tear on your vocal cords.

Unfortunately, you may have fallen into the woman-as-maid syndrome. I never once heard my husband, in all the years we were married, apologize for the condition of the house, no matter how horrendous, and I seldom if ever heard myself *not* apologize, no matter how neat it was, how tired I was or busy I had been. You may need to get out of that house. Get a job if you don't have one, so all of your energies aren't devoted to neatness. Pay someone else if you have a paying job; don't try to be superwoman. One of the nice things about dirt is that it's terrifically stable. It just sits there and waits for you. Maybe you could be a bit less neat. If you're out more, you can use your paycheck to hire someone or bring home some prepared bacon or let someone else take charge. If your whole sense of identity isn't tied up with waxed floors and polished silver, the clutter may not bother you as much. If you're still concerned, either you're the only one who cares or it concerns the rest of the family too. If the way the house looks matters to them, they'll pitch in eventually; perhaps not cheerfully or pleasantly, and maybe they won't do a "professional" job, but do you care that much? If nobody else in the family cares about the house being as neat as you do, you can either back off or do it because it matters to you. If it is that important to you, understand that you are the only one who does care that much and you're cleaning to make yourself happy. So whistle while you work—or scour or vacuum or whatever.

However, if you're going to change your behavior and the rules around the house and go to work for instance or leave the laundry undone or go on strike, you'll save yourself a lot of wear and tear if you tell everybody what you're doing and why, rather than just springing it on them. Remember, you're the one who's taught them you're the maid. It's important for them to understand why things are changing and what's in it for them to go along with the new order: You'll be more available for talks or cookies, or there will be more family vacations or movies on Friday night or a new VCR with your paycheck.

Ask anybody you know in a union. Strikes are very expensive. They do get everybody's attention and brings things to a screeching halt, but usually the new benefits don't make up for what has been lost. Confrontation is an expensive way to do business. Sounds to me that you need to do a little of what Lyndon Johnson used to call jawboning or to paraphrase him, to "grab 'em by the private parts, and their hearts and minds will follow." I've cleaned up this phraseology a bit, but you get the point. If you don't know where the family's "privates" are, who does?

My kids treat me like a doormat. It's all give and no take. Any suggestions?

Unfortunately if you write *welcome* on your forehead, somebody is going to step on your face. Do you blame them or yourself? Part of parenting is taking care of our kids, especially when they are small and helpless. As they grow older, our parenting needs to become more sophisticated and involves teaching them more and doing less. There is an old Chinese proverb that says if I'm hungry and you feed me, you've taken care of my hunger for the day. If you teach me to fish, I can take care of my own hunger for the rest of my life. Parenting is initially about feeding and eventually about fishing. The hard part is finding the crossover point. It sounds as though you may have passed it.

Four-year-olds are more trouble than they're worth in the kitchen; but if you start them at four "helping," they won't resent it when they're fourteen, since they will have been doing it for ten years. A fourteen-year-old asked to help wash or dry for the first time will give you a lesson in righteous indignation you are not soon likely to forget.

This is not to say that if you haven't started early all is lost. It just means it's going to be a bit more difficult; and from their standpoint, you're asking something totally unfair. After all, you've been doing it for all these years, why change a good thing? Which brings us to the point. You're going to have to help them understand what's in it for them, what you're going to offer or stop offering in return for some help. I guarantee you, an appeal to their sense of fairness will not work. You've taught them that fair is you doing everything while they get to loaf.

You need to get real specific before you even approach them. Compile a list of what you want from them (loading the dishwasher—not being more helpful and considerate) in return for which you are willing to offer certain things (half hour later curfew or a ride to the swimming pool on Tuesday mornings—not less hassle around the house). You are about to become the Henry Kissinger of parenting. You are going to be cheerful, diplomatic and firm, not necessarily in that order. And it's going to take some time. After all, they're not rotten kids. You've taught them to treat you this way, and you might as well start now to help them understand your needs. Don't expect compassion or cheerfulness from them, just compliance. But in the long run, once you get started, you may find that you like them better and you're a lot nicer person to be around. Martyrdom looks terrific on vellum, but as a life-style it makes you a pain in the neck. Think how nice it will be when you all like each other and treat one another with mutual respect. It won't happen for a long time, but it will most likely not happen at all if you don't start now.

You will otherwise find yourself a nagging, unhappy old lady whose kids never come to visit unless you apply maximum guilt while hating yourself for doing it.

I just read my daughter's diary and I found out she's having sex. Do I confront her and admit I'm a snoop or just ignore the whole thing and pretend I don't know what's going on?

If you tell your daughter you've been reading her diary, she is going to point out that there's no reason for her to try and earn your trust, since she can't trust you, and she's right. It's not that I don't think it's important for a parent to 'fess up when they've made a mistake; but in this situation it does no good, may do some harm, and the two of you have some important business to transact that has nothing to do with snooping.

If you haven't already sat down and had a heart-to-heart beginning discussion and an ongoing series of continuing educational updates about sex, now is the time and then some. You don't have to admit that you've read her diary (she may have fantasized or hoped you'd find it), but you do have to make sure that your daughter knows the basics. She needs to know about how you get pregnant, how you *don't* get pregnant, how to protect herself from unwanted venereal disease (which means using a condom and spermicide *every* time to protect against AIDS) and most importantly that her body is her own to do with as she wishes, when she wishes with whom she wishes. You need to explain to your daughter that there is only *one* reason ever to make love with someone and that's because she wants to, not because everybody else is doing it or because it's time or because if she doesn't he'll find somebody who will or to hold on to a failing relationship or to make you angry. She can say yes, but she can also say no. No kid ever asks a parent for permission to have sex, and your daughter is no exception. It's also okay to pass along your value system, understanding that she's most likely going to evolve her own.

And please don't tell your daughter that the only time to have sex is when she loves someone. It's okay to tell her that it's best when we love and lust after someone simultaneously, but an awful lot of lousy marriages could have been

avoided if women especially understood the difference between love and lust. Seeing a stranger across a crowded
room, tingling fingertips, sweaty palms, breathless kisses are
symptoms of lust. Love takes time and luck and probably
some degree of maturity. Don't teach her how to seduce
herself by confusing lust and love.

This is also a terrific time to share some personal experiences if you can remember them and not preach and not
judge. Kids don't think that we were ever young and scared
and dumb. Most people feel that they had sex for the first
time either too early or too late. It's okay to confess to your
daughter some of your own misgivings and mistakes. It will
make her feel less alone and crazy. (No confessions of anything since you married her father, thank you.)

This is also not a bad time to involve her father in talking
about sex with his daughter. When only mothers talk to
daughters and sons talk to fathers, it perpetuates the notion
that sex is a dirty little joke. Think of how interesting it would
be for all three of you to know a little more about what goes
on in everybody's mind then and now. Why is it we can
show what the bodies are doing quite explicitly but hide what
is truly the erotic and human and warm part—what's going
on emotionally?

An ostrich approach to your daughter's sexuality may be
comfortable for you, but it's dangerous for her. Tell her what
you need to have her know. Don't scare her or lecture her.
Kids are having sex earlier and earlier, which isn't the best of
all ideas, but they're still not asking our permission. It's okay
to say that you wish you'd waited and that you wish she'd
wait (I told my daughter that forty is a good age for her first
sexual experience; she shouldn't have a date until I do), but
understand she's going to do what seems right to her. Educate her, love her, support her and pray.

My kid comes home drunk a lot. When I criticize him, he says his father and I drink, but we just hide it better. Is there any way to make him see that it's different when you're sixteen?

My dear, is it really so different when you're sixteen? We live in a society that is ambivalent about drinking; we say it's okay, that everybody does it, but we kill thousands of people on the highways every year, and at least *half* of those deaths are directly attributable to alcohol. That doesn't count health problems, missed work, broken families and hearts. We live in a country of alcoholics. I'm certainly not suggesting that everyone who drinks is a potential alcoholic or even has a drinking problem, but I am saying that your son's drinking is a family problem and so is his parents' drinking.

First let's look at why you're right. Drinking as an adult is legal, drinking at sixteen is not. You're also right that behavioral patterns learned at sixteen can be awfully hard to break at sixty. You're also right that it's important to learn to deal —unnarcoticized—with stress, peer pressure, the need to relax, temptation, anger, sadness and all the other excuses to drink in order to become a balanced, successful adult.

You're wrong that it's okay to get drunk at any age. You're wrong that hiding a problem with alcohol makes it go away and you're wrong to pull rank and suggest that drinking too much or drinking to solve problems is an acceptable idea at any age. Most importantly, you're wrong to say, "Do as I say, not as I do."

The three of you have a wonderful if scary opportunity to sit down as a family and really hear one another talk about how it feels to have so many issues revolve around alcohol. Your son has learned some of his attitudes about booze from you and his dad. Maybe the three of you could mirror not only how each of you appears to the others but how all of you view drinking for yourself as well as how it feels and looks when the other guy drinks. All of you may want to attend an AlAnon meeting together.

Once all three of you have looked at the family tendency to imbibe, the underlying motivation may be discovered. Is your son unhappy in school, frightened of growing up, alienated from his father, unclear about his own sexuality? (Please don't suggest any of these possibilities to him; you'll scare the daylights out of both of you. These are hypothetical questions. Let him search through his own heart with your coaching, not directing.)

Do you and your husband drink together to have something to share? Do the two of you talk with one another? Are you bored? Unhappy? Frightened? How is your husband's work going? His health? Is it a family tradition to hide in a bottle and watch the rest of the world go by? Is alcohol the family's way to anesthetize the pain?

Your son may be coming home drunk to get your attention, because he doesn't know any other way to relax, because all his friends think it's cute or because he's trying to convince you and his dad to watch your drinking. Whatever the reason, it's a great opportunity to do a little soul searching, a little family counseling and a little intervention.

Just for the "fun" of it, all three of you might ask yourselves to describe the first time you had alcohol. Most people either can't remember or describe it in fuzzy detail. Alcoholics remember it vividly and use exceptionally graphic and emotional terms. See what happens in your family. Whatever else happens, you have a wonderful opportunity to get to know one another a bit better without blame, recrimination or guilt. How bad can that be?

My son wants to have an end-of-school party with beer, but he's under age. He wants us to supply the beer and then disappear. I want him to be happy, but I'm a little nervous about his party plans. Do I have to follow his suggestions?

Parenting is a tricky job. We need to give our kids roots and wings, and the tough part isn't the roots. Admittedly your son is too young to drink. On the other hand, he is not sneaking around or planning to go behind your back. Between the two of you, you may be able to effect a compromise. What if the two of you decided on a guest list that included five or six of his best friends, not a mob. You contacted each of their parents so they would know that the party was going to include beer as well as adult supervision. In addition to your presence, I would have the cherubs all agree to stay on the premises all night, sleep over and not go home in the morning until everybody was sober; absolutely no driving.

Between the two of you, you might also be able to negotiate your son and his friends into coughing up the cash for the beer (it might very well limit their consumption), and you supply the food. You and your son may want to figure out a food menu (lots of carbohydrates; they are growing boys) and a beer menu as well that you would then purchase.

In this way you are able to tune in to the fact that your son is growing up, that he has friends and they are important to him, that he's done a good job during the school year and that he indeed has something to celebrate. You have also helped him to bridge the gap between complete independence and complete dependence.

It is not your job as a parent to make your son happy. It is your responsibility to help him grow and learn to take responsibility for his own behavior. It may also be a good opportunity to discuss responsible drinking behavior. If you simply tell him no, that he's too young to drink, he will have a wonderful opportunity to act out and make you the overly strict, insensitive bad guy. If you allow him a drunken brawl, you are being an irresponsible parent and could very well find yourself criminally liable should something happen to any of his friends while at your home or under the influence of your beer.

By enlisting other parents (perhaps as potential chaperones and sponsors) you are sharing the responsibility and giving other parents the right to say no. It is crucial that at least you and your husband as well as other parents, if possible, hang around. You may also want to have an agreement about clean-up and any potential breakage that might occur (outside parties are less accident-prone but noisier).

Basically, you can emphasize to your son that you are willing to meet him partway, but if he wants to be treated as a more mature person this is his opportunity to prove himself by organizing and conducting a reasonable fun party for himself and his friends.

(I personally am not a great believer in alcohol as a necessary party ingredient, and if you feel strongly about it you may want to offer an alternative; but to sixteen-year-old boys beer is as important as a beard in establishing masculine identity.)

It is also not such a bad idea to remember how it felt to be sixteen and desperate to impress your friends and prove how cool you were.

If nothing else, you may find that your willingness to offer a compromise buys you a slightly more pliable teenager, at least temporarily.

My child is seeing a therapist, but I feel I should know what's going on, since I'm paying. Where is the line between confidentiality and ripping off a parent?

Good question. Sounds like you're the parent of a teenager. A family member seeing a therapist is always a tricky situation for the other family members. *Everybody's* fantasy is that all the family secrets are being exposed and *you're* the one who's being blamed. Honest, that's everybody's fantasy no matter who the family member or what the topic. It's one dependable thing about family; it brings out the paranoia (read guilt) in all of us.

If the therapist is any good at all, the therapy is focusing on the family member who's there, not the ones at home. When the client is the child, the therapist has at least two "masters"—the client and the person who's paying the bills. There is no question that, if the therapy is to work, the first loyalty has to be to the client, no matter how young or how poor, since if your kid doesn't trust the shrink, no work will ever get done in therapy, which means you're wasting your money.

The fear of having therapy as a means of ripping you off is not without justification, however. It's expensive, time-consuming and private. Again, a good therapist realizes this and will make some attempt to make sure that work is being done in therapy (if for no other reason than it's boring for the therapist when nothing is going on). You, however, are well within your rights to ask for an initial interview and periodic updates and even conferences when both you and your child are present with the therapist.

One of the deals I would arrange with my teenage clients was some form of responsibility for their therapy coming from them, whether it was family babysitting, additional chores, actual monetary contribution, a loan or whatever. The therapy is to benefit the child, and the child should bear some of the responsibility. Nobody expects a kid to be able to shoulder the financial burden of ongoing therapy, but the experience should have some value to the client regardless of age. On the other hand, you have to remember I'm an adult therapist, and when I treated kids, they were adolescent and I made it very clear up front that I wasn't interested in what their parents or teachers were doing but what they were doing and what they could do to change their situation. As adults, we can't change our bosses or our landlords or the world; we can only be responsible for our own behavior. If the child was too young or unwilling to adopt that perspective, I would refer him to a child psychologist. The cornerstone of my work with clients is their willingness to take responsibility for their own behavior.

In this context I would point out that realistically a parent who was footing a major portion of the bill had the right to be informed from time to time of progress or lack thereof. I would ask my clients how they would prefer my handling of that briefing. Often they would ask to be there or ask to read a report ahead of time or discuss with me what was or was not okay to be discussed. Any therapist's major responsibility is to the client and the confidentiality of his or her remarks. It has always seemed okay for me to discuss my comments, since those weren't confidential. I would also point out to the client that if a parent stopped paying that therapy would stop, and therefore it was in everyone's best interest to feel informed. At the same time I would remind the parent that if their kid couldn't trust me this whole thing was a glorious waste of time. Also, progress from my point of view might not seem apparent at home, and in fact the opposite might be true; but if they felt about ready to pull the plug to let me know. Often the whole family could be involved in therapy as the kid began feeling better about himself and trusted me a bit.

If you're getting the idea that this whole thing is a bit hazy, you're absolutely insightful. Therapy is a process of discovery, and the discoveries aren't always pleasant or neat; but with knowledge comes the ability to make clearer and more responsible and therefore ultimately better choices. And if you think about it, choices are what we try and offer our kids. That's the whole point of education—more options, more choices based on more knowledge. Isn't that why we want money or power or prestige, for the choices that are opened to us?

Think of yourself as enabling your kid to make some choices based on more complete knowledge of self. You probably wouldn't require a syllabus or a close outline or reading list from your child's teacher; and although this knowledge is a great deal more personal, it is still most likely centered on your kid, not on you or your failings. Your child's therapist is used to hearing kids bad-mouth adults, at least in the initial sessions. If the therapy is to be valuable to anyone, both will have to move beyond that point and will. See if you can be unself-conscious, moderately secure and figure out a way for your kid to take some responsibility for the cost of the therapy so you can be reassured that the whole thing isn't just an expensive rip-off. Then the next most difficult step will be to refrain from asking what did the two of you talk about in therapy today or saying, "I'm going to tell your shrink about this," or not flinching when your kid says, "Dr. Browne says you can't say that to me anymore."

Really the hardest part will be to watch your child change and grow and to realize that some other adult is masterminding the change and you have to be a spectator rather than a participant; it's tough, but an important realization for you and an important gift to your kid.

All of this may cause you to seek out your own therapist, and then you'll realize how self-absorbed and non-blaming the whole process is. Growth is a terrible and wonderful and painful and important process. The question of who pays is always determined by who is contributing the most. In therapy, that's never a question of money.

My son just told me he has a homosexual lover. He's seven-
teen. Two years ago I took him to a psychiatrist because he
thought he was gay. His father hates homosexuals. I've of-
fered to take him to a psychiatrist again and he says no.
What do I do now?

Love him. At this point I don't think your son is asking for
your permission or your approval. He is asking for your acceptance. We don't necessarily have to support our children's behavior or choices to be able to offer them our love
and support in their independence. We don't have to approve of every choice they make, just as our parents didn't
necessarily approve of everything we did, but we do have to
figure out how to get along in this world and make ourselves
happy.

If we could choose, most of us would choose more appropriate sexual partners than the ones we end up with, and our
lives would very likely be much simpler. We're not responsible for who turns us on, just how we respond. The whole
idea of sexual preference is a misnomer. Sexual orientation is
a complicated multifaceted process. Nobody has ever asked
what makes a heterosexual, so it's a bit confusing to understand what makes a homosexual long for someone of the
same sex. It is undoubtedly partly chromosomal, partly ex-
periential and heaven knows what else.

The point is that your son seems to have decided for himself and he doesn't appear to want to change. He just wants
to be honest with you about who he is and how he behaves
rather than living a lie. You don't have to like his choice, but
it doesn't seem fair or smart to assume he is crazy or sick. He
too has to make his own way through this life in the best way
he knows how. Good love is hard to find under the easiest
of circumstances. Granted, his choice of love object may
make his life a bit more complicated, but then whose life is
simple these days? If he can acknowledge who he really is
and find someone who loves him for what he is, not what he
pretends, how bad can that be? He's not robbing banks or

shooting heroin or stealing from little old ladies. He's loving someone with whom he won't have children.

With respect to his dad, that has to be between the two of them. You sort through your feelings and love him in the best way you know how and let him and his father negotiate what is necessary for the two of them. You don't have to choose. You can love them both and they will have to find their own way to one another. I would assume that these days, your son is aware of safe sex practices; and if he's not, you should find out so you can tell him regardless of his choice of partner. You must talk to your other children about the same thing regardless of their sex or sexual orientation. Sex is fine, but it's not worth dying for. Don't be squeamish; it's part of good parenting.

All of us want a perfect life for our kids, but what works for us may or may not work for them, and it's important to reassure them of our love if not our approval. Your son could have lied to you or just not confided in you. Instead, he's only asking for your love. If you can, offer it to him. It is complicated to be a grownup, and if we can find someone who helps us feel less alone, so be it. Admitting to homosexuality is a difficult task—perhaps even more now than ever before—but we have to face squarely who we are and what we are willing to do about it in order to function as healthy, happy human beings.

Perhaps you can find some comfort in the fact that although what he told you doesn't make you happy, the fact that he did choose to tell you is an enormous act of trust. He confided his scariest possible secret to you, praying that you would understand and love him, perhaps not even in spite of it but because of it.

And speaking of you, please don't start combing your conscience to find a reason for his homosexuality—something you could have done differently. Most likely it is nothing you did or said (as I mentioned, nobody knows what "causes" sexual orientation), and even if at some point we discover that saying boo to a three-year-old when he's about ready to take a drink of water is the culprit, what's done is done. Blame is as inappropriate here as everywhere else in life, and it has the added nastiness of denying your son his own mind and body and soul and choice. Love him and allow him to find his own happiness.

My son is almost old enough to get his learner's permit. I'm scared silly, but all his friends are learning to drive. I don't even like the thought of his being with them, but it seems like it's either them or him. Do you think he'd buy the idea of a chauffeur, except that I don't want to do that either. What now?

Now we know why parenting is such a tough job. It's one thing to give our kids wings, quite another to give them wheels. The statistics on teenage drivers, especially male, are horrendous and frightening. On the other hand, boys without cars feel like they're not male. What's a parent to do other than pray?

First, make sure your son takes a driver's ed course. I highly recommend the ones offered at most schools for a number of reasons. They're free or at least cheap, taught by people who are used to teaching kids; they reinforce the idea that it's okay to be a good driver as opposed to a hot-rodder (his peers are in the back seat); and it takes longer than a commercial course.

Second, talk with your son about the obligations of driving —moral and financial. Many high schools have a couple of horrifying films that they show which may be too shocking to do much good, but at least talk with him about how much it costs to buy a car, own a car, repair a car and insure a car. Presumably you have already decided that he must be willing to assume part or all of the obligation.

Third, you need to talk with him about his best, most adult self and the part of him that is going to be tempted to go along with the guys. This mostly has to do with drinking and driving or using other drugs and driving or using the car as a toy. You may want to get in touch with your local Mothers Against Drunk Driving chapter, which will provide you with statistics, videos and most importantly a contract that parents and kids can sign that says if they find themselves drinking at a party, they will call the other for a free no-lecture, no-recriminations ride home. The tendency to act like a jerk in a car is much diminished when drugs are absent. You may also want to talk with your son about the designated driver rule, which says that somebody abstains—not stays sober but abstains—at a party, so the abstaining one can drive home. Not the soberest one, the one who hasn't had *anything* to drink.

Which brings us to the other part of your question. Even if you could keep your kid from driving once he has reached the legal age, how are you going to keep him out of other kids' cars? You can make an arbitrary rule that he can't go with any drivers under the age of eighteen, but it's hard to enforce and may encourage him to lie. It may also not do all that much good. Young drivers are inexperienced, but the real problem has to do with their judgment about drugs and driving and playing with a car.

With luck, without sounding judgmental or like an old fogy, you can instill enough regard for his own life into your son and give him some reasonable, practical alternatives so that he can spread the word among his friends about careful, responsible driving rules. The two major problems as already mentioned are the diminished faculties due to drugs and the flawed judgment that thinks chicken on the highway is cool. Obviously the two are related. By giving your son some information, some education and some leeway, you may find you've raised a good driver as well as a thoughtful human being. As for the rest, like all mothers of teenagers, pray.

My eighteen-year-old son has been living with his mother since we divorced seven years ago. He is sullen to me, doesn't come to visit, never answers my letters or phone calls. He has decided he wants to go to Harvard and expects me to foot the bill. What do you think?

I think you should do whatever makes sense to you. I do think it is a parent's moral and financial obligation to provide the necessities for children while they are unable to provide for themselves. I don't think a college education for an eighteen-year-old falls into that category. It is not a necessity, he's not a child and in theory, at least, he can provide for himself.

If your son were living with you, would you feel more of an obligation or more of a wish to provide for him? If you would view it as an obligation if he were a more dutiful son, then you may want to focus on his duty as well as your obligation. If you would feel the some reluctance regardless of his rather snotty behavior, then you need to clarify your reasoning and explain it to him as well.

Whether you decide to foot any or all of the bill for Harvard, you do have an opportunity to negotiate the basis for a better relationship with your son. I'm sure you feel that his mother has poisoned his mind, but it is time to hold him responsible for his behavior. A bank would and so should you. You may want to set this out to him in a letter, not a sermon in which you set up some new ground rules for interaction. This kind of thing is best done face to face, but it is better done in a letter than not at all. Decide what you want from him in specific terms and what you are willing to offer in return. This part doesn't even have to deal with monetary issues. Think in terms of time spent together, visits, phone calls, attitude, with emphasis on the first three as a reflection of the last. If you don't feel he's been fulfilling his obligations as a son, you may feel less obligated as a father, but he needs to know this.

If you decide you want to discuss college and his expenses

with him, you might want to have some idea ahead of time about how much if anything you feel comfortable contributing.

It is a good time to encourage our kids to think of us as a bank; a bank would want some collateral, some sense of a repayment schedule and some idea of reasonable performance. You might be willing to advance him some money on the basis of a loan to be paid back at some future (specified) date, or forgiven on the basis of a certain grade point average or graduation. Speaking of banks, it is also possible to encourage your scholar-to-be to approach a bank for a student loan, the financial aid office about a loan or a work-study program, to get a job or go to a less expensive school.

Parenting is about helping our kids to walk and then to walk away. It seems that your son has learned to walk away geographically if not financially. You can decide what is important for you to teach him at this point. You can't use the money to make him love and respect you, but you can use the issue as an opportunity to get his attention and tell him what you want him to know about you, about himself, about your hopes for a future relationship, about money and responsibility and respect and exploitation. He may not be at his most charming, but you will have his attention at least momentarily. It's crucial that you decide what you want to do and what you want to say before you meet with him. You can certainly afford to listen to him, but a blanket no or a blank check are both tempting but inappropriate alternatives. Negotiating with someone we love who is giving us a hard time is never easy and seldom pleasant but very important to both parties. Your son is beginning his struggle to be a man; you're his dad, and no matter how rotten he's been, if you can help him in the struggle, you both win. The question is how to use the issue of tuition as a teaching tool. Depends on what you want to teach him and how.

Try to remember, if you can, how awful it really is to be eighteen. Make sure there aren't two of you trying to be eighteen. Be your calmest, fairest, kindest, most generous self, and then decide what you want to do about the money. Be clear about your own motives, expectations, wishes and resources. Be willing to listen as well as talk. You are obligated to be his father, not his banker.

My daughter is a college freshman and she wants to go to Europe this summer. She's saved her own money, but it's so dangerous these days. Is there any way to convince her that terrorists are dangerous, not romantic?

My dear, I doubt very much that your daughter thinks terrorists are romantic. If she does, I would seriously question forwarding any more tuition to her college, because somebody has been filling her head full of dumb, dangerous nonsense. I think it is more likely that she is having a difficult time confronting your negativism. She's probably a little nervous too. After all, Europe is far away and big and foreign and a little intimidating. But isn't there a tiny part of you that is proud of her for her gumption and independence and sense of adventure? Isn't there a part of you that wishes you would have dared the same thing at her age? Again, we need to teach our kids to walk and then walk away from us. She has absorbed enough of your good sense and confidence to want to partake of some of the best that the world has to offer, the chance to explore and learn from other people, other places, to appreciate what she has and where she's from even more dramatically.

She's not leaving you, she's just asking you to be proud of her and support her independence even if you can't approve of her specific decision. She's set a goal and worked for it and planned for it, and even if it doesn't turn out to be a terrific trip, at least she planned it and did it.

It's perfectly normal to want to protect our kids and to see danger before they can anticipate it, but it's also important to help them learn to find their own way.

You may be able to assuage your own fears by setting up a weekly collect-call schedule—once a week, not daily—or ask her to write once a week or get in touch for a good dinner with an old school chum of yours who's now living in Paris.

It's not inappropriate for you to figure out how to make yourself a bit more comfortable about her trip, but don't rain on her parade and absolutely no tears at the airport and no last-minute recriminations.

It's also important for you to make sure that you're not fighting your daughter's growing independence. It's the path to making our children dependent, fearful and justifiably resentful. You've got a neat, self-sufficient, responsible, independent kid here. You've done a good job. Now remember, the easier you make it for her to walk away from you the more likely that she'll come back.

(If it doesn't rain on her parade, it might not even be such a bad idea to meet her at the end of her trip for a weekend someplace exotic. Might be fun and grown up and reassuring for both of you.)

I'm not sure it's much comfort, but, basically, anything that can happen to your daughter in Europe can happen at home, just without an accent. Wish her a lovely summer, lots of wash-and-wears and a bon voyage. Mom, you're growing up.

I think my kid is doing drugs. Do I call the police?

Lots of kids are at least experimenting with drugs these days. It's not smart, but then being a kid was never much about being smart. You need to get some specifics. What are the signs that lead to your suspicions? Have his grades dropped precipitously? Are all the people he is hanging out with doing drugs? Have you found paraphernalia in his room? Does he come home smelling funny or walking funny or talking funny? If you're unsure about some of the signs of drug usage, you can call your local rehabilitation center or teen center and they will send you an informative pamphlet; but you're the one who knows your kid best, and if in your own mind you can point to specific changes in behavior, you may very well be on the right track.

The next question is What drugs? It may seem to you that they're all the same and that one drug is as bad as the next, and while that may be true in some abstract sense, it's not true in this context.

The abuse of prescription drugs is stupid and widespread —but at least legal. The use of the other kind of drugs, if that's what your kid is doing, is not only stupid and widespread, but also illegal and carries not only the physical and emotional penalties, not to mention some rather unsavory associates, but the possibility of jail. Don't be distracted by either your child's or your own rationalization that drugs are a national pastime, or what's the difference between drugs and alcohol. Abusing either is not very bright, but street drugs are illegal and therefore carry a whole different set of penalties.

Within that context, however, various drugs carry various weights metabolically, psychologically, addictively and legally. A majority of kids in this country have tried marijuana by the time they have graduated from high school. That's not to say it's right, but it is common. Trying is also not the same as daily usage. Heroin, on the other hand, is a much more serious, much less commonly used drug. Crack is a parental and societal nightmare because of its low cost, highly addictive properties and potency. If you're not sure which drug your kid is using, you may want to get some factual information before you begin.

Once you're armed with some general information, it's time to start to gather some information about your offspring. Asking your kid if he's using drugs probably won't work. Most kids, let alone adults, will deny wrongdoing when confronted. Gather your data and sit down prepared not to convict your kid but to share the seriousness of your concern. If you're not completely certain, it is probably wiser to have a discussion about your general feelings about drugs than an accusatory shouting match. Part of being a parent is passing along important information; part of being a kid is wanting to find out information on your own.

If you haven't already had a talk with your kid about his changing behavior pattern, grades in school, friends, seeming unhappiness, what have you been waiting for? Again, this isn't a hearing in the judicial sense but in the wider sense. You need to know what is going on in your kid's mind. I know kids are close-mouthed and sullen when they're unhappy and sometimes even when they're not, but if your kid's in trouble, he might welcome a chance to talk, especially if he doesn't have to confess anything illegal first.

If your child is older than twelve, you should have already given him or her a drug lecture. Waiting any later is tempting fate. You probably want to mention that you know that curiosity about—and being tempted by—drugs is normal and natural. You may even think about suggesting that, if the temptation to try grass or coke or beer just once becomes overpowering, you are willing to supervise the experimentation once at home, in the same way many parents are willing to allow a young person's first real taste of liquor to be in the home. It doesn't imply permission but restraint and supervision.

This is a risky proposition, but less risky than simply ignoring the fact that kids are trying and using drugs in unprecedented numbers. Assuming your child is devoid of curiosity or temptation is unrealistic. The approach suggested here allows you to make some distinctions in your kid's mind between the more and less dangerous concoctions, and it takes some of the forbidden fruit aspect out of experimentation. Your kid might also be safer experimenting with you than with friends; don't worry that your offer will be taken as permission. Adolescents do not need nor do they seek parental approval for drug usage, especially if they know you are adamantly against it. (My kid, for example, knows I don't drink or use any kind of drug and am reluctant to take an aspirin for a headache or vitamin C for a cold.)

Most of us as parents are interested in keeping our kids out of jail and having them think about what they're doing and take responsibility for their actions. Most kids know the effects, both highs and lows, of the major street drugs. Even if your kid doesn't take you up on your offer (and I wouldn't expect him to), you may—by being calm, informative and logical—increase the probability that any experimentation is done with a little more knowledge and a bit less of a feeling of daring. After all, how exciting can it be if Mom was willing to go along?

Sounds like it might be a bit late for this approach with your kid.

As long as you're playing detective, think about money. Drugs cost money, and if your kid is doing drugs on any sort of regular basis, there has to be a money source. Does he have a job? Interestingly enough, most kids who work don't seem to have as high an incidence of drug usage, perhaps because earned money is hard to come by and harder to part with; perhaps because kids who work have some outside source of stimulation, gratification and identification; perhaps because it's hard to keep a job if you're high. This isn't foolproof, but it's one more reason why jobs are a good idea for kids. Is your kid stealing from you and you just haven't wanted to admit it? If so, this might be an avenue to pursue. First, lock up your money; second, talk with your kid about the disappearance without confrontation—any kid or adult will deny stealing when confronted—but with an eye to discussing a problem around the house. If your kid isn't working or stealing, best hope he isn't dealing. Both the penalties and the ramifications are nastier.

At the very least, it's time to talk with your kid about what's going on in his life. If school is still under control, you've got less of a problem than if it's not. If he will still talk with you, you've got a different problem from the one you have if you're locked out. Is your child coming home at night? If any part of his behavior seems normal, you've still got some hope of reaching him. If there is an older brother or sister around or a cousin or other family member who might be able to talk from recent experience about drug use, that rather than a lecture might work. If you have anything to contribute about your days of experimentation, it might help. If your kid is still reachable, give it your best try, not in the form of a lecture or a threat, but as a dialogue in which you share your information and your concerns, and then you listen.

If your kid is beyond dialogue, you've got some serious thinking to do. The issue isn't confrontation or punishment but helping your kid out of a dangerous and unhappy situation. Calling the police in takes the matter out of your hands, but it's a last resort and not one likely to endear you to your child now or forever. It is a last resort and better than ignoring the problem, but it has to come at the bottom of a list that includes talking, family intervention, a visit to NarcAnon (for family members of drug users), a phone call to the local detox center. The police can only enforce the law, they cannot cure or counsel or even negotiate. They can arrest, and prisons aren't great places for anyone. I would call the police on my child only after I had exhausted all other possibilities, but I would call the police before I would let my child drift away forever. I would call the police to save her life.

My thirty-year-old daughter is still living at home. She's sullen and nasty, and I think she's using drugs. Her father says if I throw her out she'll turn to prostitution; I say at least she'd be paying her own way. Who's right?

As parents, we need to give our kids roots and wings, and the hard part isn't the roots. Your daughter is a chronological grownup but still living as a child, which must be difficult for all of you. You haven't told me whether or not she has a job or a child or is in school, although presumably if she is really on drugs she at least has some source of income.

You also haven't told me whether or not you are charging her more than a nominal room and board. (If I can come and live with you, get three square meals a day, a phone, maid service and clean sheets for twenty-five dollars per week, I'll be right over.) By charging a realistic room and board, at least a hundred and fifty dollars a week, you may encourage her to find her wings. Why pay a hundred and fifty to be harassed, when for a little more you can share an apartment with a less demanding roommate? If your daughter needs a few weeks to find herself, is going through a crisis or just needs a bit of non-stressful time, then you may want to explain to her that she is welcome for a specified length of time under specific circumstances, then it's back to the real world for her.

You are not helping her find the road to adulthood by making it easy for her to be a child. Believe it or not, she won't thank you for it, nor should she. Your time and effort and money and concern are more appropriate to helping her to move toward more independence.

This doesn't mean you have to throw her out immediately or be a doormat, but it does mean that you and your husband have to sit down and agree on a plan that both of you can present to her, one which gently but firmly includes a timetable. All parties would probably be happier if you agreed to underwrite her living elsewhere for a couple of months until she could get on her feet.

It isn't clear whether or not she contributes to the functioning of the household in any way at this time. Does she clean or cook or contribute economically? Does she adhere to the household routine and time schedule? Does she share meals as well as chores? My guess is that the answer is none of the above. She most likely feels at age thirty that she deserves some privacy and independence and consideration. She certainly does, and that's why kids leave home. If she continues to live under your roof, both you and she will see her as a child. This isn't realistic or healthy for either of you.

Her father's concern may be legitimate insofar as her ability to earn a living, but again, isn't it time to offer her a tangible incentive to get her life on track? Don't help your daughter become a couch potato or a bumette. It may make you and her dad feel strong but it weakens her.

Once you two are living in separate households, you may find that you can learn to like one another again, and Sunday brunch can be a wonderful opportunity to keep in touch when the telephone just won't do.

She needs to get on with her life, and you and your husband need to get on with yours. Which brings me to another topic. Is it possible that your husband's reluctance to give your daughter a shove out of the nest has to do with misgivings about the strength of your marriage or at least your ability to communicate with one another? Many American marriages are child centered, and the idea of no child around to keep the conversation going can feel terrifying to one parent or the other. Keeping your daughter around as a hostage isn't fair to her or to the two of you. Talking with your husband about supporting your daughter's move toward independence may be the beginning of a new life and a new relationship based on both of your needs as adults rather than as parents. Scary, but exciting. On with it. It's not who's right or wrong but what's best for all three of you, and in this instance it all comes down to the same answer.

My son never calls. How can I make him keep in touch?

Time is one of those funny commodities that mean very little to us at the beginning and end of our lives because we seem to have too much time and too little to do. In the middle of our lives the opposite is true—so much to do, so little time. Your son is now as busy with his life as you were when you were his age. And just as self-centered and just as self-involved. He's busy with his career, his social life, his friends, his home and his kids, his car, his errands. If the most important thing in your life is still him, you're bound to be disappointed and after a very short while embittered, which means that when he does call the first words out of your mouth are going to be "Why haven't you called?" Not much motivation to call again soon.

The problem is with your life and your time—too little life, too much time. What are you doing to keep yourself busy and happy and involved? You need to feel connected, that you matter to someone, but your son is not the best choice. Do you have your own friends? They don't necessarily have to be the same age or sex, but they should be people you have cultivated on your own who care about you and with whom you share an equal relationship, which means they may not be family (unless you've worked out old inequalities) and they won't be work related (unless you've cultivated independent interests together apart from work) and they won't be your husband's friends (unless you've pursued them independently). If nobody you can think of falls into the category of independent, equal, adult, cherished friend, you're in trouble and you're going to be very lonely. If your friendships are based on proximity or function or convenience or another person, they're really acquaintanceships, and when the situation on which they're based changes, so will the relationships. They will wither and die unless you nurture them. Friendships take time and effort and work, not convenience.

You know how to make friends; you probably lectured

your kids about it when they were young. Take yourself off house arrest and get out there and join the Y or smile at someone at the supermarket or comment on somebody's new baby or volunteer some time or see if there's a senior citizens' club that needs some new blood or lead a Girl Scout troop or start a bridge club. Nobody's going to knock on your door and offer to be your friend. Get out there.

In the meantime, when is the last time you called your son to invite him for a special dinner or tell him a quick (emphasis on the quick) tidbit or joke. Communication is a two-way street. Take some initiative, but don't be a nag. Once a week is probably often enough for a quick howdy from you to him. And when he does call, be cheerful and pleasant and bite your tongue before you ask him why he hasn't called. Whining is hard on stomach linings as well as ears. All of us move toward pleasure and away from pain. If you're a pain . . . you get the point.

Figure out fun things you can do together—no more than once a month—that may be on neutral turf. If he likes baseball, get a couple of tickets and take him rather than asking him to help you fix the leaky washer in your sink. If the time he spends with you is fun, he's more likely to want to be with you.

You raised him, and the way you treated your parents may very well be his role model. But even if you were a terrific kid and he's not, you do the best you can in terms of running your own life and being pleasant to be around and as undemanding as possible. If you treat your son's visits as icing on the cake rather than the most important thing in your life, it will be much easier for both of you. Great suffocating, overwhelming clutching and panicky need are tough to tolerate. If you've ever had somebody who has been desperate for your presence you know how rotten it can feel—first because it is suffocating and your impulse is to escape quickly while you still can and second because you hate yourself for feeling that way. Nobody likes to feel needed that much. Loosen up a bit. Independence is attractive in everyone at any age.

Just in case you're tempted to try that old standby, guilt, don't. Guilt is not a very good motivator. You will feel ashamed of yourself and fall into your own trap; he will feel angry and manipulated, and things will be worse, not better, between the two of you.

If you're happy and busy, he will either visit more often because you're more fun or he won't, but you won't be home to notice.

My daughter is making so many mistakes with her child. When I offer my suggestions, she's downright rude. How can I make her listen? It's for her own good.

Do you remember being a brand-new mother and having your mother offer her unsolicited advice? Do you remember how it made you feel, especially if the advice was right on the money? You were probably ready to wring her neck. It's really no different with your daughter. The important word here is "unsolicited." If your daughter asks for your opinion, it is appropriate to offer it gently, cogently and once. Because she once asked doesn't mean you can consider it carte blanche and continue to offer advice.

As you undoubtedly remember, parenting sometimes feels like an overwhelming responsibility, and most of us feel ill equipped to handle it. Most of us also aren't crazy about the way we were raised, and yet we find ourselves falling into the same patterns because it's all we know.

I grew up the oldest of six kids, and my sister and I shared a room from the time both of us were toddlers. We were never very close, but I can remember several times when we whispered after lights out, sharing secrets and thoughts and affection, and sure enough, my father would holler up, "One more word out of you two and I'm coming up there and then you'll have something to cry about." I swore I would never do that to my kids ever. Then I started babysitting (I didn't even have to wait for the real thing), and I can remember yelling the same thing up the stairs at my charges. I was tired, it was past their bedtime and I wanted some peace and quiet. So much for resolve. Often we are horrified to find ourselves trapped in our role models.

If your daughter wants your advice, she'll ask for it. Unless you feel that she's a genuinely unfit mother—not incompetent, unfit—keep your opinions to yourself. If you feel she's unfit, you need to think in legal terms to protect the children.

If you're getting the idea that I don't think your daughter wants or needs somebody peeking over her shoulder second-guessing her, you're right. You have a much more important role to play, that of grandparent. You get to be warm and supportive without criticizing or making rules or being fair. You get to be just plain loving and there for your grandkids. My grandmother is one of the emotional pillars of my life. She didn't spend much time with me when I was growing up and definitely favored other siblings and cousins, but as adults we've discovered that we have a very similar outlook on life and share secrets. We giggle a lot, and when either of us needs to be reassured or just loved, we visit or call and occasionally write and send each other goodies for no earthly reason.

She will patiently listen to my complaints about anything in this world except my mother, since we both love Mom; and Gram shouldn't have to take sides between her daughter and her granddaughter. She always has time to listen to my latest triumph or broken heart or grand scheme.

You too can be a grandparent once you stop being a critic. Love your daughter, support her emotionally when you can, keep your mouth shut unless she asks your opinion, and offer your grandchild what you can't offer your daughter—unconditional, non-judgmental love.

I gave my child up for adoption when I was sixteen. Now I'd like to see how she's doing. Should I go search for her or leave well enough alone?

I have no idea how old your daughter is now, which would obviously make a difference to her, to her new family and perhaps even to you. Once a child reaches her majority, she is a great deal freer to indulge her curiosity without needing parental permission. Let me try and walk you through some of the considerations before you make your decision.

Your daughter may or may not know that she has been adopted. Assuming that you could obtain her records and find out where she is living, what would happen if you showed up on her doorstep one day and disrupted her life? This leads very quickly to your motivation in searching for her. Are you looking for her sake or yours? Are you curious? Jealous? Lonely? Remorseful? You're the adult and you must make sure that your needs are not going to damage your child. What are your expectations? Fantasies? If you are anticipating a tearful reunion, you may want to rethink your scenario. Your daughter has been raised from birth by people who justifiably feel she is their daughter and they are her parents. Your role, to say the least, is ambiguous. None of the parties might welcome you with open arms.

This isn't to say that you shouldn't look but that you should be aware that it may not turn out the way it does in the movies.

There is now a national organization (ALMA) that allows biological mothers to list themselves, and if the child decides that he or she wants to search, the offspring can get in touch rather than the other way around, which seems a bit less dangerous to me. Most kids if they are going to search do so either during the teenage years or after they leave home, often before they begin their own family and feel the need or curiosity to fill in their history a bit from a medical as well as personal standpoint.

It's important to remember that parenting is more than

giving birth. You had the sense at sixteen to realize that you could do one but not the other. I'm sure it was a very difficult decision then and probably hasn't gotten a whole lot easier through the years, but your curiosity about who she is, what she looks like, how she would relate to you, has to take second place to your daughter's well-being today just as it did when you were sixteen. If you are concerned about her current welfare, do get in touch with someone who can put you in touch with the national link-up. In the meantime consider what you want to say to your daughter, your friends, your family, people who may not be aware of this part of your past. Make sure that you are not asking this long-lost child to fill in some blank in your life. She may or may not be willing to do it, and it's not fair to ask at this point. Get your own life in order and then see about registering so she can begin the search if and when she wishes to.

It took real courage to realize your limitations when you were sixteen. See if you can remain strong enough at this period in your life to give your daughter the gift of choice. Not easy, I know, but very important to both of you in the long run.

SUMMARY
KIDS

Kids are often the repository of both our hopes and fears. Through them we hope to be vindicated as not only parents but also as giving, thoughtful, worthwhile people. Once we believe that they're the truest reflection of our most private selves, their behavior becomes a great source of pride, not to mention terror. If they're not perfect, what does that say about us?

They are not ours. They are their own people and have been from the moment of birth if not conception. They are loaned to us to teach the best we can, but they are neither our possessions nor reflections. Sometimes we will end up loving them, sometimes not. Liking is even more problematical, but most of us do the best we can and develop a bit more compassion about our upbringing once we have our own kids.

We start worrying how to mold them when we worry about their feeding schedule, ours or theirs, solid food or milk, cup or bottle. The first misgivings may not come when they holler through the night and can't be comforted but when we're convinced that they will be the only winner of the Nobel Peace Prize to be wearing a Pamper. Resistance to toilet training need not be viewed as a lifelong problem, even though it may seem like it at the time of hastily trying to get your kid to use the potty before Grandma arrives for a two-week visit.

If toilet training revives old hidden memories, the first day of school summons the long-buried bugaboos about having no friends. We go from worrying that they won't have any to hating the ones they have. And even if the friend could earn the Good Housekeeping Seal of Approval, his brother picks his nose, his toes or the locks to his grandmother's safe deposit box, and our kid will learn those most valuable and irritating skills. And just wait till their friends are old enough to drive.

In between the first day of nursery school and your daughter's hoody first boyfriend who can drive and do other adult things come the issues of crime and punishment, when and how to punish and for what, and how to figure out who really did it. How can you make sure that that cute little tyke who used to crawl up on your lap with sticky fingers and swear, "Mummy, I wove you" can be cured of lying, stealing, picking her nose and awful friends; and if so, what can you do to alter her behavior short of reform or military school?

Other questions that come up during the intervening years are "Why did I do this?" "When do I tell them about sex?" "If I don't tell them, will they abstain?" and "Why don't they ever listen to me or appreciate anything I do?" or more succinctly "Is a grateful child a contradiction in terms?"

Your versus your child's responsibilities in school will be an ongoing issue as long as there is a PTA and a teacher, a principal and a school guidance counselor left on the face of the earth. Sorting it out for yourself only lasts for twelve years per child unless you decide to finance college.

Ten years ago parents used to worry about the empty nest syndrome: "How do I cope with the loneliness of my kids' departures?" Now it's much more likely to be "How can I get them to depart?" The economy has changed, the demand for higher education has changed; and unfortunately the demand for comfort, security and money has stayed pretty much the same. Where there was once only one set of parents to bug, there are now multiple sets with blending and coupling and uncoupling and regurgitated families. Divorce has rendered the two-parent family nearly obsolete as well as the phrase "Wait till your father comes home." He may very well not ever be coming to that particular home, and if he is he may not be *your* father but merely *my* husband. The possibilities for a lot more interaction, support, confusion, manipulation and, of course, blame exist.

The extension of the extended family to include divorce and new families may make the issue of early sex education even more important than it once was.

In many households adults and children who are unrelated by blood are often living under the same roof with fewer of the societal taboos that tended to suppress curiosity and experimentation. Sex education usually works best when it is undertaken early, not only for the information of the child but for the comfort of the parent. It's a lot easier to tell a four-year-old about sex than a fourteen-year-old. At four, embarrassing questions are a way down the road, and by then you've had a long time to practice answers.

In addition to our value system about sex, our kids need to know our stance about drugs, including alcohol. Before you go righteous on either me or them, remember it's hard to convince a kid of our sincerity when we do one thing and say another. Rules are important, but they are most effective when coupled with a whole viable explanation that includes a value system. It doesn't mean they will accept our system any more than we accepted our parents' system in total, but they need formal exposure to it. The earlier you begin talking to your kids about the hard stuff—sex, drugs, rock and roll —the firmer footing your values will have in their mind before their friends get to them. Peer pressure, as you may recall, is an unbelievably powerful influence. Pretending to be perfect as a parent doesn't give you much room to maneuver with your kids, let alone for them to deal with you.

If I'm making parenting sound like an awful lot of basically unrewarding work, you're setting yourself up for much less of a jolt. I'm trying to offset the Gerber phenomenon. Don't worry; all is not lost or futile. Being a grandparent seems to be wonderful by all accounts if you can wait that long and resist the temptation to criticize once it is upon you. Just hope that it doesn't come to pass when your chicklets are still teenagers. Giving them information now is the best protection you can buy against becoming a grandparent before you're ready.

PART V
WORK

INTRODUCTION
WORK

The idea of work definitely isn't what it used to be. When our grandfathers talked about work, they were talking about their destiny. They toiled in the mines, at banks, in law offices or on the farm, often as had their fathers and their fathers' fathers and before that, whether in the old country or the new. The legacy was passed with the idea of betterment. For most, betterment meant more money, cleaner fingernails and fewer hours. And work was something you did for a lifetime, no matter how short and dangerous and dingy or safe and prestigious and gold-watched. Grandmother's work was also of the lifetime variety and centered on keeping grandfather's shirts clean, likewise his house and kids and keeping the man efficient and able to work by providing nutritious meals and a calm and stable and healthy environment on the home front. If this all seems hopelessly old-fashioned, think about what preceded Grandfather's conception of work.

If you can trace your lineage back to the *Mayflower*, your menfolk were likely farmers, at least once they got here, since that is what better than 90 percent of the male population busied themselves with. If your family came a bit later, they may have been merchants or studied or robbed banks. Once they got here, the menfolk may have found themselves without a job, needing to send the womenfolk to work. Once men could speak the language, they often joined the women, and once the Industrial Revolution hit, there wasn't really the need for men and women to work alongside one another anymore either in the fields or in the shops. Machines replaced lots of people, and women went home to treat children as their work. This whole idea is a relatively modern one in the history of human civilization, even though it seems old-fashioned now.

The purpose of this mini-tour through the corridors of offices and sweatshops is to give you the sense that even though the whole notion of who works and what they do and for how long and for what price seems very different from the way it was fifty years ago; it was very different fifty years before that and for the fifty years preceding.

Work is a society's idea of how people should spend their time. Until recently, that included all able-bodied people, including children. Today we feel that children should learn and adults should work. (For just a moment let your mind wander over how this dichotomy between children and adults has affected women and their willingness to work and/or acceptance in the workplace. In a society that doesn't allow children to work, making it difficult for women to work makes them more childlike.)

Work has been considered necessary for much of human history but not always important. We are probably now in the midst of a pendulum swing. Our grandfathers felt that what they did defined their existence; our fathers tried to better themselves through education, so working would be more pleasurable and less physically demanding although often more intellectually challenging and emotionally stressful. Today both men and women seek personal fulfillment as well as a paycheck and often change jobs as well as careers. The mid-life career change has become symbolic of the changing position of work. We want to be happy at work. The whole idea of work as necessary and drudgery and expected has been transformed into the idea of work as providing for leisure and pleasure and being a means to an end.

The emergence of women into the work force is not unprecedented, but when combined with the changing nature of work has altered the workplace irrevocably. The idea of work as something plodding and blood sapping and soul draining has been undone by the number of people who are clamoring to work voluntarily. How bad can it be if people want to do it rather than have to do it?

Never before has the word "work" conjured up the idea of office space rather than laundry, farm or mine. It's not that those alternatives don't still exist, but they consume the time and energy of fewer and fewer people. If we were once a classless society (probably never were), we certainly made distinctions on the basis of money and how you got it, which gets us right back to work.

We want work to define our existence, which is a legacy from the primarily male workplace. Ask a man to describe himself and he will tell you what he does to pay the rent. In theory, women's emergence into the workplace with their historical emphasis on love and family might have been expected to dilute that. We are certainly more than what we do to pay the rent. However, because work has become so intimately tied with status, women too seem to have acquired the tendency to define themselves in terms of the work they do, to the horrifying extreme of the embarrassed statement "Oh, I'm only a housewife." A capitalistic society has done its work and convinced both sexes that we are worth as much as we get paid. Whether it's right or not, it is prevalent, easy to measure and tangible.

It is not surprising that, with the increasing importance we place on our self-definition, we are investing more and more emotional energy, if not actual time, in the workplace. Believe it or not, this tendency has been snowballed by one of the most popular (and longest-running) television shows ever produced in which work replaced every other institution. The "M.A.S.H." philosophy of life suggests that the workplace offers us all that we need in this life: family, companionship, employment, stimulation, sex, love, friendship, excitement, hobbies, philosophical discussions, food, exercise, clothing, enemies, something to believe in (a home away from home) and in this case a place to sleep. The fact that the TV series is fiction, a comedy and set in an era and place about which few of us know much (the Korean war, of all things) has done nothing to diminish the intensity of the rosy package and nifty thought of getting all of our goodies in one place. It's so terrifically efficient. Few jobs can measure up to that kind of intense longing based on a fantasy.

This section would probably be a great deal shorter and less complicated if all of us could get used to the notion that work is the place to work. We have lost that thought with some obvious advantage. Sweatshops don't exist anymore. Work as productive and important and useful isn't a bad reason to get up in the morning. Work as all consuming, all important, self-defining and constantly pleasurable is unrealistic for most people. The temptations and pitfalls of the new work ethic are detailed in the pages to come. Maybe some of the more obvious and common pitfalls can be avoided. Some are modern and trendy and unique to the changing role of men and women at work. Some are as old as the necessity to get things done. As work continues to remain crucial to men and becomes more important to women's self-definition, the opportunity for misunderstanding, misbehaving or mismanaging will increase.

When all is said and done, Freud said it all when he stated that the two things all of us need are work and love. Believe it or not, work is the easier of the two for most of us, since it can be negotiated on our own. Easier is not easy as you will see in the coming pages.

QUESTIONS
WORK

1. I'm supposed to start college in the fall, but I've got a great job offer that will pay me gobs of money. How important is a college education anyway?

2. I'm having a terrible time finding a job. They all want me to have experience. Do you think it's okay to fudge some experience?

3. I've got a chance to move up in the company, but I'm not sure I'm ready, and besides I'd have to move out of state. Do you think it's okay to tell them I'm not really ready yet?

4. I've become so passive in my life. Every time I think about making a change, I become terrified. Can you recommend any medication that might help?

5. I feel like I'm under constant pressure. I never seem to get reports in on time and my boss gets furious. When I get around to it, they're pretty good, but I'm not sure whether it's me or him. Should I change jobs?

6. There are not enough hours in the day to get everything I want done. How can I get better organized?

7. I've started my own business in the last year and the struggle seems to finally be paying off. A couple of competitors have offered me a job. Should I tough it out a bit longer or join up with them?

8. I keep getting fired. They just don't understand that I'm a sensitive person and I don't need this hassle. Any fields you can suggest that might appreciate my talents?

9. I haven't been working for a while, and I'm afraid a prospective employer is going to wonder why not. Should I just not put dates on my resume?

10. I just got fired. I'm tempted to tell my boss what I really think of her. What do you think?

11. I've got the world's dumbest boss. He's really incompetent and it's hard taking him seriously. Any suggestions?

12. There's one person at work who's a gossip and a liar and really disruptive. She's old and entrenched. Isn't there anything we can do?

13. My boss is really adorable and I'm sure he's interested in me. Should I risk an office romance?

I'm supposed to start college in the fall, but I've got a great job offer which will pay me gobs of money. How important is a college education anyway?

What a lovely situation to be in, an embarrassment of riches. No matter how much money somebody is throwing at you now, you're comparing it to what you've been making so far, which probably isn't much. What seems like a huge amount of money now will probably seem much less in the next few years. This doesn't mean you should turn it down, but be careful about being seduced by what in retrospect may not be such a lot of money.

Whether or not you go to college depends on why you were going to college in the first place. If you're going because your parents think it's a good idea, any amount of money may seem huge. If you're going to meet girls and you think a fat wallet may be a better avenue, money may seem seductive. If you're going to college to learn something, can you learn it equally quickly or effectively in the work world? If you're going to college for the experience or the degree, there is probably no substitute, so it gets down to a question of timing. Is school important now? Would working satisfy a yearning for independence? Would being out of school for a while be refreshing or a derailment? If you think I'm suggesting that the issue has more to do with who you are and what you want rather than how much money somebody is willing to pay you, you're right.

Think for a moment. Somebody is willing to pay you a fair amount of money without credentials not because you have cute dimples but because they think you're worth it. This means that you may not have to choose between alternatives that seem black and white. What about the possibility of a little negotiation that would offer you the best of both worlds.

If you're valuable to them now, presumably you would be at least as valuable to them with a bit more information under your belt. Maybe they would even be willing to subsidize the acquisition of that information. Most companies have some sort of tuition reimbursement program for employees. It's good for them because they get better-educated, often more grateful, hence loyal employees—and they can take it off their taxes.

There are weekends and holidays and vacations during which you could presumably work at a portion of the salary they are offering you. You could have school, some work experience and a bit of spending money as well. You are in the catbird seat if you decide to check out the possibilities a bit more carefully.

What do you want? You may not get it, but it seems as though you'll seldom have a better opportunity to explore your options. As long as you're polite and specific, the likelihood of your potential employer being offended is small and they may even be impressed by your ingenuity and at very least your self-confidence. They want you because you're useful. Find out how useful and then fit it into your plans. You're going to be working for a long time. If you can learn to figure out what you want as well as offering a prospective employer what he or she wants, your work career will be much more profitable emotionally as well as economically.

Don't assume the world is all black and white. Often we end up dealing with shades of gray. Figuring out what you want means you'll get a lot closer. No guarantees, but it'll be a lot more fun and a lot more interesting. You may not be able to have it all, but then again, with a little careful planning, you just may be able to, or at least come awfully close.

I'm having a terrible time finding a job. They all want me to have experience. Do you think it's okay to fudge some experience?

Do not under any circumstances fudge some experience. You are using a cutesy word to mask lying. It's hard enough not to have experience, but if you get tagged as a liar or fired for lying on a job application, no experience in the world can redeem you. Everybody starts out in your shoes. At some point everybody has had no experience. Stop feeling sorry for yourself and figure out what you have that makes you valuable or worth risking giving a job to.

If you haven't had much job experience, you probably haven't had much experience lying about your lack of experience, and the interviewer has probably had a lot of experience with people who have no experience and no experience lying, so you're most likely to be found out. A no-win situation any way you look at it, so please don't even think about it.

Obviously you have nerve and an imagination or it would never occur to you to fudge your experience. What have you done that is unusual or unpaid? Experience isn't limited to paid work, but just meaningful work. Did you do something interesting in school for which you received recognition but no pay? Do you have any interesting hobbies? What makes you an unusual human being?

Remember, an interviewer can't read your mind or know the right questions to ask. You must go into an interview with some interesting things to share about yourself that have at least some vague relevance to the job. Your prospective employer wants to know what you can do for her. She cares less whether you're a nice person than if you're a competent one. Experience is one way to demonstrate usefulness, an unusual constellation of abilities is another.

If there's nothing you can point to that is likely to whet her interest, think about offering her a trial of your services during which for a period of several weeks you would work for no pay or for a reduced salary so she could evaluate your performance. Obviously this doesn't cost you anything, and you get a foot in the door as well as points for aggressiveness, ingenuity and self-confidence.

Maybe you've been smart enough to have done a little research on the company, so you can make a suggestion or offer an unusual way of doing a job. If you can create a job that suits your talents, you don't have to worry about the competition, just selling them on the need for a new way of doing something.

Even if you don't get this job, if you're pleasant, candid and a little off the beaten track, the person may remember you if something does come up or recommend you to someone else or call you back if she can't find anyone who does have experience.

In the meantime, have you considered part-time work? Sometimes temporary work is a way to gain some experience and find out about different work situations and positions as well as letting a prospective employer find out about you. Volunteer situations that are related to your field or skills are also a good way of gaining some experience as well as valuable contacts.

Everybody has to start someplace and everybody is inexperienced at some point. It's a one-time problem, so treat it as a temporary but important obstacle to be overcome and get on with it. The only way to make it a permanent problem is to lie about it.

I've got a chance to move up in the company, but I'm not sure I'm ready, and besides I'd have to move out of state. Do you think it's okay to tell them I'm not really ready yet?

I think you can tell your employer anything you want. The question is What is their response likely to be? If you are assuming that if you're offered an opportunity once, you'll be offered it again, you may want to rethink your position. If you genuinely feel that you don't want the position and you can live with the possibility that the offer was a one-shot deal, then figure out what makes sense to you. Assuming you'll be offered the same chance at a more convenient time may be a fatal assumption.

Before you decide to turn down the opportunity on the basis of convenience or opt for it on the basis of fear, you may be able to glean some more information. What exactly is the job? Why does the company think you're ready? Why don't you think you are? What assurances or guarantees might make you feel more comfortable? Does your company have a hidden agenda? Do you have some unvoiced fears or concerns?

You are not a helpless pawn in a powerful game whose rules you don't know. This is your life and your career you're talking about. Sooner or later you have to make a decision, and even if the decision turns out to be wrong in the long run or even if it turns out to be right on the money, you will feel better in either case if you have carefully considered your alternatives, collected all the information you possibly could, asked all the questions of yourself and your employer, tried to discern their motives as well as your own, carefully made a list of pros and cons and then decided.

There may be a compromise you haven't unearthed, assurances you haven't requested, subtleties you haven't uncovered. Don't assume your employer is either a good guy or a bad buy who knows you better or less well than you know yourself. Ultimately you're responsible for your own decision, so get out there and do some homework. Don't be passive or angry or scared. You've got a very exciting re-search project on your hands. Would more money make any difference? A cost of living increase? A housing allowance? A guarantee that you could return to the home office if you didn't like the new job? A two-year grace period? A schooling allowance? A trip for you or your family to the new location? A relocation allowance? A travel budget? An entertainment budget?

Start thinking of yourself as a valuable resource both to your company and to yourself. Figure out what would make you feel prepared for the new job. Are you sure you under-stand the job description? Would there be somebody there to train you?

If you possibly can, you're probably better off accepting the promotion now if you're not completely convinced you'll fail. This may be a good time to remind yourself of what Helen Keller said: "Life is daring risk or it is nothing at all." If she, blind, deaf and mute, could allow herself to dare, maybe so should the rest of us. What most people regret with their final breath is not the mistakes they made but the chances they didn't take.

If you're 100 percent *sure* that you can't do it, then you're not taking a risk to take the job, you're courting disaster. If you're positive you can do it, you're a fool and a fraidy cat not to dare it. If you're in between, you've got to balance your fear with your realistic concerns and figure out a way to tip the balance one way or the other so you can live with your decision. Don't wait too long, and keep your own counsel in terms of your insecurities. Get all the specifics you can and then decide what makes the most sense to you.

You can only make the best decision which you're capable of, and it will take some time to know if the decision made sense. Just make sure you assume as little as possible and find out everything you can about the job, the risks, your employer and, most importantly, yourself.

I've become so passive in my life. Every time I think about making a change, I become terrified. Can you recommend any medication that might help?

My goodness, talk about passive. What's more passive than looking for the magic pill? Let's assume for a moment that you've had a complete physical in the last couple of months to rule out any treatable cause of lassitude. Allergies, thyroid problems, not to mention low grade fevers, flus and the like, can all cause you to feel so pooped that getting out of bed is a problem. Depression also causes you to feel lumpish and inert. Assuming that you have a clean bill of health and you don't have any of the physical symptoms of depression—sleep disturbance, eating disturbance, suicidal thoughts, lack of concentration, a change in your sexual behavior or appetites, an overwhelming sense of sadness, as well as that feeling that you just can't motivate yourself—let's talk about your passivity.

By the way, if you are feeling one or more of those symptoms of depression and have been feeling them for a month or two and you have no idea what may be causing them, you do need a psychiatric consult. You're most likely not going to just "snap out of it." You may need medication and some therapy. You're probably talking about a chemical imbalance. Don't scare the daylights out of yourself. Everybody feels one or more of those symptoms occasionally for short periods of time and those feelings do go away. We're talking about a difference in severity and duration. Besides, you were talking about passivity. If you feel you have a problem, you're probably on the right track. If you feel you are a problem, you're more than likely depressed.

To your passivity then. It sounds like you weren't always so passive. What happened? What changed? When is the last time you can remember feeling active and on top of things? Are you unconsciously mourning a loss of some sort? Is this the anniversary of a death? Sometimes our bodies remember even when our heads don't.

Your fear about changes may be a clue. What kind of change are you contemplating? In what area of your life? Most people are frightened of change, since we are taking a leap into the unknown, and we are conservative creatures, we humans. Your fear may give you a clue to the reasons underlying your passivity. Most of us do things for reasons; and if your behavior seems illogical to you, it's because you're missing some of the pieces of the puzzle. Look for them.

If you've been in a lousy situation for a while, work or love, you may have so undermined your sense of self that it's hard for you to conceptualize anything better or that you deserve anything better. Prisoners in concentration camps in World War II were reluctant to allow themselves to be liberated by the Allies because at least they knew what to expect, no matter how horrendous and unthinkable, in the camps. Their sense of self and rightness with the world had been so destroyed, their confidence in themselves and a safe good world so undermined, that they were unwilling to take the leap of faith to believe that things could be better. Inmates in institutions will often violate the rules just before their scheduled release in order to be kept on longer. However awful the terms of their confinement, freedom to choose and to lose feels too terrifying to even contemplate. Have you somehow gotten yourself into that kind of predicament?

The clue lies in the specifics of your fear. You have to find the courage to at least look at your fear so you can understand the nature and cause of your passivity. What is the worst thing that could possibly happen? Be specific and graphic with yourself. Are you waiting for someone to lead the way or to save you? Are you angry, and somehow you've turned that anger inward on yourself? Are your goals specific enough to be helpful and comforting and guiding?

You can't conquer your passivity until you conquer or at least channel your fear. You can't deal with your fear until you know its shape and definition, and you won't know that until you are willing to look. It's all there for you to see once you decide to look. Paper and pencil or a tape recorder are the way to start; paper and pencil are better than the tape recorder, since all of us have been talking for longer than we've been writing, and sometimes it's a lot easier to fool ourselves verbally than with the written word, unless you're a poet. If you're a poet, use no adjectives and try and limit yourself to three- or four-word phrases, but be specific.

Nothing is as scary in the daylight as it is in the dark of night. Daylight is when you bring the light of your understanding to bear as opposed to letting the scary stuff sit there in the dark of your closed eyes. Open up those big baby blues and look at yourself, your life, your fears, your behavior, and realize that most people are afraid. That's not the problem. The problem is Can you control your fears or will you let them control and immobilize you? Get to work. You don't have to do anything until you're ready. But you might as well have the information at your disposal should you decide you want to take more control of your life.

You're in an information-gathering phase. Decision making and policy have to be postponed till you have more information. You need to know the whys and wherefores and specifics, not just the symptoms.

Once you know what you want, where you want to be, it's a matter of beginning. For you, doing anything is better than doing nothing. Don't wait too long—don't play it too safe, don't be too sure—just do it. As you change one area of your life, the positive energy can be channeled to other areas. You may want to start with work rather than your love life because it may be less complicated. Don't change everything at once, and don't expect everything to change overnight, but get on with it. Don't try. There is only doing and not doing. Do it!

I feel like I'm under constant pressure. I never seem to get reports in on time and my boss gets furious. When I get around to it, they're pretty good, but I'm not sure whether it's me or him. Should I change jobs?

Before you change jobs, you had best try to figure out whether it's you or him. If it's you, it's not going to do much good to change jobs. Let's get organized about this. It sounds as though you're quite capable of doing the work, assuming that both you and your boss agree that the reports are good once you finally get around to them. What's keeping you from getting to them? Too many phone calls? Bad work habits? Too much socializing at work? Unclear priorities? Too much work to do? Too many distractions?

If it's your work habits and this isn't your first job, you've probably run into the problem before. If it's your first job, you may have found yourself with the same problem at school: putting things off to the last moment, a lot of late papers, grades that would have been better if you'd finished on time. If this is so, we can assume it's not your boss. Either you're a perfectionist, a procrastinator, or you have a problem with authority figures (maybe a passive-aggressive) or some combination.

If you find yourself putting things off to the last moment, ask yourself why. Do you enjoy the pressure? Do you think you can use the excuse that if you had more time you could have done better? Are you afraid to commit yourself to the project? Are you disorganized? Are you hoping you won't have to do it after all? The best way to tackle this personality glitch is to set yourself up a schedule that allows you lots of time. Adhere to it rigidly and give yourself a reward when the job is done. You may find yourself getting a lot more done and enjoying it.

If you're not getting things in on time, changing jobs probably won't do you any good. It usually takes about six months to get the hang of a new job, and during that adjustment time you would most likely be less rather than more efficient. You haven't mentioned your own organizational skills and whether or not getting things in late has been a lifelong habit or a recent occurrence.

If you have always had a problem with procrastination, waiting until the last moment, it may be time to face up to how expensive your habit is in terms of trouble for you and everybody else, stress, negative anticipation and just plain hassle. Obviously you are capable of doing good work. What's stopping you from doing it at the appropriate time?

Procrastination can be a symptom of disorganization, letting time get away from you, underestimating the time it takes to get things done, a wish to have all the information, to be perfect, to be unwilling to take risks. If you've always been a procrastinator, make yourself a schedule, estimate the time you think a task will take, how pleasurable you think it might be on a scale from one to ten, then time how long the task actually takes and how much pleasure it actually affords. You are most likely unrealistic about time and pleasure both. You may find that you actually like doing some things you thought you didn't enjoy, especially when you allow yourself enough time so you're not doing it in a frenzy.

Let's assume for a moment that you're not a habitual procrastinator and you're not a perfectionist who needs to have *all* the facts before you begin writing (for a perfectionist, there is no such thing as *all* the facts, so you just keep putting off committing to paper until the last possible second, and then it's often too late). Let's assume for a moment that the pressure you're feeling is unique to this situation. It's either you or your boss. If it's your boss, it's up to you to make the situation more tolerable, since he has the power and you have only a limited ability to negotiate. You could go to him and ask for a clearer definition of your job, less work, more help. None of these techniques is guaranteed to raise your stock in his eyes. You had the best be sure that you can point out specific inequities in your situation or you may find yourself out of a job. On the other hand, if you're ready to quit anyway, it may be worth the risk.

There is another unsettling possibility, unsettling because it is more deep-seated and therefore more difficult, but more important, to tackle. Is it possible that you have a difficult time with authority figures? Do you and your dad have an unresolved relationship in which you feel that no matter what you do you can't please him or get his attention, so either you don't try at all or you try by trying to annoy him to get him to notice you?

If you do have a problem with authority figures, it's time to work out your relationship with your dad or your mom and get on with your life. You can decide that you're being childish and the only person it's hurting is yourself, and if you still find yourself resisting authority you may want to invest part of your paycheck in a therapist before you find yourself collecting unemployment. This kind of acting-out is self-destructive, futile, and expensive.

It sounds as though you are capable of doing the work, but something is getting in your way. Might that something be you? If you're disorganized, you may as well learn to get organized now. The next job won't be any easier and may be more difficult because it will be unfamiliar. If you're a pro-crastinator, you will probably put off looking for a new job, and the same pattern will repeat itself. If you're a perfection-ist, ditto.

If you have trouble with authority figures, you can begin to work out your relationship with your dad and simulta-neously make a decision to see your boss as your boss, not your dad. You don't have to love him or please him in the same way. Get your work done to please yourself, to show yourself that you can do the work. Stop trying to make your boss love you because you feel your dad doesn't. If you can improve things with either your dad or your boss, both situ-ations will likely improve. If you can't improve either, you had best find yourself a therapist, because otherwise you will find yourself miserable at work as well as at family reunions. Even working for a female boss probably won't help. You could go into business for yourself, but sooner or later you may want to lessen the emotional burden under which you are struggling. You may or may not ever be able to please your father. You will have receptive and unreceptive bosses in your lifetime. If you learn to work to make yourself proud within an appropriate time frame, you can find a workplace environment that will suit you and a serenity both at work and at home. You are an adult and can set your own standards without having to act out a self-destructive pattern of rebellion.

If none of this applies and you think all the pressure is from an unreasonable boss and you're sure it will never happen again, get your resume in order and find another job, but be very clear from the beginning about pacing yourself at work. If there is any doubt whatsoever in your mind about rebellion, procrastination, scheduling, perfectionism or just plain snottiness on your part, I would try to work it out first so the same thing doesn't happen time after time.

There are not enough hours in the day to get everything I want done. How can I get better organized?

I think you've just put your finger on it or at least part of it. If you're not getting enough done, either you're unrealistic in terms of how much is do-able or unrealistic about how much time everything takes or unrealistic about how many hours there are in a day.

The first place to start is with a list. Sit down right now and write down everything, and I do mean everything, you are planning to do tomorrow. Include meals, brushing your teeth, licking stamps, everything. Nothing is too trivial to be left off that list. Also write down how long you think each of those tasks is going to take and on a scale from one to ten how much satisfaction you are going to derive from each task.

Tomorrow you are going to follow yourself around with a stopwatch and note how long everything actually takes and how much satisfaction you actually get from the task. You are also going to write down in red ink any task you had not written down and how long it takes. By the end of tomorrow you are going to be exhausted but much wiser.

You will find one of several things to be the case. You may find that your list is incomplete, and the reason nothing ever gets done is that other things are getting in the way, ghostly things that don't occur to you but take time nonetheless. If this is the case, it's time to set priorities. Do what's important first so you're sure it gets done. Then you may want to combine, but that will come more readily when you move onto the weekly and monthly lists which we will discuss in a moment.

If you have written everything down, it is most likely that your error lies in time estimation. Things very likely take longer than you thought, so you're always running behind and always being distracted by running behind, so you're never quite focused. This is an incredibly inefficient way of doing business. If that is the case, you're very likely back to step one, which is to figure out priorities and groupings.

The third possibility is that you're just plain unrealistic about how many hours are in a day. Are you playing Superperson? Nobody can get everything done if they are counting on more than twenty-four hours in a day without time off for good behavior. If this is what is happening, you probably didn't total your hours when you first made your list; and had you done so, you could have saved yourself some time. Are you cutting corners so that things have to be redone? Are you not concentrating because your mind is on your next task? Are you a human being that needs rest periods and not a machine? Are you mortal and pretending not to be? Who are you trying to impress or kid? Why are you feeling the need to do so much?

The key to getting organized is deciding what to organize. What's important to you? If you tell me "everything," take three giant steps backward. Are there things other people can do almost as well for you? Are you lousy at delegating responsibility? Are you afraid to have quiet time to think and be with yourself? If you haven't decided what's most important to you, make a list and organize it from least to most important. If you're unrealistic about task time, get into the habit of timing yourself at a realistic, not breakneck, pace. If you're distracted and stressed, try focusing on what you're doing and clear your mind of the next task. Make lists and cross things off so notions aren't bumping around in your head. If you're stressed, allow more time between tasks.

Do you have a weekly agenda? A monthly one? Do you know what you want to be doing five years from now? Do you know what you want written on your tombstone? If getting your tasks organized is the problem, a careful schedule, lots of lists and a stopwatch should do the trick. If the issue is getting your life organized, you're going to have to sit down and figure out who you are, what you want, what's important to you and perhaps most importantly what's not crucial to you, or at least what's not worth your time.

I've started my own business in the last year and the struggle seems to finally be paying off. A couple of competitors have offered me a job. Should I tough it out a bit longer or join up with them?

My dear, no man I know would ask such a question. From the time they are Cub Scouts, many boys understand that the only way to make any money in this world is to steal it or be self-employed. Most women don't even start thinking about their careers as anything but a job until they are somewhere in their thirties at earliest, no matter how independent or seemingly self-sufficient. By then their male counterparts have become millionaires or are well on their way. This is not to say that money is the measure of all things, but it does mean that it is time women got serious about themselves and their careers. Most independent, clever, smart, creative men either own or wish to own their own concerns by thirty-five. Women are still being flattered when somebody offers them a job with security. We just don't believe in ourselves enough to realize that we are the only security we will ever have. Men come and go in our lives, kids do the same. We will have only ourselves to count on forever. I swear to you the lesson must be in the testosterone, and we just don't get it.

Why do you think these guys are so interested in offering you a job now? My guess is that a year ago they wouldn't have given you the time of day, let alone offered you a job, which is more than likely why you went out on your own to begin with. Now that you've suffered through that first scary year and survived, they can see your value; and by offering you a salaried position, in one fell swoop they get a valued employee and remove the competition. Very clever of them. What's in it for you?

I know, I know. You get a paid vacation, sick leave, health insurance and a few paid holidays. Have you computed how much those goodies are going to cost you? Not only this year but next year and the year after that? I'm not even talking about independence or the possibility of being fired. I'm talking strictly about money. Don't be embarrassed. All of us do it. We are so unused to thinking of ourselves as being alone, when somebody comes along and offers to take care of us, we crumble. We are grateful and happy. It may even be worse than that. It may be that we so doubt our essential femininity and lovability that we take someone's hiring us as an affirmation of the fact that we can be successful and loved too. We are selling ourselves not only short but out.

There is nothing wrong with this guy offering you a job. Before you take it, ask yourself why he's offering it and why you would take it. Be honest enough to look beyond the obvious into your own perceptions about yourself, what it means to be successful and what it means to be female as well as feminine. If the job still makes sense, by all means take it. Before you do, have you ever thought of the possibility of asking him to come work for you?

It's time for you to figure out what you want, both immediately and for the long term. Another female problem: We seldom get beyond the white knight in shining armor. I can remember thinking a few years ago that I shouldn't buy a house because then it would be my house and difficult for us to live in and there was no "us"; or that I was waiting for someone to whisk me away from all "this." I would kill anybody who tried to whisk me away from my life, which is fun, exciting, stimulating, rewarding and mine. We may build a life together that will successfully incorporate both life-styles, but whisk away . . . Not on your life, or mine. You need to sort out your goals and then decide what to do. You're not a little girl playing dolls and Daddy has told you to come in and set the table. You're an adult, a skilled—yes, let's say the terrible word—successful woman. Deal with it, sweetie.

I keep getting fired. They just don't understand that I'm a sensitive person and I don't need this hassle. Any fields you can suggest that might appreciate my talents?

When we begin to see the world in terms of "they," we're in trouble. You say this is not the first time you've been fired; and unless you change both your attitude and your behavior, it probably won't be the last.

Some of us work for fun, most of us work for money and we realize that we'll be happiest when we like what we're doing, even if we're doing it primarily for the money. Not surprising, the more we like it the better we're likely to be at it and the more money we're likely to make.

Sensitivity is not usually a requirement on most job descriptions, although it can help if you are working with the public. I suspect when you say you're sensitive you mean you either don't like getting yelled at or you're not working fast enough or you're not very efficient.

The first question to ask yourself is What would you like to be doing? Are you equipped to do it? Do you have the training, the skill, the access, the talent, the will, the drive? If the answer is yes to all of these questions, why aren't you doing it? If you are already doing it, why isn't it working out better for you? You are only responsible for your own behavior. You can't change the world, the workplace or your boss, but you may be able to think in more useful terms about yourself and what you do.

If you don't like what you're doing, you are less likely to do a good job of it. If you can find something to like about it for even a short period of time, you will be able to move on with better feelings about yourself, your boss and the workplace environment itself.

Right now your attitude is probably your biggest obstacle. Saying nobody understands you might be accurate, but it is also a self-fulfilling prophecy that will leave you unhappy, embittered and unemployed. If you need more education, your current position might give you the time and the money to take night courses. If you need additional skills, perhaps you are acquiring them now. Figure out something that is valuable to you about your current situation other than the paycheck, so you feel better about your next job, better about the job you're doing and better about yourself.

If you've placed yourself in a position that is wrong for you because you have a lot of energy and the job is slow or you're slow and the job is high pressured, figure out how to change your attitude or your situation. Perhaps there is another job in the same office for which you're qualified and better suited. The best way to take the next step up the ladder, especially if you need some help, is by doing a good job in the position you now hold.

For the last nine years I have worked with screener/producers in radio, the person who answers the phone and asks the caller about their question to me. It is either the best or the worst job in the world depending on the screener's attitude. In most cases I have inherited my screener. The deal I have made with each of them begins with our agreeing that a monkey could do the job, but it takes real interest and willingness to do the job well. If they will do the job well, even if they hate it, I'll help them get on to doing what they really want to do. If they do a lousy job, I will correct them until I get tired of it. If they are nasty or incompetent, I will get them replaced if I can. If they take the money, they should give it their best, again not for my sake but for theirs. Doing a mediocre job makes you feel mediocre, unappreciated and unhappy.

I'm as good as my word. Some of my crew have performed exceptionally well for short periods of time and I have helped them to go onto bigger and better. It's hard for me actually to fire somebody, so there are still some folks in various parts of the country doing lousy jobs for my successors. You need to sit down and clean up your act, not for your boss's sake but for your own. If your work life isn't going well, it's hard for the rest of your life to be happy.

I haven't been working for a while, and I'm afraid a prospective employer is going to wonder why not. Should I just not put dates on my resume?

Very few people have a completely unbroken work history. People get fired, sick, tired. We take time to go to school, go to Europe, have babies, mid-life crises, affairs, breakdowns, contemplation periods and respites.

I assume from the tone of your questions that you're not wildly proud of the reason for your hiatus and you assume that your prospective employer would feel the same way. While I think it's important never to lie on a resume, not everything has to be included either.

You mention the possibility of not including dates. If you have a consistent work history up to a certain point, it may be okay to include the dates and then decide how you're going to explain the omission. The gap may not loom so large, but somebody at some office is going to want to know what you've been doing lately. If you're changing fields, for example, a gap is easier to explain in terms of taking time out to rethink your goals, to retrain yourself, to give priority to family or personal issues.

Most employers are looking for a reason to hire you, not to pass over you. They want the best possible candidate for an opening; and if you seem a bit more interesting in a non-threatening way, you just may find yourself with an inside track.

Were you doing anything during the time you weren't gainfully employed? Volunteer work counts, as does research or writing. You probably weren't sitting around doing absolutely nothing; and if you were, perhaps you can describe it as an inner journey or sorting through your options.

How you describe your time off will go a long way to making it interesting and compelling to your interviewer or confusing and a bit scary. The biggest step you can make toward the former is to clarify in your own mind why you haven't been working. When in doubt, the truth does offer simplicity. If you have been hospitalized or jailed, you may as well 'fess up, since an employer can check on it quite easily; and if it makes a difference to the company, they probably will. Being honest also has the added advantage of labeling you as a trustworthy soul from the very beginning. If the reason will make a difference, you're not going to get the job anyway and you certainly wouldn't be able to keep it once they found out, so why not figure out a neutral, non-inflammatory way of being if not brutally honest then at least straightforward.

Most employers would rather not take a chance if they don't have to, so figure out a way to describe your time off that makes sense to you, and then you may not have much of a problem helping your prospective employer to understand as well.

If you still feel at a huge disadvantage, is there a way of gaining some bedrock experience in your field in the next year or so by doing volunteer work, part-time work, temporary work? A partial salary or even no salary may be a better investment in your future and self-image than going around being turned down. What about some schooling? If you need to fill in some gaps, you may want to think of your long-term work goals rather than just getting a job.

If nothing else, if you can convince yourself that you're starting a brand-new chapter in your work history, you may be able to convince an employer as well. Good luck and positive attitude.

I just got fired. I'm tempted to tell my boss what I really think of her. What do you think?

Beware the seduction of the exit interview. You got fired for a reason. If the reason was justified, you probably owe your employer an apology—not an excuse, not an explanation—just an apology. The time for reconciliation or discussion is over. Keep your head up and your mouth closed.

If you were fired unfairly, you may want a clarification; maybe there's something you didn't understand or know. Do not under any circumstances unload. This is the world of work, and it is a very small world indeed. The person you are thinking about lambasting isn't going to be flattered by your candor or impressed by your guts, and she may very well know your next employer. At the very least you are going to have to admit to having worked for this person; and whether you use her as a reference or not, your next employer will very likely check you out with her.

If there is some constructive comment you can make about the work environment, you very likely should have made it before this point; and if there is a comment that you wish to make about a fellow employee, it had better be complimentary, unless you want to be viewed as not only incompetent but vindictive as well.

If you have been unjustly fired, the best revenge is keeping your mouth shut and going on to get a better job at more money and doing terrific work at the new one. Anything you say now will be viewed as sour grapes and petty. Keep your dignity intact.

If there is information you need, this is probably the time to ask for it; and if you are leaving on anywhere near good terms, ask for a letter of recommendation at this point. Your boss is human, even though you may not want to admit it at this point, and she very likely feels even worse than you do. If you can find it in yourself to be gracious, she may feel guilty enough to either give you a good letter of recommendation or at least not bad-mouth you to your next prospective employer. At the very least she may question her decision at some future date based on your mature and dignified exit. It won't do you much good right now, but at the very least it may bedevil her in the future.

I hope I have convinced you beyond the shadow of a doubt to keep your mouth shut and go quietly. It can only work in your best interest, even though you may be tempted to blow off steam. It's a cheap, expensive temptation. Resist it.

Which brings us to your next decision. Should you lie about being fired on your next job application? Again this is why being calm and dignified at your exit interview can pay off. If you can find out *why* you were fired—presumably not for dipping into the till—you may be able to find a more tactful but nonetheless honest description of your leave-taking. It is never a good idea to lie on a job application. You will most likely be found out sooner or later. If it's sooner, you won't get the job and you may get a reputation as a liar, especially if the industry in which you work is small; and they're all small when it comes to gossip. Also, in most companies you can be instantly dismissed for lying on a job application. Even if you're not caught for a while, it will be hanging over your head the whole time you're there; and then what do you tell your *next* employer about why you were fired this time? Lying as an adult has roughly the same consequences as lying as a child, only more so. Some people only seem to get away with it.

Almost everybody gets fired at least once if they hang around long enough. It is no sin, but you'd best be prepared with at least a neutral explanation that bears some relationship to the truth, since you will no doubt be asked. This is another opportunity to resist the temptation to unload. Saying terrible things about an ex-employer always raises the unpleasant specter in the prospective employer's mind about what you might say about her. Resist the temptation by reminding yourself that nobody's perfect and that it is not up to you to point out an ex-employer's obvious flaws or your own perfection.

Doors open, doors close. This one has just closed. Make sure your mouth follows suit, and prepare for the next exciting challenge behind door number two.

I've got the world's dumbest boss. He's really incompetent and it's hard taking him seriously. Any suggestions?

The first thing to remember about dealing with a boss is that the power is on his side. You may be terrific, but he's in charge. Unless he's the chairman of the board's nephew, he probably knows something, and anyway you have limited options.

If he is making your life miserable, you need to figure out specifically the ways he's doing it and ways around this. For example, if his instructions are unclear, you could ask for clarification or send him a memo following every meeting outlining what you think he wants you to do. This way imprecisions can be rooted out before they become disasters. If his demands on you are unfair, again you can ask for clarification and point out discrepancies between what you think you're supposed to be doing and what he wants you to do. Thinking he's an oaf is not very good for your morale; and unless you're one terrific actor, it probably shows and will do nothing for your career advancement. He may not be exactly the kind of person that you would like to emulate, but that doesn't mean that you can't learn from him, work for him and get on with your career.

If he's making mistakes and attributing them to you, make sure your own work can withstand scrutiny, and then be very clear and careful about memos that outline what you've done. (Any time you write a memo about anything, you should keep a copy. It is also a good idea to keep a copy of anything that might be lost or disputed, for your own peace of mind and well-being.)

Remember, if it comes to a showdown you will probably lose even if you're right. Your goal is to avoid a showdown unless absolutely necessary until you've got your resume in order. Going over his head is tricky business unless you've got a very tight, very good, indisputable case; and even then, if he loses his job, you may lose yours.

A good boss isn't necessarily smart, and he may not be

able to do what you can as long as he can motivate you to do it. Your boss may be a good manager rather than a good technician. Unfortunately in our society there are often better rewards for managers than technicians, and your boss may have been a good technician who was promoted into managerial duties for which he is ill-equipped. He may very well have reached his level of incompetence, which may be irritating to you, but it need not be limiting. Learn what you can from him, do your job, keep the complaining to a minimum, especially at the office, keep good accurate memos and keep your resume up to date.

This will probably not be your last job, and learning to get along with the boss is as important a job skill as any other and in fact more important than most. Having a competent, smart, sensitive, savvy boss is a rare event, a blessing to be savored, not a commonplace to be anticipated. If nothing else, he may be a terrific case study for how not to be a boss when your time comes.

There's one person at work who's a gossip and a liar and really disruptive. She's old and entrenched. Isn't there anything we can do?

Anybody who's worked for any length of time has run into the office looney. She has been there since the doors first opened, is there first thing in the morning and is the last person to leave, often has no home life and can make everybody's life miserable. I once worked with one who went around making sure all the phone buttons were up so that the alien forces couldn't come through the telephones. This was alternately amusing and terrifying until she disconnected an overseas phone call; then it was just plain infuriating.

We live in a society that expects everybody to produce and be perfect and happy at all times. For some people this is not only unlikely but impossible. As they become less and less capable of meeting society's standards, they often retreat farther and farther into their own world—often of fantasy, not infrequently of paranoia. The beaten are on the streets, the stronger are in offices, sometimes making life miserable for the better adjusted. If it sounds to you that I'm making an argument for tolerance, you've read me loud and clear.

If this woman is just lonely and embittered, befriending her might help. An invitation to lunch, a smile, a nod, a brief conversation of the sort that might normally occur between friends might be a lifeline for her. Feeling like an outsider doesn't bring out the best in any of us.

If she is truly beyond the pale, it might be appropriate not to report her but to see if it's possible that the company physician could see her and evaluate her. It sounds as though she is a very lonely person who lives for her work and has nearly no human contact outside of work. I'll bet she has never even been to a company outing.

We are all touched by the plight of the needy at Christmas. It sounds like this woman is needy all year round, 365 days a year. Maybe a group of you could ask her out for lunch, begin a campaign to at least try to get to know her. At the very least you may find that she isn't quite so awful. You might make her feel less paranoid, less prone to gossip and lies. We talk about one another because we are interesting. The question is what we say and why. If she didn't feel so left out, she might be happier, less prone to malice and better informed. Even if she has a life outside the office which is functional, it is possible but unlikely that a bit of kindness at work couldn't hurt.

If she's been around since before you arrived, she may outlast your tenure. If you could make her life a little better, you may find your work environment improving significantly; if you can't, you may as well adjust to the fact that it's more her turf than yours. You may want to change jobs; she won't be at the new place, but there are no guarantees that you won't find a reasonable facsimile. The world is full of strange and wonderful things and some of them end up in the workplace.

My boss is really adorable and I'm sure he's interested in me. Should I risk an office romance?

At first blush, the idea of an office romance seems all things American: sexy, efficient, logical and profitable. Don't you believe it.

For most of us, finding love relationships at the office is dangerous if not downright disastrous to both heart and bank account. In a recent study of office affairs, it was found that 80 percent of the affairs culminated in the women being fired, transferred or demoted. Sex does not look good on your resume.

Because there are more women in the work force than ever before and they are in higher-level positions, the opportunities for office liaisons have flourished, but as you can see, so have the casualties.

There is something sexy about liking a person for the job they do, feeling comfortable and at ease around them, admiring their competence, staying late together, being part of the same team, sharing thoughts and dreams and aspirations and typewriter ribbons. The temptation is obvious. However, please think down the road a bit and consider some of the glitches.

First, your romance will *never* be a secret. Think of all the times you've giggled at someone else's sophomoric attempt to avoid eye contact and to brush by one another seemingly accidently or to keep that sparkle under control. Believe that everyone but the most obtuse will know, and somebody will tell even that poor soul.

If you're in a position of power, you risk being sued for sexual harassment—not only by your friend if the romance goes sour, or if he or she fails to receive a promotion, but also by other co-workers who feel your love received special treatment. If you're the subordinate, your ability to do the job will be undermined by everyone's perception of how you got the position in the first place, regardless of the facts. (You may eventually have the same worry.) At work you're hired for your competence; any hint of sexuality (unless you're a stripper) will undermine that sense of competence. You will be distracted as well as being a distraction, and that's just if the affair is going nicely.

If the two of you have a fight, it will carry over into the workplace. If work is a mess, it will make a shambles of the bedroom. Logically, many of us throw ourselves into work when love goes sour and less often into love when work goes sour. You will not have that option. I know, "M.A.S.H." says that feelings get hurt but never for long, jealousies are trivial and relationships will work forever. Don't believe it.

You are focusing on the fun of the sharing, the headiness when everything is going well, and overlooking the fact that you are choosing to let someone directly threaten your livelihood and sense of self-esteem and employability.

I'm sure that your boss is interested in you—as a pleasant, efficient, competent member of the office team. Don't embarrass yourself or him by assuming anything else. And don't wear sexy clothes to work. You said it all when you said risk. There is no possible long-term payoff for you in this. If you really think he's terrific, find yourself another job and invite him to lunch. In the meantime find another boyfriend so you can continue to afford to buy yourself lunch. If the boss should be foolish enough to make a pass at you, ask him to guarantee your position in writing to give both of you enough time to cool off. Bedroom and boardroom don't mix.

SUMMARY
WORK

Looking for a job is one of the most terrifying human experiences. When we ask someone to hire us, we are saying, "Do you want me?" "Do you need me?" in their most basic form. What we feel is "Do you love me?" Obviously if there is more than one candidate for a job, the possibility of rejection is high; and that's why looking for a job puts hair on your chest, male or female. Some of the terror of the situation can be reduced if you remember that they are also looking for an employee. I know it sounds obvious, but just as your prospective employer can ask you questions and make some decisions about you, you have the same option. You can ask questions, not to appear interested but because you're talking about spending a large chunk of your waking hours and available energies with this person; and if you're not interested, you don't understand what's going on.

Granted they are paying you the money, but you're offering your loyalty, energy, ideas and most importantly your time; and time is the only really precious commodity in the universe. There's no more where that came from. When yours is used up, you're done, so don't underestimate your value.

Any job needs to be considered in context. What do you want now, what will you want soon? Is this a temporary stop to accumulate some experience, some money, some skills? Your employer can't read your mind or determine your destiny. You're in control of your life. This guy can only offer you a job. And you can always say no or yes. When to say either depends on who you are and what you want, not to mention the question. There is no such thing as the perfect job, the perfect employer or the perfect employee, but you can make some intelligent choices once you figure out what you want.

There are some questions to which the answer is always no. If the question is Are you willing to lie, break the law, cheat, hurt somebody? think long and hard about your answer. People in positions of power are the only ones who can ever ask those questions, and if they have the power they can always use the answers against you. Only you know what's best for you, even at work.

What I guarantee is not best for you at work is an affair. I know you think everybody's doing it and nobody will know and just this once, but you're kidding yourself in a very dangerous way. As for other relationships at work, you will probably be safest if you can remember that work is the place to work. It doesn't mean you can't be friendly or cheerful or forthcoming, but putting all of your emotional eggs in a workbasket may be shortsighted and uncomfortable if not dangerous.

Information you give other people about yourself purposely or accidentally is likely to make the rounds. Office gossip is as old as the first person able to process a word—not because people are rotten but because people who spend a lot of time around one another sharing time and space are curious about one another and share the knowledge. Just how much and what kind of knowledge is up to you. There will always be gossip; its accuracy and intensity and depth are up to you. You can't stop people from talking about you, but you can give them precious little to go on.

Precious little to go on should only be your motto when it comes to interpersonal business relationships. Getting the information you need to make decisions may be the single most important part of any job. How do you know whether to take a position, a promotion or a vacation without knowing who you are, what you want and what's going on in the boardroom as well as at the water cooler. It's amazing how few people take the time to find out how their own company is run, from table of organization to labor policy to promotion policy. This is your work; find out.

Speaking of finding out, don't ever be tempted to lie on a

resume, because someone will find out; and not only is it grounds for instant dismissal but often criminal prosecution. Besides which, you'll get a terrible reputation overnight, no matter how sterling your record. That doesn't necessarily mean you have to admit every glitch in your work history. Between honesty and duplicity is silence. Nobody is perfect, and nobody has a perfect work history. Blanks can be tolerated if they're few and far between. If you keep losing jobs or can't hold a job, maybe it's time to figure out why. Are you in the wrong position or wrong frame of mind? Don't expect anybody to be as interested in your career as you are, but don't assume that anybody is out to get you either.

There are going to be some terrific people with whom you work and some louses and some people who are just going through a bad time. We are not robots who can leave all of our feelings at the door; but having seen how disruptive it can be to the workplace, be careful if you're tempted to let non-work issues spill over unless absolutely necessary; and if you feel they are, you're best off telling someone in authority before they figure it out for themselves.

Authority is also one of those mixed blessings. It always seems as though it would be fun to be the yeller rather than the yellee, but for some of us managing is not our best skill. As we get older and more experienced at our work, we can begin moving toward our strengths and, if not avoiding, at least countering and compensating for our weaknesses. (I'm a terrible manager. I always expect people to do what they're supposed to do and tell me before I find out if something is wrong or about to go wrong. It always hurts my feelings when people don't do their job and then complain about money or how hard it is or they just don't like it. Clearly the Harvard Business School isn't going to ask me to lecture any time soon, although they do use my study of used car salesmen as a textbook on bargaining behavior. Sigh. Guess you can't have everything. I told you nobody's perfect, and I mean nobody!)

Keep in mind that most of what you do at work will be

noted and recorded. If you're doing a good job, maybe you want to make sure that you do at least some of the recording in the form of a memo detailing your latest triumph to your boss, and don't forget to keep a copy. In fact, memos can be a terrific way of keeping track of all sorts of things, including discrepancies in what you thought you heard and what your boss thought she said. Do make sure you are careful what you put in writing. As one of my friends once remarked, make sure you never put in writing anything you aren't willing to defend in court. That doesn't mean you shouldn't take chances or risks; it does mean that you need to think things through.

It is worthwhile to think through one of the major temptations of any job: the exit interview. If you are in the workplace long enough, odds are that sooner or later you will lose a job involuntarily. You will get fired. It is not the end of the world, just the end of that job. The way to keep its pain from spreading is to avoid being seduced into unloading all of your frustrations and anger on your last day. Don't do it. You're not going to get your job back and you may want to work in the same field again. Angry, impassioned, ill-advised statements have a habit of finding immortality and finding their way to our next job interview before we do. You never know who knows whom or who works for whom.

If you feel you've been treated unfairly, write it all out in a letter, read it and burn it and keep your mouth shut.

We are more than what we do to pay the rent, but how we earn it takes up a lot of time and a lot of effort in our lives. We can be as assertive and in control in this area as in any other once we know who we are, what we want and how we're going to bring those two factors together. It may be very good work indeed.

CONCLUSION

There is an ancient Chinese parable about an approach to feeding somebody who's hungry. You can cook him a fish and take care of his hunger for that day or you can teach him to fish, which takes a lot longer and is a good deal more frustrating for both of you, but then he can take care of his own hunger for a lifetime. This book is about fishing. It's not the perfect book. I'm not the perfect teacher and you're not perfect either, but if you can find some solace, information, fun or philosophy here, well then I'm pleased. If you can't, ask for your money back, assuming that you haven't made notes in the margin.

The message of this book is that nobody's perfect. And if you've gotten that idea, a conclusion seems redundant. You may not be perfect, but you're not simple either.

What remains to be said is a word about how this book may be used once you've read it, about how to use it for reference. I said in the beginning the book is not meant to be an exhaustive discussion covering problems that might arise in life, but rather an overview of likely issues, general situations and common problems. The best way to use this book may be to think specifically about a problem and then look in the index to see if there is a heading that deals with the specifics of your concerns. For example, if you're concerned about telling your child about a planned move, you may want to check out "Kids," "Moving," "What's in it for me?" "Bargaining." If your problem doesn't fit any of the headings, try turning to the section that primarily concerns you, whether it's "Family" or "Kids" or "Work." Perhaps a similar situation has been discussed. Can you use any of the information? How might you use it to change your behavior? Even if the situations aren't identical, are there sufficient similarities? If not, either you need to get more specific, can't see the forest for the trees or may need a professional to help you sort things out. It is also possible that I haven't included the subject, in which case, write to me and I'll put it in the next book or try to become a bit less specific (Now how often do you hear me say that?) and see if there mightn't be a close enough question. If not, maybe the book isn't perfect either.

If you can find yourself or your situation within the text, then at least you know you're not alone. If you can't, it may be because the book is limited or you need more guided insight. At the very least, by now you have most likely gotten the hang of asking specific questions and looking for concrete solutions as well as taking responsibility for your own behavior rather than asking other people to change or assigning blame. Those are hard habits to break, but if you can the result is guaranteed to offer a bit more calm as well as control in your life. The point is not where or how the insight is acquired, or even the insight itself, but to see yourself as responsible so that blame becomes irrelevant (even to the point of blaming yourself), so that you are motivated to change your own behavior and get on with your life.

Here is an example. My editor said her sister had called with a question about her fourteen-year-old daughter who had gone away to camp and sent a letter home with a note on the outside of the envelope saying, "Don't be mad." Upon opening the letter, she found that her daughter had gotten her ears pierced against the express wishes of her parents. Nancy said, "Let me read you something," and read the beginning of the section on adolescence and independence. Her sister said she'd already made three of the mistakes I had mentioned. While the problem was not identical to anything I had discussed, the overlap was close enough to be helpful. If there is something that is troubling you or about which you are curious, try the index; and if that doesn't work, you can always reread the whole text or think about it overnight or make some notes.

If you think about it, there are at least three possible ways to use this book: You can read the whole thing through to get a flavor for the philosophy that indeed nobody is perfect. Or you can look for specific problems, i.e., rotten little kids with a tendency to write on walls. Or you can try for an overview, i.e., rotten little kids. Or you can always do all three at one time or another. Once you have the feel for the book, you can use it as a reference book for specifics, an overview of a particular problem or a relaxing overview of the human condition. In theory, you can also use it to press leaves. As I said, I want this book to be useful, but how you use it is up to you. As you may have already surmised, there isn't a perfect way to use it. I'm just delighted I got you past the front cover. Please take it and me with a grain of salt. Please enjoy learning more about yourself and your world.

In the meantime, don't give up the search for perfection. It's fun and important to try and be more than we currently are, to do well, maybe even to be the best, but realize that if getting there isn't half the fun, we're wasting our time. We need serenity, pleasure, sharing and rest in our lives. If your search deprives you of any of those, you may want to rethink your quest. It's okay to try for perfection as long as you are willing not only to tolerate but also to embrace a lack of it in others as well as yourself. If the word "failure" popped into your mind even once during the last sentence, reread this entire book immediately. You've missed the whole point. Life indeed should be daring risk, but perfection is only an abstract goal, so our reach can exceed our grasp and we won't get bored. Next year we can all try and be perfect. This year let's focus on cleaning up our act, smiling more often, sharing more with friends, offering a kindness to strangers and enjoying the fun of walking around on the planet. Deal?

Besides, if we're perfect, what do we do about chocolate?

INDEX

abuse, of kids, 37–39
activities:
  meeting friends in, 98
  shared by spouses, 160–61
adolescence, 12, 108
  see also teenagers
adoption, 124
  reunions between child and
    birth parent, 274–75
Adult Children of Alcoholics, 32
adultery, *see* affairs
advice:
  repeatedly ignored, 163
  unsolicited, from
    grandparents, 272–73
affairs, 137, 166, 168, 172–76,
    185–88, 192, 193
  combating of, 172–73
  confronting spouse about,
    172–73
  ending of, 186–87
  kids and, 182, 185–86
  married men's lies in, 185
  mistresses in, 185–87
  prenuptial, 144–45
  spousal jealousy and, 174–75
  telling spouse about, 176
  at work, 315–16, 318
aging:
  fear of, 54
  of parents, 15, 52–54, 61
AIDS (Acquired Immune
    Deficiency Syndrome), 70,
    105–7, 137, 244
  antibody tests for, 105
  condoms and, 105, 107, 244
AlAnon, 32, 33, 246
AlaTeen, 32
alcohol, *see* drinking
alcoholics:
  bargaining with, 33
  first drink of, 247

  parent as, 31–33
  support groups for loved
    ones of, 32
allowances, for kids, 239
anger, expressing of, 38
anxiety attacks, 40–42
  breathing technique for, 41–42
  heart attacks vs., 42
arguments:
  techniques for, 177
  withholding sex after, 177–78
  yelling in, 115–16
attention, kids' desire for, 234,
    236–37
attitude problems, at work,
    304–5
authority figures, difficulties
    with, 296, 298–99
automobile accidents, alcohol-
    related, 31, 246

bargaining, 101
  with alcoholic parent, 33
  about college expenses, 259
  about holiday or weekend
    visits to in-laws, 148–49
  to improve communication
    with spouse, 160
  about rules for teenagers, 26–
    27
  about teenage drinking
    parties, 248
  see also bribery
being oneself, 108–9
best man, affair between bride
    and, 144–45
birth control, 201, 226, 244
blame, 322
  assigning of, in family, 62,
    63, 64
  for homosexuality of kid,
    254–55

ABOUT THE AUTHOR

Dr. Joy Browne is heard nationally every weekday on WABC Talkradio. She has been a media psychologist in San Francisco and Boston and has also appeared on television on "Good Morning America," "Phil Donahue," "The WABC Morning Show," "The Regis Philbin Show," and "The Alan Thicke Show." Dr. Browne has had a private practice, been director of Social Services for the Boston Redevelopment Authority, and taught at Northeastern University. Weekends she can be seen on television on "I.D."